# Improving
# BASAL READING
# Instruction

# Improving
# *BASAL READING*
# Instruction

PETER N. WINOGRAD
KAREN K. WIXSON
MARJORIE Y. LIPSON

*Editors*

**T**EACHERS
**C**OLLEGE
**PRESS**
Teachers College, Columbia University
New York and London

Published by Teachers College Press, 1234 Amsterdam Avenue, New York, NY 10027

*Library of Congress Cataloging-in-Publication Data*

Improving basal reading instruction / Peter N. Winograd, Karen K.
  Wixson, Majorie Y. Lipson, editors.
      p.   cm.
  Bibliography: p.
  Includes index.
  ISBN 0-8077-2932-9 (pbk.)
  ISBN 0-8077-2933-7
  1. Basal reading instruction.   I. Winograd, Peter N.   II. Wixson,
Karen K.   III. Lipson, Marjorie Y.
LB1050.36.I47 1989
372.4′1—dc19                                              88-29756
                                                              CIP

ISBN 0-8077-2932-9 (pbk.)
ISBN 0-8077-2933-7

Manufactured in the United States of America

94  93  92  91  90  89        1  2  3  4  5  6

# Contents

# Preface

The original idea for this book came from a 1984 preconvention institute on decision making in basal reading instruction, presented at the International Reading Association, organized by two of the editors and including many of this book's contributors as participants. The institute made us acutely aware that although basal programs are the dominant means of reading instruction in the United States today, there were no texts available to provide teachers with constructive suggestions about how to use basals as part of a more complete, balanced, and effective program of reading instruction. This awareness, combined with the knowledge gained from the research on reading and reading instruction during the past 10 to 15 years, made clear the need for a theoretically sound text on basal reading instruction.

This text is designed to apply current theory and research in reading and reading instruction to basal instruction and, in so doing, to provide teachers with usable, conceptually sound guidelines for improving basal reading instruction. The book is intended for use with inservice teachers and as a supplementary text in undergraduate- and graduate-level courses in reading methods. In addition, researchers will find it a useful example of how theory and research can inform instructional practice.

The introduction provides an overview of current thinking about reading, readers, and reading instruction. Part I of the book (chapters 1–3) focuses on the effective use of the basic components of basal instruction: teaching the selection, grouping and pacing, and seatwork activities. Part II (chapters 4 and 5) considers effective means of evaluating students and individualizing instruction within a basal program. Part III (chapters 6–9) examines ways to integrate and expand basal instruction in the important areas of beginning reading, children's literature, writing, and content-area reading. The book concludes with a summary that examines the role of basals in American classrooms and provides guidelines for evaluating basal reading programs.

The authors wish to acknowledge gratefully the assistance of Kathleen Hric and Cheryl Gaylock in preparing the figures for chapter 1, and the assistance of Lindell Ohia who provided the examples of fifth-grade lessons and seatwork assignments for chapter 3.

Thanks also to the teachers enrolled in the 1987 summer session of *EDC 600: Workshop in Reading,* at the University of Kentucky, for their thoughtful responses to early drafts of many of the chapters in this book.

Finally, the authors thank editors Sarah Biondello, Nina George, and the other folks at Teachers College Press for their support, encouragement, and patience.

*Improving*
**BASAL READING**
*Instruction*

# Introduction:
# Understanding
# Reading Instruction

## PETER N. WINOGRAD

The thesis of this introduction and of all the chapters in this book is that basal readers are most effective when they are used flexibly and as part of a comprehensive, balanced program of reading instruction. Moreover, the converse is true: Basal readers are least effective when they are used as the total reading program and children spend all of their allocated instructional time in the basals program, reading selections and completing various exercises. To be sure, the better basal reading programs are designed and intended to be used as part of a comprehensive reading program. As we shall see, however, there is legitimate concern that, too often, basal reading series become the total reading program. Thus, the purposes of this book are to examine why it is important to use basal readers flexibly and how this can be accomplished.

This introduction will focus on what recent research has taught us about reading, readers, and reading instruction. Each of the chapters that follow looks at specific aspects of reading instruction as they relate to basal reading programs.

## EXPANDING PERSPECTIVES ON READING

Research in the area of reading has grown tremendously in the 1970s and 1980s. The number of research articles in the last fifteen years equals all of the published research in the past ninety years (Weintraub et al., 1982). This research has confirmed some long-standing assumptions, provided new insights, and caused us to revise many of our theories and instructional suggestions. Any attempt to summarize all this research runs the risk of overemphasizing certain findings or theories while oversimplifying or ignoring others. Nonetheless, some aspects of the research are particularly pertinent to improving the instructional use of basal readers. In this introduction, I will examine research related to both the processes and the purposes of reading.

## Processes of Reading

Perhaps the most radical change in recent years has to do with our understanding of the processes involved in reading. The essence of the change has been a shift from the view of reading as a set of hierarchically arranged subskills to a more interactive view.

The subskills view can be characterized by a number of questionable assumptions (Johnson & Pearson, 1975). The first is that reading is comprised of a number of discrete skills, including those involved in decoding, vocabulary, language, and comprehension. Second, these various skills should be learned in a certain sequence; usually the decoding skills are emphasized first, and comprehension skills are emphasized later. Third, fluent, skilled reading comes about when the reader has mastered each of the subskills.

The subskills view of reading has been the dominant one. If one examines the objectives lists of almost any of the standardized reading tests, or the scope-and-sequence chart of almost any commercial reading series, or the curriculum guidelines of almost any school district, then one will encounter the subskills view of reading.

It is essential to note that the idea of reading skills plays a useful role in reading instruction. Certainly it makes sense to spend some time with children talking about the vocabulary they are encountering in their science books or the themes of the literature selections they are reading. Researchers who have been critical of the subskills view have not argued against skills in reading, but rather how they have been defined, organized, and taught (Johnson & Pearson, 1975; Rosenshine, 1980). Their concerns can best be examined by presenting the interactive view of reading.

Wixson and Peters (1984) provided one of the clearest statements about the shifting view of the processes involved in reading.

Recent research holds that reading is a dynamic process that involves the reader's ability to construct meaning through the interaction between information suggested by the written language and the reader's existing knowledge. In other words the reader is an active participant in the process. This interactive dimension focuses on how the reader derives meaning from print; what the reader brings to the reading situation in terms of experience, skills and ability; how the information is presented in written text; and what effects context has on reading. As a result, difficulty is no longer viewed as an absolute property of a particular skill or task, but rather as a relative property of the interactions among specific reader, text, and instructional factors. [p. 4]

The differences between the subskills view and the interactive view are substantial. Fluent reading still involves skills, but we have come to appreciate the importance of other factors as well. Fluent reading also means integrating those skills with one's prior knowledge in a flexible and strategic manner, depending upon one's purpose, the nature of the material, and the context. As we will see in the rest of the chapters in this book, the instructional implications of this shifting view of the processes involved in reading are considerable.

## Purposes of Reading

The changes in how we perceive the processes involved in reading really represent some new ways of thinking about reading. The changes discussed in this section are not new insights as much as they are reaffirmations of some of the things that we have known all along about reading. Perhaps the most important of these changes is our appreciation of the fact that reading is a communicative process. What this bit of common sense means is that reading is intimately related to the other language arts, especially writing (see chapters 3 and 8). This also means that reading instruction should involve children reading authentic materials for authentic purposes, rather than spending their time completing drills and exercises that focus on skills devoid of authentic context or legitimate purpose.

The relationships between reading and writing have received much attention in recent years (Hansen, 1987; Tierney & Pearson, 1983). Some of the work has focused on the similarities and differences in the underlying processes involved in comprehending and composing (Tierney, Leys, & Rogers, 1986), but the work most pertinent in our discussion here concerns the importance of what Connie Bridge in chapter 6 and Taffy Raphael and Carol Sue Englert in chapter 8 call a "literate environment."

A literate environment is one in which students learn to be both readers and writers, both authors and audience. Its key characteristic is that children are responding to and creating authentic texts for authentic purposes. Children spend much of their time working on projects that they and their teachers have chosen, and they are doing so in a climate that is cooperative and collaborative, rather than competitive in nature. Children may be writing and reading notes, bulletin board information, stories, social studies or science reports, full-length books, or short articles in a class newspaper. In any and all cases, the children's attention is on how well the message is communicated. Reading skills and writing skills are important because they are a means of helping the children communicate, not as ends in themselves. Moreover, the more children write, the better they read; the more they read, the better they write.

The recent emphasis on the importance of purpose has another dimension that is relevant for our discussion on the expanding perspectives on reading. This dimension is best captured by Rosenblatt's (1978, 1980) distinction between efferent and aesthetic stances in reading. According to Rosenblatt, when readers adopt an efferent stance toward reading, they focus their attention on the ideas, the meaning, that they will need to remember and use later on. In other words, the reader is attempting to take information away from the text after the reading is completed. Clearly, the ability to take an efferent stance toward reading is important, especially in the content areas of science, social studies, health, and so forth. But there are other reasons why people read.

When readers adopt an aesthetic stance during reading, they are intent on experiencing the ideas and feelings suggested in the material. During aesthetic reading, readers are not trying to learn from the text but rather to become involved in the experience of reading. Aesthetic reading is performed for the sheer pleasure of the experience itself, as when someone voluntarily reads a novel or a poem. Rosenblatt (1978) describes aesthetic reading this way:

> In aesthetic reading, we respond to the very story or poem that we are evoking during the transaction with the text. . . . We listen to the sound of the words in the inner ear; we lend our sensations, our emotions, our sense of being alive, to the new experience which, we feel, corresponds to the text. We participate in the story, we identify with the characters, we share their conflicts and their feelings. [p. 270]

A broader view of reading, then, suggests that both efferent and aesthetic reading are important. The point here is that sometimes the most important information in what children read is not information at all; rather it is responses, emotions, feelings, imagery, and reactions. Teachers need to be concerned about both efferent and aesthetic reading. Children need to learn the information necessary for success both in school and in life. But children also need to experience the pleasures that derive from aesthetic reading, for these are the key to developing lifelong readers. Fortunately, children spend a great deal of time in schools engaged in efferent reading. Unfortunately, they spend too little time enthralled in aesthetic reading. Lesley Morrow will examine specific ways that teachers can involve children in aesthetic reading in chapter 7, but for now it is sufficient to say that children need opportunities to experience both efferent and aesthetic reading.

## EXPANDING PERSPECTIVES ON READERS

Clearly, the more we learn about reading, the more we learn about readers. Indeed, the interactive view of reading emphasizes the essential role that various reader factors play in reading. In this section we will discuss what the reader brings to reading in more depth by examining what recent research has revealed about prior knowledge and strategic readers.

### Prior Knowledge

Perhaps the dominant theme to emerge from recent research is the importance of background knowledge or schema. Indeed, an entire school of thought about reading has been identified as schema theory (e.g., Anderson, 1977). The central tenet of schema theory is that what an individual knows already exerts a powerful influence on how she will understand new information.

> Whether we are aware of it or not, it is this interaction of new information with old knowledge that we mean when we use the term comprehension. To say that one has comprehended a text is to say that she has found a mental "home" for the information in the text, or else that she has modified an existing mental home in order to accommodate that new information. [Anderson & Pearson, 1984, p. 255]

Let us consider some of the important ways that a reader's schema influences reading comprehension. First, background knowledge enables a reader to organize incoming information in such a way as to make it comprehensible (Bransford & Johnson, 1972). One popular example that illustrates this effect is the sentence, "Because the seams were split, the notes were sour." Most people find this sentence difficult to understand, even though they understand the individual words. The problem is that most readers don't know how to organize the information in a meaningful way until they hear the word *bagpipes*. The ability to organize incoming information should not be underestimated, by the way, because readers use background knowledge as one way of determining which ideas are more important and which are less important (Prichard & Anderson, 1977). For example, a reader familiar with the way that mysteries are organized will pay attention to details like the location of the murder weapon, because she knows that such clues will be essential in identifying the killer. Researchers are adept at reading technical reports and chefs are adept at reading recipes because they are familiar with the kind of information presented and the way it is organized.

A second way that background knowledge is important is that it enables the reader to make inferences during reading (Anderson & Pearson, 1984; Paris & Lindauer, 1976). Authors are unable to explicitly communicate all of the information they want the reader to understand; even if they could, such texts would be too boring to read. Instead, readers must make inferences as they read, to fill in gaps and to add depth to the writer's words. Researchers have identified a surprising number of different kinds of inferences, ranging from filling in the correct referent for a pronoun (Baumann & Stevenson, 1986) to making conjectures about the main character's motives and plans (Omanson, Warren, & Trabasso, 1978). Clearly, the ability to draw inferences is crucial to understanding what is read, and background knowledge is essential to drawing inferences.

A third way that background knowledge is important has to do with what makes a text easy or difficult to read (Rubin, 1985). Recall that a key difference between the skills view of reading and the interactive view of reading is that difficulty is no longer defined as a fixed characteristic of a particular text but rather as a "relative property" of the interaction between the reader and the text. The research into the importance of background knowledge has taught us that one of the things that makes a text easy or hard to read is what the reader knows about the topic. Thus, we are oversimplifying and distorting the picture when we rely too heavily upon readability formulas and say that a certain book is at the fifth-grade level and is too hard for third graders to understand. It may be hard for some children at any grade to understand, if they are unfamiliar with the topic. Conversely, it may be easy for other children at any grade, if they are familiar with the topic. We have come to appreciate that the readability level of a text cannot be estimated from the material alone; we must take the reader into account as well. The educational and diagnostic implications that derive from this are very important, as will be shown in chapter 1 by Karen Wixson and Charles Peters, chapter 4 by Marjorie Lipson and Karen Wixson, chapter 6 by Connie Bridge, and chapter 9 by Donna Alvermann.

Our discussion of the various ways that a reader's background knowledge influences reading comprehension has really only touched the surface of this important topic. However, even this brief examination should illustrate why so many of the activities and techniques mentioned in later chapters deal with building and activating background knowledge.

## Strategic Readers

In addition to the importance of a reader's schema, research has also emphasized the importance of readers taking an active and strategic role in reading. This is the second theme that has emerged from recent research on readers (Brown, Bransford, Ferrara, & Campione, 1983; Paris, Lipson, & Wixson, 1983). Strategic readers approach the tasks of reading in a flexible manner that depends upon their purpose and the nature of the text. Strategic readers are skilled, of course; but, more important, they are capable of using those skills appropriately and willing to use them to achieve purposes they consider important. In contrast, many poor readers do not approach reading in a strategic manner. Their purposes for reading are often imposed and thus not their own; indeed, many open books only under duress. They display little sensitivity to differences in texts or tasks. Many lack skills and, in addition, fail to make good use of the skills they do have or the skills their teachers are trying to teach them.

Researchers interested in how good readers are able to be so strategic and why poor readers encounter so much difficulty have focused much of their attention on the construct of metacognition. While it is difficult to define exactly, *metacognition* usually refers to an individual's ability to appraise and manage his own thinking (Paris & Winograd, in press). When an older student decides that a particular chapter on chemistry is too difficult to understand without a teacher's assistance, he is displaying an instance of metacognition. So is the student who pauses to consider what she knows about dogs before reading an article on pet care, or the young reader who substitutes one word for another and then self-corrects because the resulting sentence did not make sense. The preceding examples of metacognition are primarily cognitive in nature. But metacognition involves affect as well as cognition (Borkowski, Carr, Rellinger, & Pressley, in press), and the interplay between the two is particularly evident when one considers the differences between good and poor readers.

Characterizing the differences between good and poor readers can be very difficult because children experience difficulties in learning to read for a wide variety of reasons. Moreover, as stated earlier, the interactive view of reading difficulties implies that reading ability is not a fixed entity, but rather that it may vary depending upon the text, the task, and the context (Wixson & Lipson, 1986). Nonetheless, a great deal of recent research has focused on comparing good readers who are actively involved in the process of reading and poor readers who are not. Johnston and Winograd (1985) characterize this latter group of children as "passive failures," who harbor misconceptions and confusion about the tasks of reading; who fail to see the relationships between their efforts and outcomes; who usually attribute their difficulties to their own low ability; and who display antagonism, apathy, resignation, and low self-esteem. Good readers are strategic in their attempts to get involved with print; many poor readers are strategic in their attempts to avoid reading.

The contrast between strategic readers and passive failures is useful for our purposes because it illustrates how any description of readers must touch upon the essential and related dimensions of cognition and affect. In terms of cognition, what a reader knows about the topic, the type of text, and the skills that pertain to that particular task all play a crucial role in determining whether comprehension will occur. In terms of affect, how a reader feels about herself and reading is essential. Readers who believe that they are incapable of learning or who are worried about appearing foolish and stupid in front of others are unlikely to become strategic readers. Such children are likely to do their best to avoid reading altogether or focus too much on inappropriate goals such as "saying all the words fast without stumbling" (Canney & Winograd, 1979).

In summary, recent research into schema theory, strategic reading, and metacognition has reminded us of the essential role of reader factors during reading. The importance of the reader seems so obvious that it is difficult to believe that we need to be reminded of it. Nonetheless, the simplicity of this point belies the difficulty we seem to have in actually keeping the reader in focus during instruction.

## EXPANDING VIEWS ON READING INSTRUCTION

Our greater understanding of reading and of readers has important implications for reading instruction. We have learned much about the strengths and weaknesses of current practice, and we have identified some promising possibilities for future practice. Let us begin this last section by examining some of the major criticisms that have been leveled against current approaches to reading instruction. This will set the stage for a brief discussion about the positive elements in reading instruction as well as specific recommendations contained in the chapters that follow.

The essence of the problem with current reading instruction, critics charge, is that children are spending too much time using contrived materials in contrived situations while working toward contrived ends, and too little time involved with authentic texts while reading for authentic purposes. Moreover, teachers are spending too much of their time managing materials and too little of their time helping children to learn how to read. Let's consider these complaints in more detail.

The charge that children are spending too much time using contrived materials comes from a variety of sources, including a large number of classroom observation studies (e.g., Fisher et al., 1978; Mason & Osborn, 1982). Researchers point to data that indicate many primary-grade children are spending 60 to 70 percent of their allocated reading time completing tasks that focus on discrete skills (Anderson, 1984; Fisher et al., 1978). The Report of the Commission on Reading presented the figures in another way: Children are spending about an hour a day on workbooks and skill sheets and seven or eight minutes a day engaged in silent reading (Anderson, Hiebert, Scott, & Wilkinson, 1985). It is important to note that these figures are for children in regular classrooms; children in compensatory reading programs spend almost all of their time completing skill lessons in workbooks or worksheets (Allington, Stuetzel, Shake, & Lamarche, 1986). Such an imbalance is difficult to defend, especially given recent evidence that time spent in free reading is consistently related to gains in reading achievement, while time spent completing worksheets is not (Fielding, Wilson, & Anderson, 1986). To expand on this point, in chapter 3, Judith Scheu, Diane Tanner, and Kathryn Au will examine how the seatwork that comes with basals can be used more wisely.

Concern over contrived materials is not limited to skills activities; indeed, a large body of research has been developed that focuses on the importance of well-written, meaningful reading selections and the detrimental effects that accrue when "stories" have been adapted to fit "readability formulas" or manufactured simply to provide exercises in specific skills (Brennan, Bridge, & Winograd, 1986; Davison & Kantor, 1982). Researchers have noted that well-written, meaningful texts are critical to learning in the content areas as well. Anderson and Armbruster (1984) and Armbruster (1985), for example, argue persuasively that students learn best from content texts that are coherent and have clear overall structures that emphasize the important ideas. Recall the point raised earlier that the purpose of reading is communication. The problem with contrived materials is that they often have no meaning to communicate. Instead, they are designed to provide practice in decoding or some other skill, without regard for meaning. We have come to appreciate, however, that the best way to practice the skills and strategies involved in reading (and other forms of communication) is with meaningful materials for authentic purposes. As the noted children's author Tommy DePaola (1987) puts it, "If . . . we want real readers, we must give them real books" (p. vi).

Researchers have also expressed concern over the fact that reading instruction is usually conducted in contrived situations. Perhaps the most widely voiced complaint is that children are grouped by ability, often permanently, and that readers in different ability groups then receive differential instruction (Allington, 1983; 1984). Data indicate that, compared to those in high-ability groups, children in low-ability groups do less silent reading, encounter more words out of meaningful context, are asked more lower-level comprehension questions, and are corrected more often for oral reading mistakes. Mary Shake in chapter 2, on grouping and pacing; Marjorie Lipson in chapter 5, on individualizing instruction; and Connie Bridge in chapter 6, on beginning reading, will examine these and related issues in more detail. For now it is sufficient to say that researchers have stressed the need for instructional situations that are more conducive to learning (Au & Kawakami, 1986; Slavin, 1983; Stevens, Madden, Slavin, & Farnish, 1987).

Criticism of current reading instruction has also focused on the contrived ends of reading instruction. Related issues here include the narrowness of current approaches to reading assessment, the pressures of accountability, and the view of reading as a competitive activity. Johnston (in press), Wixson & Lipson (1986), and Cross and Paris (1987), among others, have written widely on the limitations of current approaches to reading assessment. Many of their complaints center on the use of standardized tests that are designed to ignore many of the factors (e.g., background knowledge, strategic reading, motivation) that recent research has indicated are essential to the reading process. Moreover, because such standardized assessments usually incorporate brief passages with little meaning and multiple-choice questions that limit and distort possible responses, they are more suited to collecting "objective" data that can be used for classification and accountability than they are to providing information useful in making instructional decisions (Johnston, in press).

This fact should come as no surprise to anyone associated with current reading instruction. Accountability—the need to prove that a program is effective—is often cited as among the strongest influences on reading instruction, sometimes the strongest (Shannon, 1983, 1984, 1986; Winograd & Greenlee, 1986). Critics argue that current forms of accountability place too much credence on standardized test scores and that teachers are pressured to abandon balanced curricula in favor of teaching the skills that are to be tested. Cautions that such tests can only sample a narrow range of reading behaviors are ignored; reading instruction comes to mean guided practice through a series of skills, and reading achievement comes to mean little more than scores on a standardized test (Linn, 1985).

Contrived situations and contrived ends in reading instruction share a common feature that many critics find particularly disturbing. Because children are often placed in groups and compared to one another, and because the goals of reading instruction are often determined by test scores, children, educators, and the public come to view reading as a competitive activity. In many states the results of reading tests are published in the newspapers so that all can see which schools are doing well and which are doing poorly. Such a view has a number of pernicious effects, especially on the self-perceptions and motivations of poor readers. Indeed, many of the problems mentioned during the earlier discussion of passive failure are caused or exacerbated by the view of reading as a competitive activity (Johnston & Winograd, 1985). Researchers have speculated that the competitive nature of reading instruction may produce able readers who only engage in reading for extrinsic rewards, such as grades, and who never develop a love of reading. An estimated 40 percent of adult

Americans who can read books choose not to (Toch, 1984), and we are coming to realize that aliterates have few advantages over illiterates.

Finally, critics charge that teachers are spending too much of their time "managing" children through materials by assigning them activities and asking questions, and too little time engaging in the kind of teaching that will help children develop into independent readers. In this regard, Durkin (1978–1979) has used the term *mentioning* to describe the inadequate way that teachers presented comprehension lessons to children, and she and others (Durkin, 1978–1979, 1981; Hare & Milligan, 1984) have documented how little support basal reader manuals and professional textbooks offer teachers in terms of teaching comprehension.

The importance of presenting clear, explicit comprehension lessons to children should not be underestimated. Indeed, a major focus of recent instructional research has been on how to teach children about the processes involved in comprehension (Duffy et al., 1986; Paris, Wixson, & Palincsar, 1986; Winograd & Hare, 1988). Terms like *direct instruction, direct explanation, cognitive coaching, scaffolded learning,* and *modeling* have become extremely popular, as educators expand their repertoire of techniques for teaching reading comprehension. As you shall see in the chapters that follow, the current emphasis on showing children why, how, when, and where to use various comprehension skills and strategies is very different from earlier approaches, which were often limited to reading the selection, asking questions to see if the children understood the content, and assigning worksheets.

A number of researchers have also argued that teachers have become "deskilled" in the sense that they no longer exercise their professional judgment in deciding what to teach, how to teach it, or when it should be taught (Shannon, 1983, 1984; Shulman, 1983; Woodward, 1986). As Shannon (1983) puts it, teachers "control only the level of precision with which they apply commercial materials" (p. 71). There has been some debate about why this state of affairs has come about. Some researchers place the blame directly on the use of commercial reading materials (Goodman, Freeman, Murphy, & Shannon, 1987), while others fault different culprits including the politics of social organizations, classroom management issues, and accountability (Fraatz, 1987; Winograd & Smith, 1987). Jean Osborn will examine these issues in more detail in her summary but for now it is sufficient to state that most researchers agree that teachers deserve more support and encouragement for using their professional judgment to make important instructional decisions about the children they know best.

Our expanding perspective on reading instruction has, in summary, revealed a number of weaknesses in current reading instruction. Children are not spending enough time reading worthwhile materials, and teachers are not spending enough time helping children understand and appreciate what they are reading. Clearly, the way to improve reading instruction is to address these problems. The chapters in this book attempt to show how that can be accomplished.

## CONCLUSION

In each of the following chapters, the authors begin by summarizing the research relevant to their particular topic. These summaries provide the necessary background and rationale for the specific suggestions, recommendations, and activities contained in each chapter. As you read the following chapters, please keep the following general guidelines in mind. First, the basal reading series is only part of a complete reading program. Such a program also involves a variety of resources including trade books, content textbooks, magazines, newspapers, and materials produced by the children themselves. Such a program involves people as well—the teachers, librarians, administrators, parents, and other caring individuals who can provide children with the incentive and assistance they need to become members of the literate community.

Second, teacher judgment is essential to a quality reading program. Teachers know more about the individual children in their classrooms than do the authors and publishers of basal reading programs. Thus, it is critical that teachers use their knowledge by selecting and adapting materials and lessons to fit the needs, strengths, and interests of their particular students. Indeed, the activities and lessons in basal readers should be viewed as recommendations rather than as requirements. If a suggested selection, activity, lesson, or test does not seem appropriate, teachers should feel free to change or drop it.

Finally, teacher enthusiasm is essential to a quality reading program. Teachers should share their love of reading with the children. Taking the time to read stories aloud to children or to engage in sustained silent reading is critical to producing good readers.

Recent research in reading has resulted in a richer understanding of how to help children become accomplished readers. This research has also provided us with a deeper understanding about the strengths and limitations of basal readers. The lesson seems to be that basal readers can be an effective instructional resource if they are carefully designed, thoughtfully applied, and flexibly used as part of a more comprehensive reading program. It is hoped that the information in this book will help teachers use basals wisely and thus make reading more meaningful, readers more independent, and reading instruction more effective.

## REFERENCES

Allington, R. (1983). The reading instruction provided readers of different ability. *Elementary School Journal, 83,* 255–265.

Allington, R. (1984). Content coverage and contextual reading in reading groups. *Journal of Reading Behavior, 16,* 85–96.

Allington, R., Stuetzel, H., Shake, M., & Lamarche, S. (1986). What is remedial reading? A descriptive study. *Reading Research and Instruction, 26,* 15–30.

Anderson, L. (1984). The environment of instruction: The function of seatwork in a commercially developed curriculum. In G. Duffy, L. Roehler, & J. Mason (Eds.), *Comprehension Instruction: Perspectives and Suggestions* (pp. 93–115). New York: Longman.

Anderson, R. C. (1977). The notion of schemata and the educational enterprise. In R. C. Anderson, R. J. Spiro, & W. E. Montague (Eds.), *Schooling and the acquisition of knowledge* (pp. 415–432). Hillsdale, NJ: Lawrence Erlbaum.

Anderson, R. C., Hiebert, E., Scott, J. A., & Wilkinson, I. A. (1985). *Becoming a nation of readers: The report of the Commission on Reading.* Washington, DC: The National Institute of Education.

Anderson, R. C., & Pearson, P. D. (1984). A schema-theoretic view of basic process in reading. In P. D. Pearson (Ed.), *Handbook of reading research* (pp. 255–292). New York: Longman.

Anderson, T. H., & Armbruster, B. B. (1984). Content area textbooks. In R. C. Anderson, J. Osborn, & R. J. Tierney (Eds.), *Learning to read in American schools: Basal readers and content texts* (pp. 193–266). Hillsdale, NJ: Lawrence Erlbaum.

Armbruster, B. B. (1985). Content area textbooks: A research perspective. In J. Osborn, P. Wilson, & R. C. Anderson (Eds.), *Reading education: Foundations for a literate America* (pp. 47–60). Lexington, MA: D. C. Heath.

Au, K., & Kawakami, A. (1986). Influence of the social organization of instruction on children's text comprehension ability: A Vygotskian perspective. In T. Raphael (Ed.), *The contexts of school-based literacy* (pp. 63–78). New York: Longman.

Baumann, J., & Stevenson, J. (1986). Identifying types of anaphoric relationships. In J. W. Irwin (Ed.), *Understanding and teaching cohesion comprehension* (pp. 9–20). Newark, DE: International Reading Association.

Borkowski, J. G., Carr, M., Rellinger, E., & Pressley, M. (in press). Self-regulated cognition: Interdependence of metacognition, attributions, and self-esteem. In B. F. Jones & L. Idol (Eds.), *Dimensions of thinking and cognitive instruction*. Hillsdale, NJ: Lawrence Erlbaum.

Bransford, J., & Johnson, M. K. (1972). Contextual prerequisites for understanding. Some investigations of comprehension and recall. *Journal of Verbal Learning and Verbal Behavior, 11*, 717–726.

Brennan, A., Bridge, C., & Winograd, P. (1986). The effects of structural variation on children's recall of basal reader stories. *Reading Research Quarterly, 21*, 91–104.

Brown, A. L., Bransford, J. D., Ferrara, R. A., & Campione, J. C. (1983). Learning, remembering, and understanding. In J. H. Flavell & E. M. Markman (Eds.), *Carmichael's Manual of Child Psychology* (Vol. 1). New York: John Wiley.

Canney, G., & Winograd, P. (1979). *Schemata for reading and reading comprehension performance* (Technical Report No. 120). Urbana-Champaign: University of Illinois, Center for the Study of Reading.

Cross, D., & Paris, S. (1987). Assessment of reading comprehension: Matching test purposes and test properties. *Educational Psychologist, 22*, 313–332.

Davison, A., & Kantor, R. (1982). On the failure of readability formula to define readable texts: A case study from adaptations. *Reading Research Quarterly, 17*, 187–210.

DePaola, T. (1987). Foreword. In B. Cullinan (Ed.), *Children's literature in the reading program* (pp. v–vi). Newark, DE: International Reading Association.

Duffy, G. D., Roehler, L. R., Meloth, M. S., Vavrus, L. G., Book, C., Putnam, J., & Wesselman, R. (1986). The relationship between explicit verbal explanations during reading skill instruction and student awareness and achievement: A study of reading teacher effects. *Reading Research Quarterly, 21*, 237–252.

Durkin, D. (1978–1979). What classroom observations reveal about reading comprehension instruction. *Reading Research Quarterly, 14*, 481–533.

Durkin, D. (1981). Reading comprehension instruction in five basal readers series. *Reading Research Quarterly, 16*, 515–544.

Fielding, L., Wilson, P., & Anderson, R. (1986). A new focus on free reading: The role of trade books in reading. In T. Raphael (Ed.), *The contexts of school-based literacy* (pp. 149–160). New York: Random House.

Fisher, C., Berliner, D., Filby, N., Marliave, R., Cohen, L., Dishaw, M., & Moore, J. (1978). *Teaching and learning in elementary school: A summary of the beginning teacher evaluation study*. San Francisco: Far West Laboratory of Educational Research and Development.

Fraatz, J. M. (1987). *The politics of reading: Power, opportunity, and prospects for change in America's public schools*. New York: Teachers College Press.

Goodman, K., Freeman, Y., Murphy, S., & Shannon, P. (1987, November). *Report card on basal readers.* Paper presented at the Invitational Conference on Basal Readers, Los Angeles, California.

Hansen, J. (1987). *When writers read.* Portsmouth, NH: Heinemann Educational Books.

Hare, V., & Milligan, B. (1984). Main idea identificational explanations in four basal reader series. *Journal of Reading Behavior, 16,* 189–204.

Johnson, D., & Pearson, P. D. (1975). Skills management systems: A critique. *The Reading Teacher, 28,* 757–764.

Johnston, P. (in press). Steps toward a more naturalistic approach to the assessment of the reading process. In J. Algina (Ed.), *Advances in content based educational assessment.* Norwood, NJ: Ablex.

Johnston, P., & Winograd, P. (1985). Passive failure in reading. *Journal of Reading Behavior, 17,* 279–301.

Linn, R. (1985). Standards and expectations: The role of testing. *Proceedings of a National Forum on Educational Reform* (pp. 88–95). New York: The College Board.

Mason, J., & Osborn, J. (1982). *When do children begin "reading to learn"? A survey of classroom reading instruction practices in grades two through five* (Technical Report No. 261). Urbana-Champaign: University of Illinois, Center for the Study of Reading.

Omanson, R. C., Warren, W. H., & Trabasso, T. (1978). Goals, themes, inferences, and memory: A developmental study. *Discourse Processes, 1,* 337–354.

Paris, S. G., & Lindauer, B. K. (1976). The role of inference in children's comprehension and memory. *Cognitive Psychology, 8,* 217–227.

Paris, S. G., Lipson, M. Y., & Wixson, K. K. (1983). Becoming a strategic reader. *Contemporary Educational Psychology, 8,* 293–316.

Paris, S. G., & Winograd, P. (in press). Metacognition in academic learning and instruction. In B. F. Jones & L. Idol (Eds.), *Dimensions of thinking and cognitive instruction.* Hillsdale, NJ: Lawrence Erlbaum.

Paris, S. G., Wixson, K., & Palincsar, A. (1986). Instructional approaches to reading comprehension. In E. Rothkopf (Ed.), *Review of research in education* (Vol. 13) (pp. 91–128). Washington, DC: American Educational Research Association.

Prichard, J. W., & Anderson, R. C. (1977). Taking different perspectives on a story. *Journal of Educational Psychology, 69,* 309–315.

Rosenblatt, L. M. (1978). *The reader, the text, the poem.* Carbondale: Southern Illinois University Press.

Rosenblatt, L. M. (1980). What facts does this poem teach you? *Language Arts, 57,* 386–394.

Rosenshine, B. V. (1980). Skill hierarchies in reading comprehension. In R. J. Spiro, B. C. Bruce, & W. F. Brewer (Eds.), *Theoretical issues in reading comprehension: Perspectives from cognitive psychology, linguistics, artificial intelligence, and education* (pp. 535–554). Hillsdale, NJ: Lawrence Erlbaum.

Rubin, A. (1985). How useful are readability formulas? In J. Osborn, P. Wilson, & R. C. Anderson (Eds.), *Reading education: Foundations for a literate America* (pp. 61–78). Lexington, MA: D. C. Heath.

Shannon, P. (1983). The use of commercial reading materials in American elementary schools. *Reading Research Quarterly, 19,* 68–85.

Shannon, P. (1984). Mastery learning in reading and the control of teachers and students. *Language Arts, 61,* 484–493.

Shannon, P. (1986). Teachers' and administrators' thoughts on changes in reading instruction within a merit pay program based on test scores. *Reading Research Quarterly, 21,* 20–35.

Shulman, L. (1983). Autonomy and obligation: The remote control of teaching. In L. Shulman & G. Sykes (Eds.), *Handbook of Teaching and Policy* (pp. 484–504). New York: Longman.

Slavin, R. E. (1983). *Cooperative learning.* New York: Longman.

Stevens, R. J., Madden, N. A., Slavin, R. E., & Farnish, A. M. (1987). Cooperative integrated reading and composition: Two field experiments. *Reading Research Quarterly, 22,* 433–454.

Tierney, R. J., Leys, M., & Rogers, T. (1986). Comprehension, composition, and collaboration: Analyses of communication influences in two classrooms. In T. Raphael (Ed.), *The contexts of school-based literacy* (pp. 191–216). New York: Random House.

Tierney, R. J., & Pearson, P. D. (1983). Toward a composing model of reading. *Language Arts, 60,* 568–580.

Toch, T. (1984, September). America's quest of universal literacy. *Education Week, 4,* L3–L5.

Weintraub, S., Smith, H., Plessas, G., Roser, N., Hill, W., & Kibby, M. (1982). *Summary of investigations relating to reading: July 1, 1980 to June 30, 1981.* Newark, DE: International Reading Association.

Winograd, P., & Greenlee, M. (1986). Children need a balanced reading program. *Educational Leadership, 43,* 16–21.

Winograd, P., & Hare, V. C. (1988). Direct instruction of reading comprehension strategies: The nature of teacher explanation. In C. Weinstein, E. Goetz, & P. Alexander (Eds.), *Learning and study strategies: Issues in assessment, instruction, and evaluation* (pp. 121–140). New York: Academic Press.

Winograd, P., & Smith, L. (1987). Improving the climate for reading comprehension instruction. *The Reading Teacher, 41,* 304–310.

Wixson, K., & Lipson, M. (1986). Reading (dis)ability: An interactionist perspective. In T. Raphael (Ed.), *The contexts of school-based literacy* (pp. 131–148). New York: Random House.

Wixson, K. K., & Peters, C. W. (1984). Reading redefined: A Michigan reading association position paper. *The Michigan Reading Journal, 17,* 4–7.

Woodward, A. (1986, Spring). Over-programmed materials: Taking the teacher out of teaching. *American Educator,* 26–31.

# PART I

# Components
## of
# Basal Instruction

Chapter 1

# *Teaching*
# *the Basal Selection*

KAREN K. WIXSON
CHARLES W. PETERS

The purpose of this chapter is to describe procedures for evaluating and modifying the lessons used to teach the basal reading selections. The procedures that are described emphasize two dimensions of basal lessons. The first focuses on teaching about the *process* of reading a particular selection, while the second focuses on teaching about the *content* of a particular basal selection. The chapter begins with background information about basal reader lessons and a brief discussion of the implications of current research for teaching the basal selection. This is followed by a description of procedures for previewing and planning and then evaluating and modifying basal lessons in ways that are consistent with current views of reading and reading instruction. Two examples from basal materials are used to illustrate the application of these procedures.

## BACKGROUND

Basals traditionally use a lesson framework known as the directed reading activity (DRA) to teach the reading selections. The DRA framework as we know it today was described by Betts in 1946 for the purposes of (1) giving teachers a basic format for providing systematic group instruction, (2) improving students' word recognition and comprehension skills, and (3) guiding students through a reading selection. The original DRAS were compiled by Betts in accordance with a set of guidelines recommended by various basal authors for teaching the reading selections, consisting of the following:

1. The group should be prepared, oriented, or made ready for the reading of a selection.
2. The first reading should be guided silent reading.
3. Word recognition skills and comprehension should be developed during the silent reading.
4. A silent or oral second reading should be done for purposes different from those of the first reading.
5. Follow-up on the reading lesson should be differentiated in terms of student needs.

The DRAS used in today's basals have not changed a great deal since Betts's 1946 description. Although there are a number of minor variations, the DRA usually consists of preparatory activities prior to reading, guided reading activities, postreading activities, and follow-up skill work. Preparatory activities often include providing relevant background, creating interest, introducing meanings and/or pronunciations for new vocabulary, and establishing purposes for reading. The guided reading activities often include silent reading focused on answering purpose-setting questions, oral reading and responses to questions dealing with short sections of the text, and/or oral rereading to clarify or verify a point. Postreading activities frequently consist of group discussion and answering general end-of-selection questions. Follow-up activities consist of a variety of skill lessons and practice exercises that may or may not be related to the reading selection.

In evaluating the DRA framework, we need to consider both *what* is being taught and *how* it is taught. With regard to what is being taught, most traditional basal lessons are primarily skill driven; that is, the stated purpose of each lesson is to learn a particular skill (which may or may not be relevant to understanding the reading selection), rather than to learn how to comprehend a particular type of text. Students are often held accountable for their skill learning through practice exercises and end-of-unit or end-of-level skills tests. However, they are rarely held accountable for their comprehension of the reading selection, except through group questioning and discussion.

The skill-driven view of reading instruction implies that skills are static and generalizable across all reading situations; however, skills simply do not operate the same way under all reading conditions. That is why students can pass one test for a skill such as identifying the main idea and fail another. Differences in text type, length, coherence, familiarity, and task requirements often account for differences in readers' performance. Getting an implicit idea from a narrative text is simply not the same thing as getting an explicitly stated idea from a short, unfamiliar expository text. Similarly, picking the best title or copying the topic sentence does not require the same skill level as generating a summary sentence.

As described in the introduction to this book, current research suggests that reading is interactive; that is, readers construct meaning through a dynamic interaction among the reader, the text, and the context of the reading situation. This view suggests that reading is a variable process and that reading instruction should be driven by the predicted interaction among reader factors such as knowledge, skill, experience, and motivation; among text factors such as the type and organization of the material; and among contextual factors such as the purposes, tasks, and settings for the reading. Skills then become a means of achieving the goal of successfully comprehending a variety of texts under a variety of different reading conditions for a variety of purposes, rather than the end in themselves. Thus, our goal is not simply to teach the content of given selections, but to develop an understanding of how to read. Therefore, reading selections should be taught as prototypes of larger classes of text types, and reading lessons need to have both content and process goals.

With regard to *how* skills and content are taught in many basals, research suggests that this is done primarily through indirect means of practice and assessment. Although basal instruction is often thought of as direct instruction, recent reviews suggest that it consists more of indirect practice than of direct modeling or explanation (Durkin, 1981). Current research also suggests that many students learn best when instruction begins with modeling and explanation from a knowledgeable other and then passes through a stage of guided practice, ending at the point where the student can operate independently. Thus, the responsibility for learning has been gradually released by the teacher and assumed by the students (Pearson, 1985).

This model of direct instruction is in sharp contrast to the model that appears in most basal lessons, which focuses on independent student practice. The instruction that most basal lessons direct the teacher to provide frequently consists of asking the students to practice or perform a particular task. For example, in the case of main-idea instruction, the manual often instructs the teacher to place a short paragraph on the board and ask the students to find the main idea. If students do not know what a main idea is or how to find one, then this instruction is not likely to be effective. Similarly, the process of comprehending the text is taught through questioning and discussion, with little initial modeling or explanation. Many students do eventually learn through indirect practice methods; however, many do not, and some are actually misled by the questions and activities provided in basal lessons. Therefore, the method of instruction should provide more direction for students in the acquisition phases of learning.

In summary, current research suggests that we need to teach lessons that are process or text driven, as opposed to skill driven; that we need to have both content and process goals for our instruction; and that our methods need to include more direct instruction. The following sections describe the application of these ideas to the process of teaching the basal lesson.

## PREVIEWING AND PLANNING

Previewing and planning of reading selections and instruction should be done within the context of classroom or school-based curricular and instructional goals. Students at almost every level are asked to read many different types of text in their basals, including fables, myths, realistic fiction, mysteries, fairy tales, historical fiction, poetry, plays, informational selections, and reference materials. It is important to determine whether a particular type of text is consistent with established curricular and instructional goals, to insure consistency within and across grade levels. If teachers proceed from one reading selection to another without knowing how and why a particular reading selection fits, then the materials become the curriculum. Consideration of the importance of the reading selection and its role in instruction refocuses our attention on teaching students how to read a particular type of text for particular purposes, rather than on the traditional instruction of isolated subskills.

### Analyzing Text

It is clear that an analysis of the text is one of the most important steps in planning a basal lesson. This step also represents the greatest change from traditional procedures for lesson preparation. The first step in analyzing the text is to preview the reading selection to determine the type of text and its appropriateness for a given group of students, in relation to a specified set of curricular and instructional goals. This information can be determined by asking questions about the appropriateness of the structure and content of the selection and about the purposes for which this type of text is written and/or read, outside the instructional context. An inappropriate selection should be omitted.

If the selection is appropriate, the next step in the text analysis is mapping the selection (Wixson & Peters, 1987). The primary purpose of mapping is to determine the overall coherence and clarity of a selection by identifying relations among important elements of text information (e.g., story events, characters, concepts). If the text is not clear or is difficult to understand, the mapping process highlights these points at the word, sentence, and whole text or subsection levels. For example, at the word level, the mapping process identifies concepts that are important to comprehending the theme of a story and the appropriate and/or inappropriate use of context in defining or clarifying unfamiliar vocabulary. At the sentence level, mapping identifies clear or confusing use of reference and/or connective terms. At the whole-text or subsection level, it identifies helpful and/or disruptive organizational patterns, notes structural features such as headings and illustrations, and determines how well the various sections of the text are linked together.

Although generic mapping procedures are often recommended and used, it should be noted that there is no one way to map text and that different types of text require different mapping procedures. For example, generic story maps are not suitable for mapping mysteries, science fiction, or historical fiction, because of differences in their literary structures. It should also be noted that a text map need not be complex to be of value. The level of specificity required in text maps varies according to the procedures used and the purposes for reading.

The following sections describe the analysis of two different types of materials, a narrative selection ("The Little Red Hen" [Durr, 1981]) and an informational selection ("The Sea Otter" [Clymer, 1979]) each of which requires a different type of map. To minimize interference from the lesson prepared by the publisher, we have used the selection in the students' reader, rather than the copy in the teacher's manual, and we recommend this practice.

*The Little Red Hen.*   The version of "The Little Red Hen" (LRH) we will be discussing is taken from primer-level materials and is presented in Figure 1.1. The LRH was chosen as a sample text because it is representative of the large proportion of narratives with a thematic focus that are found in basal readers. As you read, think about what you would want your students to learn from and understand about this type of material. Also, ask yourself what type of text it is, and for

**Figure 1.1**   Pupil's Edition of *The Little Red Hen*

---

| | | |
|---|---|---|
| One day the little red hen said, " Come see what I have found! I have some wheat. I am going to plant it." <br><br> (Hen pointing to wheat seeds.)* <br><br><br> 34. | (Animals leaning over the garden wall watching the hen at work.) <br><br> "Then I will plant it myself," said the little red hen. And she did. The wheat grew and grew. It grew into a big plant. <br><br> 35. | "Who will help me plant the wheat?" asked the little red hen. "Not I," said the duck. "Not I," said the cat. "Not I," said the pig. <br><br> (Duck, cat, and pig, looking at the hen.) <br><br><br> 36. |
| "Who will help me cut the wheat?" asked the little red hen. "Not I," said the duck. "Not I," said the cat. "Not I," said the pig. "Then I will cut it myself," said the little red hen. And she did. <br><br> (Duck, cat, and pig looking at the hen cutting wheat.) <br><br> 37. | "I will take the wheat to the mill," said the little red hen. "The mill will make the wheat into flour. Who will help me take the wheat to the mill?" "Not I," said the duck. "Not I," said the cat. "Not I," said the pig." Then I will take it myself," said the little red hen. And she did. <br><br> (Animals watching hen carrying the bag to the mill.) <br><br> 38. | (Animals watching hen pound the wheat.) <br><br> "Who will help me pound the wheat?" asked the little red hen. "Not I," said the duck. "Not I," said the cat. "Not I," said the pig. "Then I will pound it myself," said the little red hen. And she did. <br><br><br> 39. |
| (Animals watching the hen make bread.) <br><br> "I will make the bread with the flour," said the little red hen. "Who will help me make the bread?" "Not I," said the duck. "Not I," said the cat. "Not I," said the pig. "Then I will make the bread myself," said the little red hen. And she did. <br><br> 40. | "Now who will help me eat the bread?" asked the little red hen. "I will," said the duck. "I will," said the cat. "I will," said the pig. <br><br> (Animals sniffing freshly baked bread.) <br><br><br><br> 41. | "Oh no," said the little red hen. "You did not help me plant the wheat. You did not help me cut the wheat. You did not help me pound the wheat. You did not help me take the wheat to the mill. You did not help me make the bread. So you will not help me eat the bread. I will eat it myself." And she did. <br><br> (Animals watching hen eat bread.) <br><br> 42. |

*Information in parentheses describes story illustrations.

what purposes average, middle-class students at the first-grade level would read this type of text, outside of the instructional context.

It is obvious to us as adult, skilled readers that the LRH is a fable. Most of us already know the story, but, even if we did not, we would be able to identify this selection as a fable, based on our knowledge of this type of text (e.g., animals in the role of people, the presence of a lesson or moral). For what purposes are fables written, told, and/or read? No doubt there is more than one reason, but a primary purpose for the writing and telling of fables is to communicate a moral or lesson, and an understanding of the moral is frequently our purpose for reading them.

The next step in the analysis of the LRH is to map it. Our story-mapping procedure begins with the identification of the problem, the conflict, and the resolution. Combining these elements provides the basis for generating the theme of the story at two levels of abstraction, the moral and the main idea. The main idea refers to specific events in the story, and the moral is more generalized. Once these components of the story map are in place, we can proceed to list the major events of the story essential to developing the themes. The final categories of the map are the importance of the setting to the themes and the traits and functions of the major characters in the story. A complete map of the LRH is provided in Figure 1.2. As you examine the map, notice how it highlights the important elements of the fable in relation to an understanding of the moral. Information that is not important to comprehending the moral has been omitted.

The completed map is then used in conjunction with the actual text, as the basis for further analyses of the selection at the whole-text, sentence, and word levels. The LRH has two obvious strengths at the whole-text level. First, both temporal sequence and cause and effect are used to organize the information, although the latter is not as clearly signaled as the former. Second, the text is very repetitive and thus predictable, thereby assisting young readers with both comprehension and word recognition. This makes it possible for them to discern clearly the important elements of information in the fable, such as the problem and its resolution.

At the sentence level, we need to identify strengths and weaknesses of the LRH in the use of connective ties and terms of reference. Our analysis suggests that there may be a problem of reference, because the little red hen often refers to the wheat as "it" throughout the text. The first time, she is referring to seeds, the second and third times she is referring to the plant, and the fourth time she is referring to the crushed grain. Students may not understand exactly what is

**Figure 1.2**  Story Map of *The Little Red Hen*

---

Theme (Moral):     If you want rewards, you must work for them.

Theme:             The animals did not help the little red hen
(Main Idea)        make the bread, so they did not get to eat it.

Problem:           The hen needs help planting and harvesting the
                   wheat, and making the bread.

Conflict:          The animals want to eat but don't want to help.

Resolution:        The hen makes and eats the bread by herself.

Setting:           Not essential to the theme.

Major Characters:

  Little Red Hen: Traits--dedicated, fair, persistent.
                  Function--to challenge the other animals.
  The animals:    Traits--lazy, selfish, inconsiderate.
                  Function--to test the hen's commitment to her goal.

Major Events:

      The little red hen finds seeds.
      The hen asks animals to help plant the seeds, cut the wheat,
      pound the wheat, take the wheat to the mill, and make the bread.
      The animals refuse each request, so the hen does it herself.
      The hen asks, "Now who will help me eat the bread?"
      The animals say they will help.
      The hen refuses their help, and eats the bread herself.

---

being referred to in each instance. On the plus side, the connectives *then* and *now* are used clearly to indicate the sequence of events.

At the word level, teachers should select both implied and explicitly stated key concepts, on the basis of the themes of a story and in relation to their knowledge about the background information of their students. Key concepts in the LRH include *wheat, plant, cut, pound, mill,* and *flour.* Students may not know what *wheat* is, how it grows, or its uses. Similarly, students may not understand the two meanings of *plant* that are used in this text. Students may also have difficulty with the specific definitions of *cut* and *pound* as they are used in this selection. In addition, students need to understand the meanings of *mill* and *flour* in this text.

Key concepts that are important for understanding the moral also must be included (e.g., *reward, lazy*). These concepts typically are omitted, because they are not directly mentioned in the text, despite their overall importance. However, by examining the map it becomes clear that, without the knowledge of these concepts, one may not be able to construct the moral of the fable.

*The Sea Otter.*   Our analysis of "The Sea Otter" (TSO) begins with a reading of the student version of this second-grade text, which is shown in Figure 1.3. Once again, we need to ask ourselves about the type of text this is, the purposes for which our students would read this type of text outside of reading instruction, and what we would want our students to learn about this type of reading. Our analysis reveals that the TSO is an informational text similar to those found in natural science trade books or textbooks written for students at this grade level. Among the purposes for which this text might be read is to learn something about the habits and behaviors of the sea otter. In addition, we would want our students to understand the differences between the characteristics and uses of this type of text and stories such as the LRH.

As we begin our mapping of the TSO, it is important to note that our procedures will change from those we used with the LRH. This is due to the differences between narrative and informational materials. The procedure we use for mapping informational materials focuses on the identification of important concepts and the relations among them (Peters & Hayes, in press). The concept map also arranges the ideas hierarchically, in order of importance—central purpose, major ideas, and supporting ideas. Concept maps are used to determine the appropriateness of an informational text by depicting the quality of the text organization, the types of organizational patterns used, and the hierarchical arrangement of the ideas within the selection.

Concept mapping begins with the identification of major concepts within the text, through reading and an examination of important text features such as headings and photographs. These concepts are then arranged hierarchically to form the first two levels of the concept map—central purpose(s) and major ideas. Then the map is expanded to include a third level of information—supporting ideas. Relations between concepts are highlighted by adding relational links specifying how the concepts are connected. The more clearly orga-

**Figure 1.3**   Pupil's Edition of *The Sea Otter*

| | | |
|---|---|---|
| (A sea otter swimming under water.)* <br><br> The sun comes up.  A hungry otter dives deep into the sea to look for her food.   Down she goes- down- down. <br><br> 115 | She catches a fish and swims up with it.  Up- up through the water. <br><br> The otter floats on her back.  And she eats her fill. <br><br> (A sea otter floating on her back eating a fish.) <br><br> 116 | (A sea otter swimming up to the surface.) <br><br> The otter dives again, but this time she is not looking for food.  She wants to find something to play with.   She finds a little rock, and she swims up through the sea again. Up-up through the green water.            117 |
| (A sea otter flipping a rock into the air.) <br><br> She flips the rock into the air and she catches it.   And if she drops it, down she goes after it, and she finds it and comes up again.  The game goes on and on.  And when at last, she is through with the rock, she lets it fall into the sea.  And she plays with the otters in the herd.   118 | They jump up from the water, high into the air. They flip over and over. They jump again. All day long, the otter plays and looks for food and plays again.  Now she dives and she finds a clam. <br><br> (A sea otter diving down to get a rock.) <br><br> 119 | The otter swims up with the clam in one front paw, and a rock in the other paw. <br><br> (A sea otter floating on her back with a rock on her stomach and a clam in her  paw.) <br><br> She floats on her  back, and she puts the rock on her stomach.            120 |
| (A sea otter eating the clam she has broken open with a rock.) <br><br> She hits the clam against the rock, and she eats bits of good food. A bit of clam shell falls on her stomach. And the otter flips over and over, and washes her stomach in the sea. <br> 121 | Night comes, and the sea otter swims to a bed of seaweed.   She pulls the seaweed around her. <br><br> (A sea otter floating on her  back in seaweed.) <br><br><br> 122 | She floats there on her back with seaweed for her bed.  She rocks with the tide, and she sleeps. <br><br> (A sea otter floating on her  back in seaweed.) <br><br><br> 123 |

\* Information in parentheses describes the photographs in the text.

nized the text, the more coherent the concept map. If the relation between two concepts is not clear, a link cannot be established.

The concept map for the TSO is presented in Figure 1.4. An examination of this map reveals that the TSO is a well-organized text. This can be seen by looking at how clearly the ideas are linked together. Each concept is connected by a linking concept which appears in

**Figure 1.4** Concept Map of *The Sea Otter*

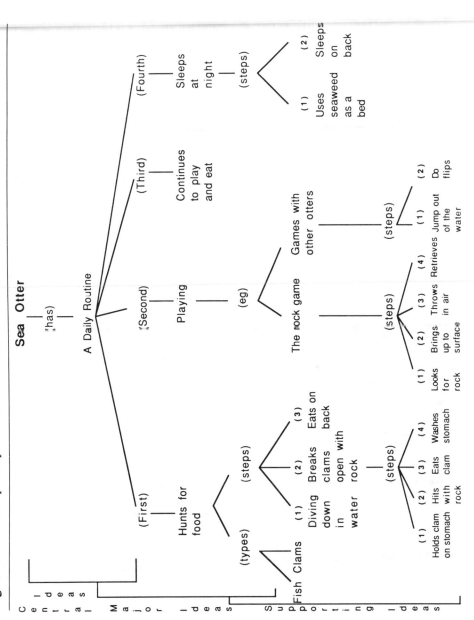

parentheses (e.g., *first, types, steps*). The links also indicate that the primary organizational structure of the TSO is temporal sequence, that is, the otter's first, second, third (and so forth) daily activities. This is a significant feature of this text, because it provides a structure that is readily interpretable by most students. In addition, there is a series of steps involved in each of the sea otter's daily activities, and these sequences provide a secondary level of temporal organization within "The Sea Otter."

The concept map also reveals a clear, consistent hierarchical relationship among the three levels of information in the TSO. The central purpose is the daily routine of the sea otter; the major ideas are the sequences of activities the sea otter engages in during one day (e.g., hunting, eating, playing, and sleeping); and the supporting ideas are the series of steps the sea otter goes through while hunting, eating, playing, and sleeping.

The features of the TSO that are noteworthy at the sentence level include the presence of several sentence fragments (e.g., "Up—up through the water"). There also is an excessive use of *and* and *both*, at the beginnings of sentences and as a connective. Given the organization of the material, better use could have been made of connectives such as *then, next, after,* and *before.*

At the word level, there are several key concepts in the TSO that may be unfamiliar and difficult to understand from context. They are *herd, clam,* and *wave. Routine* is another key concept that appears on the map and is important to understanding the central purpose, although it does not appear directly in the text itself. In addition, it is important to note that *rock* has two meanings in this text.

### Establishing Goals

The information obtained from the text analysis is used to establish content and process goals that are appropriate for the selections and consistent with your curricular and instructional goals. Content goals refer to what you want students to understand and/or learn about the specific content of the selection. Process goals have two components: *knowledge* about a specific type of reading and its relevant skills and *application* of this knowledge to the specific selection. Knowledge goals should reflect what you want students to learn about the particular type of reading, and application goals should reflect how you want students to apply this knowledge to a specific reading selection.

*The Little Red Hen.* Our text analysis established that the LRH is a fable and that fables are often read to communicate a moral. Therefore, our content and process goals must focus on (1) knowledge about fables and how identifying cause-and-effect relationships aids in understanding morals and (2) the application of this knowledge to the LRH. The following are the process and content goals for our revised LRH lesson:

A. Process Goals
   1. Knowledge
      a. To understand characteristics of fables, including that they teach a moral, that they were originally oral tales, and that they frequently have animals play the roles of people
      b. To develop awareness that fables often describe cause-and-effect relationships, and that linking these events together can help identify the moral of the fable
   2. Application
      a. To understand and describe LRH as an example of a fable (e.g., animals play the roles of people; it tells a lesson)
      b. To practice identifying cause-and-effect relationships as an aid to understanding the lesson of the LRH
B. Content Goals
   1. To understand how the animals' unwillingness to help the LRH caused her to do everything by herself (effect), including eating the bread
   2. To understand the moral of the LRH, namely, that you must share in the work if you wish to share in the rewards

The knowledge goals focus on knowledge both about the characteristics of fables and about cause-and-effect relationships, a skill that is relevant to understanding the moral in many fables. The application goals focus on knowledge about the characteristics of fables and the role causal relationships play in understanding the LRH. The content goals focus on the information that is important to the holistic interpretation of the fable, that is, the information that appears on the story map.

*The Sea Otter.* Our text analysis established that the TSO is a natural science selection, whose central purpose is to describe the daily routine of a sea otter. Therefore, our content and process goals must focus on knowledge about natural science texts and how a sequential organization aids understanding, and on the application of this knowledge to the TSO. The following are the process and content goals for our revised "Sea Otter" lesson:

A. Process Goals
   1. Knowledge
      a. To understand the properties of nonfictional natural science texts (e.g., describe real objects and events, use more photographs and charts than fictional materials, may use headings and subheadings), and when, why, and how we read them.
      b. To increase awareness that an organizational pattern such as temporal sequence can exist at different levels within this type of text.
      c. To understand how to identify different levels of temporal sequence and how they can help readers understand and remember important ideas in text
   2. Application
      a. To understand the TSO as an example of nonfictional natural science text and how it uses photographs to support the major ideas of the selection
      b. To apply knowledge about text organization to identify the different levels of sequential organization in the text
B. Content Goals
   1. To understand that the major sequence of events in the daily routine of a sea otter is hunting, playing, and sleeping
   2. To understand how the sequence of events within an individual activity (e.g., hunting consists of diving, breaking clam open, then eating) contributes to understanding the habits of a sea otter
   3. To understand what these sequences of events indicate about the intelligence of the sea otter

The knowledge goals indicate that students need to develop further their understanding of why it is important to read this type of material, how material like this is organized, and the types of strategies they would use in reading the selection. The application goals focus on how to identify the different levels of sequential organization that appear in the text and their importance to understanding content. The content goals focus on the specific information about sea otters in the text. The purpose is not merely to learn a lot of details about sea otters, but to understand how the various daily activities reveal certain behavioral characteristics about sea otters, such as that they are very smart animals. These goals place the emphasis on the integration of information to form the central purpose of the text, rather than the understanding of a series of isolated facts.

## EVALUATING AND MODIFYING THE EXISTING LESSON

The existing lesson in the teacher's manual should be evaluated and modified, when necessary, to make it consistent with the established content and process goals. In evaluating and modifying the lesson, we need to be concerned with both what is taught and how it is taught. The methods of instruction should reflect current research and theory, which suggest that the acquisition phase of learning be characterized by teacher direction in the form of modeling and teacher explanation. As students become increasingly knowledgeable and proficient, the responsibility for learning is gradually shifted from the teacher to the students. This is accomplished through an intermediary stage of guided practice, which is gradually phased out, to the point where students are ready to assume primary responsibility for their own learning, through independent practice. Most current basals appear to be stuck at the practice end of this continuum, providing for only minimal direct instruction. Although the newest basals are incorporating more teacher explanation and modeling, it is important to be aware that too much modeling when students are ready to take some responsibility for their own learning is no better than too much practice when students need more teacher guidance. The decision about the appropriate level of instruction must be made by the teacher in relation to the knowledge and skill of the students and the demands of the reading situation.

This section emphasizes the evaluation and modification of the first three parts of the DRA: preparation for reading, guided reading, and postreading. Since seatwork is discussed in more detail in chapter 3, this part of the DRA is addressed only briefly.

### Preparation for Reading

Our major concern is that the prereading activities prepare students for the type of reading that is assumed in our goal statements. This means that we would expect to see instruction that informs students about the type of text they are asked to read and its properties, the purposes for which it might be read, and the strategies for reading it. In addition, there might be activities related to the particular skills and strategies relevant to this type of reading, although these may also be placed at the end instead of the beginning of the lesson.

In preparing students for reading a specific selection, we would focus on information and/or activities that activate or build the meaning of key concepts, not simply instruction in how to decode difficult or phonetically regular words. We would also expect information or activities designed to provide background information and set purposes for reading. These concerns become the criteria by which we evaluate the prereading activities in both "The Little Red Hen" and "The Sea Otter."

*The Little Red Hen.* In Figure 1.5 are shown, side by side, the original preparatory section of the teacher's manual lesson for the LRH and the revised lesson plan. The prereading phase of the original teacher's manual lesson for the LRH is divided into sections entitled "Summary," "Introducing New Words," and "Setting the Scene." The "Summary" section emphasizes that the LRH is a fable and identifies its moral. Although this information is consistent with some portions of our text analysis and the goals we established for teaching the LRH, it does not provide any information about important elements of the fable, such as character traits, the problem, conflict, or resolution. There is also no background information about fables and why they are written and/or read.

The "Introducing New Words" section focuses exclusively on decoding new words and does not activate or build knowledge of key concepts. This section needs considerable revision to be consistent with our goals. Although we agree that new and important words should be introduced, this should be done in a context that is consistent with the fable. In addition, the criteria for determining which words to include in this section must be expanded. As the text analysis indicated, important concepts that are implied in the moral and appear on the story map are also essential. For this reason, the words *reward* and *lazy* have been added to the "Key Concepts" section of the revised lesson. The emphasis here is on activating and building knowledge of key concepts, rather than decoding unfamiliar words. In the revised lesson, students are helped to understand the specific meanings of words such as *wheat* and *pound* as they are used in the LRH. They are also helped to understand the two different meanings of the word *plant* used in this fable.

The "Setting the Scene" section of the original lesson suggests that the LRH is about making bread. This is not consistent with either

(*text continues on p. 40*)

**Figure 1.5** Original and Revised Preparation Activities for *The Little Red Hen* Lesson

| Original Lesson | SKILLS | Revised Lesson |
|---|---|---|
| UNIT 5<br>THE LITTLE RED HEN | N Noting Correct<br>  Sequence<br>R Clusters<br>  fr,  br,   gr | **Objectives for the Little Red Hen**<br><br>**Process Goals** |
| **Spring Planting** | | *Knowledge* |
| **Summary** | NEW WORDS | a. Understand characteris-tics of fables including that |
| For generations young chil-dren have been fascinated by the old folk tale "The Little Red Hen."  Today's young children will be no less delighted to read this story of the plucky Little Red Hen who shows her lazy barnyard friends that she cannot only plant, harvest, and process the wheat in order to make bread; she is quite capable of eating the bread by herself as well. The age-old theme that, "If one wants to eat, one must work," is beautifully portrayed in this old tale. | HIGH - FRE-QUENCY WORDS: plant, who, my-self, into, cut, pound, eat, so<br>STORY WORDS: hen, wheat, duck, grew, mill, flour, bread<br><br>RESOURCES<br><br>= BASIC<br>Sunshine:    pages 33-43<br>Practice    Book: pages 15, 16, 17, and 18 (word rec-ognition test) | they teach a moral or lesson, were originally oral tales, and frequently have animals play the role of people.<br><br>b. Awareness that fables often describe a series of cause and effect relations that can help identify the moral of the fable.<br><br>*Application* |
| **READING THE SELECTION**<br><br>**Introducing New Words**<br><br>The story you will read to-day is about a little red hen and some things she did. Before you begin reading, let's look at some words that may be new to you.<br><br>TEACHER'S NOTE | = OPTIONAL<br>Instruction Charts: Unit 5<br>Assessment: Forms A, B<br>Noting    Correct Sequence<br>Reading    Bonus: Unit 5<br>Language    Bonus: Unit 5 | a. Understand and describe LRH as an example of a fable (e.g. animals play the role of people, it has a moral or a lesson).<br>b. Practice identifying cause and effect relation-ships as an aid to under-standing the moral of the LRH.<br><br>**Content Goals**<br><br>Understand the animals' unwillingness to help the LRH caused her to do |
| If children are to become skilled readers, they must develop, as soon as possible, the ability to independ-ently decode new words as they meet those words in their reading.  Therefore, we recommend that from this point on, children reading *Sunshine* be given the op-portunity to decode most new words independently as they meet them in the closely directed first reading of the remaining stories in this book.  At this point, most children should have a sufficient number of words in their instant-recognition vocabulary to enable them to use context together with well known letter-sound as-sociations to decode words unfamiliar in their printed form.  However, for words that exhibit letter-sound irregularities or that appear in relatively weak context, introduction before the reading of the selec-tion continues to be recommended. | | everything by herself (effect), including eating the bread.<br><br>Understand the moral of the LRH--i.e., you must share in the work if you wish to share in the rewards. |

**Figure 1.5** (*continued*)

| Original Lesson | Revised Lesson |
|---|---|
| Setting the Scene | Setting the Scene |

Setting the Scene

The story that you are going to read today tells about making bread. Have any of you ever watched someone making bread? Discuss with the children their various experiences with bread making.

One thing that you need when you make bread is flour. There are many kinds of flour. How many of you have seen flour before?...What does it look like?...(powdery; grainy; white; yellow; light brown; answers will vary depending on children's individual experiences) Some flour is made from wheat. Wheat seeds are crushed and made into flour by machines in a place called a mill.

In this story the Little Red Hen takes some wheat to the mill. Open your books to page 33.

**Page 33**
Here is the title of the story. Read the title to yourself ....Who will read it aloud? ...Who do you see in the picture on this page?... (a hen, a duck, a cat, and a pig) Turn to page 34 and let's begin the story.

The Little
Red Hen

(Illustration of a pig, duck, cat, and hen on a farm.) *

33

* Information in parentheses describes story illustrations.

Revised Lesson

Setting the Scene

1. Introduce the concept of a fable as a make-believe story that teaches a lesson or moral. Discuss the features of a fable (e.g., "old," animals talk, passed down from generation to generation) and how these features can be used to understand it.

2. Have students give you examples of a lesson or moral. If they cannot provide examples, list several for them on the board. Discuss the critical features of a moral, i.e., it establishes a "rule" for what is right or what is wrong. If students provide statements that do not qualify as morals, state why they are non-examples. Discuss how the moral forms the basis for writing and reading fables.

3. Explain to the children that fables often describe a series of cause and effect relations that help them understand the moral. Put a series of cause and effect statements from other familiar fables on the board (e.g., "Boy Who Cried Wolf"), and ask children to identify the causes and effects. Put the moral(s) on the board and ask students to explain how they relate to the cause-effect statements.

4. Tell the children to look at the title page of the LRH. Ask if they know this fable. Discuss with them whether it is easier or harder to understand a story if they already know it and then tell why. Ask the students to identify the characters from the title and the pictures.

**Figure 1.5** (*continued*)

| Original Lesson | Revised Lesson |
|---|---|
| For teachers working with children who appear to need the additional support of having *all* new words introduced before story reading, context sentences are provided beginning on page 234 of this guide.<br><br>See pages 5-8 for model.<br><br>**> wheat**<br>Print: The pig wants some lunch.<br>It wants wheat for lunch.<br>Checking words: corn *(wrong sounds)*<br>white *(no sense)*<br><br>**> who**<br>Print: I need some help.<br>Tell me who will help.<br>Say: In this word the *w* and *h* together stand for the sound for *h* .<br>Checking words: somebody *(wrong sounds)*<br>hay *(no sense)*<br><br>**> myself**<br>Print: I do not want you to help me.<br>I'll do this myself.<br>Checking words: alone *(wrong sounds)*<br>mice *(no sense)*<br><br>**> grew**<br>Print: Look at my dog.<br>See how big she grew.<br>Checking words: became *(wrong sounds)*<br>gray *(no sense)*<br><br>**> pound**<br>Print: I don't want this box to open.<br>I'll have to pound on it.<br>Checking words: step *(wrong sounds)*<br>pond *(no sense)*<br><br>**> flour**<br>Print: Father will make that.<br>All he needs is some flour.<br>Checking words: dough *(wrong sounds)*<br>floor *(no sense)*<br><br>**> bread**<br>Print: Maria will have lunch now.<br>She wants some bread.<br>Checking words: soup *(wrong sounds)*<br>braid *(no sense)*<br><br>If you prefer to introduce all the new words in advance of the reading, see guide page 234 or the pages for Teaching Unit 5 in the Instruction Charts. | **Activate/Build Key Concepts**<br><br>**> wheat**<br>Wheat is grown by farmers and can be used to bake bread.<br>Students should understand that it is a grain; it comes from seeds; when a seed is planted, it grows into a tall grass-like plant; it is used for different things (i.e. cereal, flour, bread).<br><br>**> plant**<br>We planted the seeds in the ground. Wheat is a type of plant.<br>Students should understand the 2 meanings of this word being used in this fable-to bury something in the ground and the name for things that live and grow (i.e. grasses, etc.)<br><br>**> reward**<br>The boy received a reward for finding the lost dog.<br>Students should understand that a reward is something you receive for doing a good deed.<br><br>**> lazy**<br>The boy did not get to play because he was lazy and did not help his father pick up the toys.<br>Students should understand that being lazy can have undesirable effects.<br><br>**> cut**<br>The child cut his finger with the knife. The farmer cut the plants in the field.<br>Students should be made aware of the different meanings of this word within various contexts.<br><br>**> pound**<br>My sister uses a hammer to pound the nail into the wall. The Indians pound the grain into cornmeal.<br>Students should be made aware of the different meanings of this word within various contexts.<br><br>**> mill and flour**<br>They took the wheat to the mill to be ground into flour.<br>Information about these terms under "Setting the Scene" can be presented here. |

the summary information or our text analysis and lesson goals. To suggest that one should read the LRH for the purpose of learning how to make bread is absurd. If we want someone to read a text that teaches them how to make bread, we would have them read a cookbook, not a fable. The stated purpose is entirely inconsistent with the purposes for which fables are created, told, or read outside of the instructional context. Therefore, we will need to alter the purpose-setting section to include information about fables.

The revised purpose-setting activities are designed to provide students with the type of knowledge required to comprehend the moral of a fable. These activities introduce the concept of a fable, define a moral, illustrate how the series of cause-and-effect relationships often found in fables aids in understanding the moral, and establish purpose-setting questions for the LRH. All of these activities are directly related to our content and process goals. This approach is in sharp contrast to the activities in the original teacher's manual lesson, which have very little to do with the type of knowledge needed to comprehend a fable.

*The Sea Otter.* The original and revised lessons for "The Sea Otter" are juxtaposed in Figure 1.6. The original preparation activities fall into sections entitled "Vocabulary," "Background Information," "Introducing Vocabulary," and "Setting Reading Purpose." The "Vocabulary" section consists of the basic, enrichment, and decodable words. As the concept map in our text analysis section reveals, only *otter* is important to understanding the central purpose of the selection. The other words listed are less important and are primarily related to the supporting ideas. The "Background Information" section of the original lesson gives an informative overview of the habits and interests of the sea otter but offers no suggestions for how this information might be used by the teacher.

The "Introducing Vocabulary" section presents the words from the vocabulary section in sentence contexts that are consistent with the selection. Additional words are written on the board for students to read and put in sentences. Although this is a good instructional technique, most of the words, as was noted previously, are relatively unimportant. Furthermore, the three questions highlighted in this section focus on isolated information, rather than providing guidance for understanding the central purpose of the selection. The revised lesson, by contrast, refocuses students' attention on an understanding of the key concepts that appear on the concept map and are important to identifying the central purpose. Some of these concepts come

(*text continues on p. 44*)

**Figure 1.6** Original and Revised Preparation Activities for *The Sea Otter* Lesson

| Original Lesson | Revised Lesson |
|---|---|
| **THE SEA OTTER**<br>pages 115-123 | **THE SEA OTTER**<br>PREPARATION FOR READING<br>**VOCABULARY** sea otter, routine, herd, rock |
| Skilpak pages 62-67<br>Studybook pages 48-50 | **PROCESS GOALS**<br>Knowledge |
| **INFORMATION FOR THE TEACHER** | a. Understand the properties of nonfictional natural science text (e.g., describes real objects and events, uses more photographs and charts than fictional materials, may use headings and subheadings), and when, why, and how we read them. |
| **VOCABULARY** | |
| *Basic*<br>otter    floats    clam | b. Increase awareness that an organizational pattern such as temporal sequence can exist at different levels within this type of text. |
| *Enrichment*<br>pulls | |
| *Decodable*<br>(words to be read independently) | c. Understand how to identify different levels of temporal sequence and how they can help readers understand and remember important ideas in text. |
| washes    seaweed    sea    tide    shell | Application |
| **BACKGROUND INFORMATION** | a. Understand why The Sea Otter as an example of nonfictional natural science text (e.g., describes real events, uses photographs). |
| The sea otter inhabits the rocky shores of the North Pacific from California across the Bering Strait into Russia. Living in groups, the otter spends nearly all of its life in the water never more than a mile from shore. Here in the kelp beds are all the elements for an enviable life; plenty of food, a floating bed of spongy kelp, and an endless playground of caves and tunnels. Quite resourceful animals, sea otters belong to that small and select group of mammals that employ tools in obtaining and opening their food. Eating up to one-fifth of their body weight in shellfish, octopi, and sea urchins keeps them diving as deep as 180 feet in the search for food. When they surface, they hammer the hard shell of their shellfish prize against a rock balanced on their chest until the shell breaks. Sea otters bear one pup each year. When mature they may reach a length of 4 feet and a weight of 80 pounds, and lead a comfortable life eating and sleeping floating on their backs. | b. Apply knowledge about text organization to identify the different levels of sequential organization in The Sea Otter.<br><br>**CONTENT GOALS**<br><br>Understand that the major sequence of events in the daily routine of a sea otter is hunting, playing, and sleeping.<br><br>Identify the sequence of events within each of the sea otter's activities (e.g., hunting consists of diving, breaking clam open, then eating).<br><br>Understand what these sequences of events indicate about the sea otter's habits and intelligence. |

**Figure 1.6** *(continued)*

| Original Lesson | Revised Lesson |
|---|---|
| INTRODUCING VOCABULARY | INTRODUCING VOCABULARY |
| Write the title "The Sea Otter" on the chalkboard. Have the children turn to the selection in their text and examine the photographs. Lead them to note that the sea otter is an animal that lives in the water. Have children suggest what sea otters might eat. Also, ask them to tell anything they may know about this animal. Then write the following questions on the chalkboard: | Write each sentence on the board and have students determine the meaning of the underlined word. |
| What does the *sea otter* do with a *clam shell*? | **The sea otter is an animal that lives by the rocky shores of the North Pacific Ocean.** Teachers should make sure that students understand the characteristics of a sea otter. Once they have read the word in context, have them look at the photographs in the book. See how much additional information they can contribute. |
| What can the sea otter do when it *floats* on its back? | |
| Why does the sea otter pull *seaweed* around itself? | **The sea otter has a daily routine. She swims, eats, plays and sleeps.** Students should understand that the sea otter is a creature of habits and that she engages in a similar set of activities each day. |
| Ask the children to read each question on the chalkboard silently, then aloud. If necessary, help them with unknown words. Compare *clam* with the known word *class*, *float* with the known word *fly* and *pull* with the known word *put*. Have the questions reread aloud. Tell the children they may find answers to these questions as they read the story. Keep the questions on the chalkboard for later reference. Write *washes* and *tide* on the chalkboard and let pupils read the words and use them in sentences. If pupils live near the ocean, guide them to use *tide* in a context referring to the rise and fall of the ocean. If children are unfamiliar with this phenomenon, a simple explanation will be necessary. | **The sea otter lives in a herd with many other otters.** Students should understand that certain types of animals live in herds. The sea otter is one of them. |
| | **The sea otter uses the rock as a tool.** Students should understand that rock has more than one meaning. See if they can tell you the other meaning of the word. |

**Figure 1.6** (*continued*)

| Original Lesson | Revised Lesson |
|---|---|
| **SETTING READING PURPOSE** | **SETTING READING PURPOSE** |
| Have pupils tell what they know about animals that live in the ocean such as seals, penguins, dolphins, clams, lobsters, crabs.<br><br>Ask pupils to read the story to find facts about the sea otter as well as looking for answers to the questions listed on the chalkboard during *Introducing Vocabulary*. | 1. Ask students what they think the daily routine of such animals as seals, penguins, and dolphins might be. Ask them to compare it to the daily routine of a sea otter. Ask how they think the behaviors are examples of intelligent behaviors.<br><br>2. Ask students to predict how information that describes a daily routine of a sea animal might be presented or organized. As students give this information, help them connect words such as first, second, next, then, finally with the concept of routine.<br><br>3. Have students write/talk about their daily routine. What do they notice about how they describe their daily routines? Do they use any connectives, e.g., first, second, next, then, finally? If so, see if they know why they are used to describe an order in which we do things.<br><br>4. Have them predict what they believe the daily routine of a sea otter might be. Place their predictions on the board and group into categories, e.g., eating, playing, sleeping. Ask them to read to confirm their predictions. |

directly from the text (e.g., *herd* and *rock*), while others are implied (e.g., *routine*).

The "Setting Reading Purpose" section of the original lesson does provide for some activation of prior knowledge about sea animals in general, and sea otters in particular. It also provides for multiple reading goals, although these are not entirely consistent with the important information identified in our concept map. Finally, as with the original LRH lesson, there is no provision here for helping students understand the nature of the text they are reading or the skills that are likely to aid them in understanding the central purpose of this type of selection.

The purpose of our revised preparatory activities is to activate and build prior knowledge about the content of the selection, its structure, and the skills needed to comprehend it. The first activity in our "Setting Reading Purpose" section asks students to think about what type of daily routine animals such as penguins, dolphins, and seals go through and to predict what a sea otter might do under similar conditions, rather than focusing on general information about the sea otter and other sea animals. The second activity is designed to get students to speculate about how material that is organized around daily routines might be structured.

The third activity helps the students use their own personal experiences to identify the words that can signal temporal sequence. The fourth activity requires students to make predictions about what they believe the daily routine of a sea otter might be. The predictions are then placed into categories that correspond to daily routines such as eating, playing, and sleeping. Students are asked to confirm their predictions as they read. Finally, students are presented with two purpose-setting questions that focus their attention on the central purpose of the selection. As you can see, all of these activities are consistent with our goals.

### Guided Reading

The next step is to examine the guided reading activities of the original lessons, and evaluate them in light of our revisions. We will focus on the extent to which the activities and questions in this part of the lesson are related to helping students attain content and process goals. To attain these goals, they must both guide students in the acquisition of important information identified in the text analysis and promote an awareness of the type of text they are reading and the skills needed to comprehend it. As a general guideline, activities and questions that are not directly related to content and process goals should be omitted or replaced. Similarly, activities and questions related to goals not addressed by the original lesson should be added. The following sections describe this process of evaluation and modification.

   *The Little Red Hen.*   The guided reading materials for the original LRH lesson consist of a series of "Motivation and Silent Reading" questions to be asked prior to reading and a series of "Checking and Developing Comprehension" questions to be asked following the reading of every one or two pages of the children's text (see Figure 1.7). Starting with the first section of guided reading questions, which focuses on pages 34–35 of the text, we find that many of the questions are relevant either to the important context or the process of deriving meaning from these pages. However, some additions are necessary to help clarify potential areas of confusion identified in our text analysis and to focus students' attention on important information. For example, instead of asking students, What do you do with seeds? we might ask, What kind of seeds do you think they are? and, What do you think the hen will do with them? Similarly, we would want to add questions that focus students' attention on the motivation behind different characters' actions, such as, Why didn't the other animals help the little red hen?
   The motivation questions for the second part of the guided reading (pp. 36–37 of the text) ask the students to draw information from the illustrations. This section might also be expanded to capitalize on the repetitive nature of this text by asking, What do you think the little red hen will ask the other animals? and, What do you think the animals will say? In the comprehension check, we would want to highlight the cause-and-effect relationships in the text by asking students why the LRH planted the wheat seeds (and later cut the wheat plant) by herself, and by discussing these events as examples of cause-and-effect relationships. Again, we would want to clarify any potentially confusing information in the text as revealed by our text analysis. Therefore, we might review the multiple meanings of the word *plant* by asking, Which meaning of *plant* is used on page 36?
   Modifications of the remaining sections of the guided reading (pp. 38–39, 40–41, and 42 of the text) should continue those established in the first two sections. Specifically, during the motivation part, students should be asked what they think the little red hen will say and how they think the animals will respond. During the comprehension check, cause-and-effect relationships should be emphasized

(*text continues on p. 51*)

**Figure 1.7**   Original and Revised Guided Reading Activities for *The Little Red Hen* Lesson

### Original Lesson

One day the little red hen said," "Come see what I have found! I have some wheat. I am going to plant it."

(Hen pointing to wheat seeds.)
34

"Who will help me plant the wheat?" asked the little red hen. "Not I," said the duck. "Not I," said the cat. "Not I," said the pig.

(Duck, cat, and pig, looking at the hen.)
35

#### Pages 34-35

#### Motivation and Silent Reading

Look at the pictures on pages 34 and 35. Can you tell what the hen is pointing to?... (some seeds) What do you do with seeds?... (plant them; eat them) If necessary, explain to children that some plants have seeds. If the seeds are planted, new plants will grow.

Who is the hen talking with? (the duck, the cat, and the pig) Hold up a book and point to the quotation marks. Who can remember what we call these marks?... What are quotation marks used for?... (They show the exact words that someone said.)

Read pages 34 and 35 to yourself and find out what happens to the little red hen.

#### Checking and Developing Comprehension

What did the little red hen find?...(some wheat) Who will read aloud the words on page 34 that tell us what the little red hen found?

What was the little red hen going to do with the wheat?... (plant it)

Who do you think the hen was talking to when she said, "Come see what I have found."... (the duck, the cat, and the pig)

What did the little red hen ask the other animals to do?... (help her plant the wheat) Who will read aloud the sentence on page 35 that tells that? If the words asked the little red hen are not read, point out that this is a part of the sentence. Remind children that when a sentence is long, it goes onto the next line.

When Little Red Hen asked for help, how many animals answered her? (three) What did they all say? ("Not I.") What did they mean when they said "Not I"?... (They would not help).

Let's read these two pages aloud. Who spoke on page 34?... (hen) Who spoke on page 35?... (the hen, the duck, the cat, and the pig) Have one child read aloud page 35 and another page 35.

Since the duck, the cat, and the pig would not help the hen plant the wheat, what do you think she will do?... (Accept any reasonable answer.) Let's turn to page 36 now.

### Revised Lesson

#### Pages 34-35

#### Motivation and Silent Reading

Look at the pictures on pages 34 and 35. Can you tell what the hen is pointing to? **What kind of seeds do you think they are? What do you think the hen will do with the seeds?** * Read pages 34 and 35 to yourself and find out what happens to the little red hen.

#### Checking and Developing Comprehension

What did the little red hen find? Who will read aloud the words on page 34 that tell us what the little red hen found?

What was the little red hen going to do with the seeds? **Which meaning of plant is this?**

**Why do you think the LRH planted the seeds?**

What did the little red hen ask the other animals to do? Who will read aloud the sentence on page 35 that tells that?

What did the animals say when the LRH asked for help? What did they mean when they said "Not I"?

**Why didn't the other animals help the little red hen?**

Since the duck, the cat, and the pig would not help the hen plant the wheat, what do you think she will do?

Let's turn to page 36 now.

* New questions appear in bold type.

46

**Figure 1.7** (*continued*)

| Original Lesson | | Revised Lesson |
|---|---|---|
| | | **Pages 36-37** |

<table>
<tr><td colspan="2">

(Animals leaning over the garden wall watching the hen at work.)

"Then I will plant it myself," said the little red hen. And she did. The wheat grew and grew. It grew into a big plant.

36
</td><td>

"Who will help me cut the wheat?" asked the little red hen. "Not I," said the duck. "Not I," said the cat. "Not I," said the pig. "Then I will cut it myself, "said the little red hen. And she did.

(Duck, cat, and pig looking at the hen cutting wheat.)

37
</td></tr>
</table>

**Motivation and Silent Reading**

Look at the picture on page 36. What do you think the little red hen is doing?

On page 37 what has happened to the seeds?

What is the little red hen doing to the wheat?

**What do you think the LRH will ask the other animals? What do you think they will say?**

Read these two pages to yourself and find out what the hen does next.

**Checking and Developing Comprehension**

**Why did the LRH plant the wheat seeds herself? (Discuss the cause-effect relationship.)**

After the wheat had grown into a big plant, what did the little red hen have to do to it? Who will read aloud the questions on page 37 that tells you that the wheat had to be cut?

**Why did the LRH cut the wheat herself? (Discuss the cause-effect relationship.)**

**Why do you think the other animals did not help the LRH?**

**Which meaning of <u>plant</u> is used on page 36?**

Now let's read pages 36 and 37 aloud.

Why do you suppose the little red hen wants to cut the wheat?... Turn to page 38 and see if you can find out.

---

**Pages 36-37**

**Motivation and Silent Reading**

Look at the picture on page 36. What do you think the little red hen is doing?...(*planting the wheat seeds*)

On page 37 what has happened to the seeds? ...(*They've grown into big plants-wheat*) Point out to the children that the clusters at the tops of the stalks are the grains that will be ground into flour.

What is the little red hen doing to the wheat? ...(*cutting it down*) What are the duck, the cat, and the pig doing?...(*watching her*)

Read these two pages to yourself and find out what the hen does next.

**Checking and Developing Comprehension**

When no one would help her plant the wheat, what did the little red hen do?... (*planted it herself*)

What happened to the wheat after the little red hen planted it?...(*It grew into a big plant.*) Who will

read aloud the two sentences on page 36 that tell what happened to the wheat?

After the wheat had grown into a big plant, what did the little red hen have to do to it?...(*cut it*) Who will read aloud the questions on page 37 that little red hen asked that tells you that the wheat had to be cut?

Who said they would help the hen cut the wheat?... (*no one*) So what did Little Red Hen do?...(*Cut it herself*)

Now let's read pages 36 and 37 aloud. **Ask one child to read page 36 and another to read page 37. Encourage children to read with good expression.**

Why do you suppose the little red hen wants to cut the wheat?...(*to get the grains of wheat; accept any reasonable answer*) Turn to page 38 and see if you can find out.

# Figure 1.7 (continued)

| Original Lesson | | Revised Lesson |
|---|---|---|

**Original Lesson**

(Animals watching hen pound the wheat.)

"Who will help me pound the wheat?" asked the little red hen. "Not I," said the duck. "Not I," said the cat. "Not I," said the pig. "Then I will pound it myself," said the little red hen. And she did.

38

"I will take the wheat to the mill," said the little red hen. "The mill will make the wheat into flour. Who will help me take the wheat to the mill?" "Not I," said the duck. "Not I," said the cat. "Not I," said the pig. "Then I will take it myself," said the little red hen. And she did.

(Animals watching hen carrying the bag to the mill.)

39

**Pages 38-39**

**Motivation and Silent Reading**

What is the hen doing to the wheat on page 38?...*(hitting it)* She's hitting, or pounding, the wheat to get the seeds from the wheat. Only the seeds are used to make flour.

On page 39 what is the little red hen holding?... *( a bag; a sack)* What do you think she might have in the sack?... *(the seeds from the wheat)*

Read pages 38 and 39 to yourself and find out what happens to the wheat.

**Checking and Developing Comprehension**

On these pages what was the first thing that had to be done to the wheat?...*(It had to be pounded.)*

Who pounded the wheat?...*(the little red hen)* Who will read aloud what the hen said on page 38 that tells you that?

Why did the little red hen pound the wheat herself? ...*(The other animals wouldn't help her.)*

On page 39 where was the hen taking the sack of wheat?...*(to the mill)* Hold up the book and point to the mill. Say: This building is the mill.

Why was the little red hen taking the wheat to the mill? ...*(to have it made into flour)* Who will read the sentence on page 39 that tells why she was taking the wheat to the mill?

How many animals carried the wheat to the mill?...*(one)* Who? ...*(the little red hen)*

Now let's read pages 38 and 39 aloud. Have one child read page 38, another read page 39.

At the mill the wheat will be turned into flour. What do you think the little red hen will do with the flour?...Turn to page 40 and find out what the little red hen does next.

**Revised Lesson**

**Pages 38-39**

**Motivation and Silent Reading**

What is the hen doing to the wheat on page 38? **What do you think the LRH will ask the other animals? How will they answer her?**

Read pages 38 and 39 to yourself and find out what happens to the wheat.

**Checking and Developing Comprehension**

On these pages what was the first thing that had to be done to the wheat?

Who will read aloud the part on page 38 that tells you that the LRH pounded the wheat?

Why did the LRH pound the wheat?

**Why did the little red hen pound the wheat herself? (Discuss the cause-effect relationship.)**

Why was the little red hen taking the wheat to the mill? Who will read the sentence on page 39 that tells why she was taking the wheat to the mill?

**Why did the little red hen take the wheat seeds to the mill herself? (Discuss the cause-effect relationship.)**

**What do you think the LRH thinks about the other animals?**

At the mill the wheat will be turned into flour. What do you think the little red hen will do with the flour?...Turn to page 40 and find out what the little red hen does next.

**Figure 1.7** (*continued*)

| Original Lesson | | Revised Lesson |
|---|---|---|

|   |   | **Pages 40-41** |
|---|---|---|

| (Animals watching the hen make bread.) | | |
|---|---|---|

**Revised Lesson** / **Pages 40-41**

**Motivation and Silent Reading**

| "I will make the bread with the flour," said the little red hen. "Who will help me make the bread?" "Not I," said the duck. "Not I," said the cat. "Not I," said the pig. "Then I will make the bread myself," said the little red hen. And she did.<br><br>40 | "Now who will help me eat the bread?" asked the little red hen. "I will," said the duck. "I will," said the cat. "I will," said the pig.<br><br>(Animals sniffing freshly baked bread.)<br><br>41 |
|---|---|

Look at the picture on page 40. What is the little red hen doing?

**What do you think the LRH will ask the other animals? What will they say?**

Read these two pages now and find out what the duck, the cat, and the pig say to the little red hen.

**Pages 40-41**

**Motivation and Silent Reading**

Look at the picture on page 40. What is the little red hen doing?... (*baking bread*) What is she doing on page 41?... (*showing a loaf of bread to the duck, the cat, and the pig*)

Read these two pages now and find out what the duck, the cat, and the pig say to the little red hen now.

**Checking and Developing Comprehension**

**Checking and Developing Comprehension**

What was the little red hen going to do with the flour? (*make bread*) Who will find and read aloud the first sentence on page 40 that tells us that?

Did the little red hen ask the other animals to help her make the bread?...(*yes*) Would they help her?...(*no*) So what did she have to do? (*make the bread herself*)

After the little red hen made bread, what did she ask her friends? (*who would help her eat the bread*) Who will read aloud what the little red hen asked her friends on page 41?... ("*I will*"; *that they would help eat the bread.*)

How do you suppose the little red hen feels? ...(*Accept any reasonable answer.*) Do you think she's going to let the duck, the cat, and the pig have some bread?... Turn to page 42 and see.

**Why did the LRH have to make the bread by herself? (Discuss the cause effect relationship.)**

After the little red hen made bread, what did she ask her friends? Who will read aloud what the little red hen asked her friends on page 41?

How do you suppose the little red hen feels? Do you think she's going to let the duck, the cat, and the pig have some bread? Turn to page 42 and see.

**Figure 1.7**  (*continued*)

| Original Lesson | Revised Lesson |
|---|---|
| | Page 42 |
| | Motivation and Silent Reading |

Original Lesson box:

> "Oh no," said the little red hen. "You did not help me plant the wheat. You did not help me cut the wheat. You did not help me pound the wheat. You did not help me take the wheat to the mill. You did not help me make the bread. So you will not help me eat the bread. I will eat it myself." And she did.
>
> (Animals watching hen eat bread.)
>
> 42

**Revised Lesson — Motivation and Silent Reading**

What's happening in this picture?
**Why do you think they are watching?**
Now read page 42 to yourself and find out what the little red hen says about the bread.

**Checking and Developing Comprehension**

What was the hen going to do by herself this time?
Why wouldn't she give any bread to the other animals?
Would you let the other animals eat the bread? Why or why not?
**What do you think is the moral or lesson of this fable?**

**Original Lesson (continued)**

Page 42

Motivation and Silent Reading

What's happening in this picture? ... *(The little red hen is eating bread by herself. The other animals are watching her.)*
Now read page 42 to yourself and find out what the little red hen says about the bread.

Checking and Developing Comprehension

What was the hen going to do by herself this time?... *(eat the bread)*
Why wouldn't she give any bread to the other animals?... *(They had not helped her do any of the other work.)*
Who will read aloud all the words that the little red hen spoke when she told the duck, the pig, and the cat why she wouldn't let them eat the bread? **Be sure that all six lines are read.** Would you have let the other animals eat the bread? Why or why not?

after questions such as, Why did the little red hen pound the wheat herself? and through the addition of questions such as, Why did the little red hen take the wheat seeds to the mill herself? and Why did the little red hen have to make the bread herself? Finally, at the conclusion of the guided reading on page 42, students should be asked, What do you think is the moral or lesson of this fable?

*The Sea Otter.*   The guided reading phase of the original teacher's manual lesson for the TSO provides before-and-after questions for every two or three pages of the reading selection (see Figure 1.8). We asked two general questions in determining the extent to which the original lesson is consistent with our content and process goals: Do the questions ask students to integrate important information? Do the questions make students aware of the text type and organizational features that aid comprehension?

The importance of the information elicited by the original questions was determined by examining our concept map for the TSO (see Figure 1.4). Information that appears at the top of the map (i.e., the central purpose and major ideas) is considered more important than the information at the bottom (i.e., supporting ideas). To be consistent with our content goals, all before-and-after reading questions should focus on information found on the concept map, preferably at the central-purpose and major-idea levels. In addition, questions were evaluated to determine the extent to which they focused on the two levels of temporal sequence identified in the text analysis and specified in our goal statements.

In examining the original before-reading questions, we find that most of them are not directed at the higher-level information in the text. For example, the first before-reading question, What does the sea otter eat? focuses on information that is at a relatively low level of importance, according to the concept map. A better question and one that is at a higher level of importance is, What does the sea otter do first in her daily routine? In addition to focusing the students' attention on information related to our content goals, this question is also consistent with the type of background knowledge that was activated in the preparation phase of the lesson.

The second before-reading question asks the students to find what else the otter dives for. Again, the focus is on a detail about playing and not on the overall activity itself. A more appropriate question is, How do sea otters spend their time when they are not eating? This question asks the student to consider other activities that are at the same level of importance as eating. In addition, it encour-

(*text continues on p. 54*)

**Figure 1.8**   Original and Revised Guided Reading Activities for *The Sea Otter* Lesson

| Original Lesson | Revised Lesson |
|---|---|
| **GUIDED READING FOR COMPREHENSION** | **GUIDED READING FOR COMPREHENSION** |

<table>
<tr><td>

**PAGES 115, 116**

**Before Reading** What does the sea otter eat?

**After Reading** Where does the sea otter look for her food? Why do you think she swims up with the fish instead of eating it under water?

**PAGES 117-119**

**Before Reading** Read these pages to find what else the otter dives for.

**After Reading** How does the sea otter hold a rock? How is the sea otter like a human child? (They like to play.)

</td><td>

**PAGES   115, 116**

**Before Reading**   What does the sea otter do first in her daily routine?

**After Reading**   Discuss the answer to the Before Reading purpose setting question. How does she go about eating? Why does she eat the fish while lying on her back?

**PAGES   117-119**

**Before Reading**   How do sea otters spend their time when they are not eating?

**After Reading** Discuss the answer to the Before Reading purpose setting question. Which words tell you the sea otter has a routine?

Who does the word <u>they</u> refer to at the top of page 119? How is the sea otter like a human? What words can be used to replace <u>and</u> that would indicate sequence?

</td></tr>
</table>

| | |
|---|---|
| (A sea otter swimming under water)* <br><br> The sun comes up.   A hungry otter dives deep into the sea to look for her food. Down she goes—down—down. <br><br> 115 | She catches a fish and swims up with it.  Up-up through the water. The otter floats on her back. And she eats her fill. <br><br> (A sea otter floating on her back eating a fish.) <br><br> 116 |
| A sea otter swimming up to the surface.) <br><br> The otter dives again, but this time she is not looking for food. She wants to find something to play with. She finds a little rock, and she swims up through the sea again. <br><br> Up—up through the green water. <br><br> 117 | (A sea otter flipping a rock into the air.) <br><br> She flips the rock into the air and she catches it. And if she drops it, down she goes after it, and she finds it and comes up again. The game goes on and on. And when at last, she is through with the rock, she lets it fall into the sea. And she plays with the otters in the herd. <br><br> 118 |

| | |
|---|---|
| They jump up from the water, high into the air. They flip over and over.  They jump again. <br><br> All day long, the otter plays and looks for food and plays again. Now she dives deep and she finds a clam. <br><br> (A sea otter diving down to get a rock.) <br><br> 119 | * Information in parentheses describes the photographs in the text. |

52

**Figure 1.8** (*continued*)

| Original Lesson | Revised Lesson |
|---|---|
| **PAGES 120, 121** | **PAGES 120, 121** |
| **Before Reading** What do you think the sea otter will do with the clam? | **Before Reading** What other ways does a sea otter use the rock? |
| **After Reading** Describe how the sea otter opens the clam shell and eats the meat inside. | **After Reading** Discuss the answer to the Before Reading purpose setting question. What steps does the sea otter go through to eat her clam? What would be some good words to describe the sea otter? (e.g., intelligent, playful) |
| **PAGES 122, 123** | **PAGES 122, 123** |
| **Before Reading** Read these pages to find out how the sea otter sleeps. | **Before Reading** What does the sea otter do at the end of the day? |
| **After Reading** What kind of bed did the sea otter have? Do you ever try to fall asleep in a way similar to the sea otter's rocking? If so, can you recall how you felt? | **After Reading** Discuss the answer to the Before Reading purpose setting question. What steps does the sea otter go through to sleep? Which words signal another step in the sea otter's daily routine? ( e.g., "night comes") |

*Original Lesson text boxes:*

The otter swims up with the clam in one front paw, and a rock in the other paw.

(A sea otter floating on her back with a rock on her stomach and a clam in her paw.)

She floats on her back, and she puts the rock on her stomach.
120

( A sea otter eating the clam she has broken open with a rock.)

She hits the clam against the rock, and she eats bits of good food. A bit of clam shell falls on her stomach. And the otter flips over and over, and washes her stomach in the sea.
121

*Revised Lesson (continued):*

Why do you think the sea otter pulls the seaweed around her? How is the meaning of <u>rock</u> different in this section?

Night comes, and the sea otter swims to a bed of seaweed. She pulls the seaweed around her.

(A sea otter floating on her back in seaweed.)

122

She floats there on her back with seaweed for her bed. She rocks with the tide, and she sleeps.

(A sea otter floating on her back in seaweed.)

123

ages the students to begin thinking about these activities as part of the sea otter's daily routine.

The third before-reading question in the original lesson is consistent with our goals. Although not high on the concept map in terms of importance, it does focus on an important attribute of the sea otter, its use of the rock. However, to emphasize that this is an example of the sea otter's intelligence, the question should ask students to find out how else the sea otter uses a rock, rather than what she will do with the clam.

The final before-reading question asks students to predict how the sea otter sleeps. Although this question focuses on an important idea, it might be better to shift the emphasis from how the sea otter sleeps to what the sea otter does at the end of the day. This changes the focus from a specific concern about the details of sleeping to a more general emphasis on another daily activity.

One would expect the after-reading questions to begin with a discussion of the answers to the before-reading questions; however, such is not the case. This is one modification that should be made for each set of after-reading questions. Several additional concerns emerge when we apply the same evaluative criteria to the after-reading questions as we did to the before-reading questions. First, many of the questions deal with information that appears at a low level on our concept map (Figure 1.4). For example, the question, How does the sea otter hold a rock? places the emphasis on a detail within an activity. A better question might be, What steps does the otter go through to eat the clam? This question helps students pull together or synthesize information about a sequence of events that is important to understanding the central purpose of the text.

A second area of concern is that the original after-reading questions do not promote an awareness of the important text characteristics that were identified in the text analysis and that contribute to students' understanding of how to read this type of text. Questions should assist students in identifying and clarifying the temporal organization of the TSO, and in understanding the importance of the text organization in comprehending this passage. Questions such as, Which words signal another step in the sea otter's daily routine? or What words can be used to replace *and* that would indicate sequence? have been added for these purposes. In addition, questions such as those referring to the antecedent of *they* or the multiple meanings of *rock* have been added to clarify other important text features identified in the text analysis.

A positive feature of the original after-reading questions is that some of them require students to integrate text information with their existing knowledge (e.g., Do you ever try to fall asleep in a way similar to the sea otter's rocking? or Why do you think she swims up with the fish instead of eating it under water?). In general these are good questions to ask; however, one must also determine if the students are likely to possess the knowledge necessary for answering them. For example, the question about why the sea otter brings the fish to the surface before she eats requires knowledge that sea otters must come to the surface to breathe, which may not be known by many students at this grade level.

### Postreading Comprehension

The evaluation of the postreading phase of the lesson focuses on the extent to which activities integrate process and content goals to promote a holistic understanding of the selection. Therefore, the activities should help students bring together all of the pieces that have been emphasized during the guided reading. At this stage, students should be encouraged to recognize the characteristics of the selection that make it representative of a certain type of text, and how the application of certain skills enhances comprehension and learning. This can best be done in the context of activities that focus on an integrated understanding of important text information. Given the specific students, it may also be appropriate to extend students' understanding to issues and events that go beyond the text, or, conversely, to guide them directly through some of the steps that model good reading behavior when comprehension has broken down.

*The Little Red Hen.* The postreading comprehension activity in the original lesson for the LRH consists of a discussion guided by a series of literal, interpretive, and evaluative questions, which are shown in Figure 1.9. The literal questions focus on identifying the characters and sequential events (i.e., steps in making bread) in the fable. The interpretive question focuses on character traits, and the evaluative questions focus on interpreting the characters' feelings and actions. These questions are largely consistent with the publisher's stated purpose (learning how to make bread) and skill objective for this lesson. However, they are not consistent with the modified process and content goals of identifying the LRH as an example of a

**Figure 1.9**  Original and Revised Postreading Activities
for *The Little Red Hen* Lesson

| Original Lesson | Revised Lesson |
|---|---|
| **Extending Comprehension** | **Extending Comprehension** |
| Now that the children have finished the story, have them close their books. Then conduct a short discussion of the story, using some of the following questions as stimuli. | 1. Discuss the reasons (causes) why the little red hen did not let the other animals have any bread. (They would not help her with the following: planting, cutting, pounding, going to the mill, making bread.) |
| L  1.  How many animals were in the story?*(four)*    What were they? *(a little red hen, a duck, a cat, a pig)* | |
| L 2.  Let's talk about all the things that the little red hen did with the wheat.  Have the children tell you all the steps that the little red hen went through to get bread, beginning with the planting of the seeds.  You may wish to print a word or phrase on the board as each step is given.  If the children do not tell you the steps in sequential order, you may then want them to go back to the reader and help them develop the correct order of events.  The steps were as follows: | 2.  Remind the children about the earlier discussion which focused on the morals of fables. Ask the children about the lesson the "The Little Red Hen" teaches us?  Discuss examples of this lesson or moral taken from the children's own experiences. |
| 1.    planting<br>2.    cutting<br>3.    pounding<br>4.    going to the mill<br>5.    making bread<br>6.    eating the bread | 3.  Remind the children of the earlier discussion about fables. Ask them to identify the features of "The Little Red Hen" that are common to fables. |
| I 3.  In what way were the duck, the cat, and the pig alike? *(lazy; not helpful)*  How was the little red hen different from the other animals? *(hardworking)* | 4.  Show the children how causes and effects are related to the moral.  Put an event on the board (e.g., the animals did not help the LRH plant the wheat).  Ask the children to identify the reason (cause) and results (effect) of this event.  Then ask them what they can conclude about the characters, and predict about the outcome. |
| E 4.  Which do you think was the hardest work: planting, cutting, pounding, going to the mill, making the bread, or eating the bread?  Why? Which do you think was the easiest to do?  Why? | |
| E 5.  How do you think the little red hen felt each time the animals wouldn't help her?  How do you think she felt at the end of the story? | 5.  Have the children read or read to them other similar fables, and talk about their similarities/differences (e.g., The Grasshopper and The Ant, Frederick the Mouse, The Judge). |
| F 6  How do you think the duck, the cat, and the pig felt when the little red hen wouldn't give them some bread? | |
| E 7.  Do you think the animals will help the little red hen if she asks for help again?  Why do you think that? | |
| E 8.  Do you think the little red hen should have let the other animals have some bread?  Why or why not? | |

fable, learning that the morals to fables often represent cause-and-effect relationships, and understanding that the lesson to be learned from the LRH is that if you do not work, you are not likely to share in the rewards.

The purpose of the revised postreading activities is to help students integrate content and process into a holistic understanding of how to read and understand the LRH as an example of the larger set of texts known as fables. The first activity helps students link the cause-and-effect relationships throughout the fable to the final event—and main idea—of the fable. The second activity moves students' attention from the literal main idea to the more abstract moral of the fable. The third activity focuses students' attention on the features of the LRH that are characteristic of fables, and the fourth shows them how causes and effects are related to understanding a moral. The fifth and final activity extends students' experience with fables and morals to other similar fables.

*The Sea Otter.* The only postreading activity provided by the teacher's manual for the TSO is a discussion of the three questions generated during the introduction of the vocabulary (see Figure 1.10). Not only do these questions not address any process goals, they simply do not provide for a discussion of content that focuses on a holistic understanding of the important text information. This activity also does not in any way address the discussion of other sea animals or the direction given to the children that they read to find facts about the sea otter, which were set forward in the section on "Setting Reading Purpose" (Figure 1.6).

The revised postreading lesson continues to integrate content and process goals by having students engage in a variety of activities. First, students are asked to discuss the accuracy of the predictions they made before reading, by comparing them to the actual content of the text. This information is then used to make a prediction about what the sea otter will do tomorrow. A second activity uses a chart of the sea otter's activities and the steps within each activity to show students how the two levels of temporal organization within the text are related. The chart is then used as the basis for a discussion about the characteristics of sea otters (e.g., their intelligence). The final activity focuses on an understanding of the characteristics of natural science text and how it differs from other selections they have read, and an awareness of how text organization aids comprehension and learning.

**Figure 1.10**  Original and Revised Postreading Activities for *The Sea Otter* Lesson

| Original Lesson | Revised Lesson |
|---|---|
| **DISCUSSING READING PURPOSE** | **DISCUSSING READING PURPOSE** |
| Refer the children to the chalkboard and the list of questions about sea otters, generated during the introduction of vocabulary for the story. Elicit pupils' answers to these questions. | 1. Discuss the predictions students made before reading and their accuracy. Ask: "What would you predict the sea otter will do tomorrow? How can you be sure?" |
| | 2. Through class discussion put a chart on the board that indicates the order of the daily activities of the sea otter. Then, list the steps within each activity. Use the chart to discuss these two levels of temporal organization within the text. Ask students what these activities suggest about the sea otter. |
| | 3. Remind students of the discussion about natural science text. Where might they find this type of text? How might their purposes for reading this type of text differ from that of a story? Discuss how organizing the information according to the sequence of events helped them understand and remember the important text information. |

## Seatwork

The final phase of the DRA typically involves some type of individual seatwork. As mentioned previously, we will only touch briefly on this here, because seatwork is covered at length in chapter 3. The most important thing to remember is that seatwork should be evaluated and modified in much the same manner as the previous parts of the lesson, especially to determine the extent to which it is appropriate to the content and process goals of the lesson. Too often the seatwork in basal lessons has little relationship to the content and/or skills that were emphasized in teaching the selection. Seatwork should focus on the application and extension of these skills, identified in the process goals, to the content of the selection. In addition, it should be used as an opportunity to extend students' experience in reading a particular type of text. Writing activities and video- and audiotapes are particularly good methods for doing this.

For example, seatwork for the LRH lesson might include exercises that list the steps in a series of cause-and-effect relationships, from this or another fable (e.g., event, reason, result, conclusion). Students might then be given a moral and a related series of cause-and-effect statements and asked to construct their own fable, either individually or in a group. Seatwork for the TSO might expand the idea of the relationship between text content and organization to include the implied comparison between the daily activities of the sea otter and those of a human child. Charts such as the one used at the end of the revised TSO lesson (see Figure 1.10) could be constructed, using the daily activities of the child as a comparison, to be filled in by students as an independent activity. Students could then be asked to compare the central ideas communicated by the different organizations shown in the charts. Although there are many other activities that might be used with these lessons, it is important to remember that the essence of all good seatwork is the integration of content and process in ways that help students become independent readers and learners.

## CONCLUSION AND SUMMARY

The purpose of this chapter has been to describe procedures for evaluating and modifying basal lessons, consistent with current research on reading and reading instruction. Basal lessons traditionally have been based on a model in which skills drive instruction, content plays a secondary role, and process is rarely addressed. Current research suggests that we need to teach lessons that are driven by the content and structure of the text and the processes necessary for successful comprehension. It also suggests that our methods of instruction should provide more direction for students in the acquisition phases of learning. Therefore, we need to prepare our lessons by analyzing the text and establishing both content and process goals for instruction. Furthermore, we need to evaluate the lessons in the teacher's manual to determine the extent to which the activities and questions relate to our content and process goals and provide for direct explanation and/or modeling of the information to be learned.

Several comments regarding the implementation of these procedures are in order as we conclude this chapter. It is important to note that the extent to which it is necessary to implement these procedures will differ, both within and between basal series. Certain lessons and certain series will require more extensive modifications than others. In fact, one might consider the frequency with which major modifications appear to be necessary as a means of evaluating both individual lessons and entire series.

It should also be noted that the amount of time required to implement these procedures can be expected to decrease with experience. Over time, these procedures are likely to become more a "mind-set" than a series of discrete steps. It is recommended, however, that teachers ease into the use of these procedures gradually. For example, teachers might begin with one lesson per month, keeping a record of their revisions for use the next time they teach at a particular level. In this way they could gradually add revised lessons to their files. As an alternative, teachers using the same levels could start by working together to revise several lessons. After these initial experiences, they could work separately and exchange materials. These are just a few of the ways teachers can begin to incorporate these procedures into their regular planning activities. The point of all this, of course, is that teachers—not materials—should be the instructional decision makers for classroom reading instruction.

## REFERENCES

Betts, E. A. (1946). *Foundations of reading instruction*. New York: American Book.

Clymer, T. (1979). *The dog next door and other stories*. Reading 720 Rainbow Edition. Lexington, MA: Silver, Burdett & Ginn, Inc.

Durkin, D. (1981). Reading comprehension instruction in five basal reader series. *Reading Research Quarterly, 16,* 515–544.

Durr, W. K. (1981). *Sunshine.* Houghton-Mifflin Reading Program. Boston: Houghton-Mifflin Co.

Pearson, P. D. (1985). Changing the face of reading comprehension instruction. *The Reading Teacher, 38,* 724–738.

Peters, C. W., & Hayes, B. (in press). The role of reading instruction in the social studies. In D. Lapp & J. Flood (Eds.), *Handbook of instructional theory and practice.* Englewood Cliffs, NJ: Prentice-Hall.

Wixson, K. K., & Peters, C. W. (1987). Comprehension assessment: Implementing an interactive view of reading. *Educational Psychologist, 22,* 333–356.

## RECOMMENDED READINGS

Au, K. H. (1979). Using the experience-text-relationship method with minority children. *The Reading Teacher, 32,* 677–679.

Beck, I. L., McKeown, M. G., & McCaslin, E. S. (1981). Does reading make sense? Problems of early readers. *The Reading Teacher, 34,* 78–80.

Fitzgerald, J. (1983). Helping readers gain self-control over reading comprehension. *The Reading Teacher, 37,* 249–253.

Pearson, P. D. (1982). *Asking questions about stories* (Ginn Occasional Papers #15). Columbus, OH: Ginn.

Ringler, L. H., & Weber, C. K. (1984). *A language-thinking approach to reading.* New York: Harcourt Brace Jovanovich.

Roehler, L. R., Duffy, G. G., & Meloth, M. B. (1986). What to be direct about in direct instruction in reading: Content-only versus process-into-content. In T. E. Raphael (Ed.), *Contexts of school-based literacy* (pp. 79–96). New York: Random House.

Spiegel, D. L. (1981). Six alternatives to the directed reading activity. *The Reading Teacher, 34,* 914–920.

Wilson, C. R. (1983). Teaching reading comprehension by connecting the known to the new. *The Reading Teacher, 36,* 382–390.

# Chapter 2

# Grouping and Pacing with Basal Materials

MARY C. SHAKE

Central to the appropriate use of basal materials are the issues of grouping students for reading instruction and determining the rate at which new skills, strategies, and materials are introduced during this instruction. Both grouping and pacing have been the object of research and practical concerns. With respect to grouping, attention has focused primarily on the criteria used for forming reading groups and on the advantages and disadvantages of homogeneous and heterogeneous grouping patterns. Attention devoted to pacing has centered on the notion that, if instruction moves too quickly, students will acquire "half-learnings," or an incomplete grasp of what is being taught. Students will only gain comfort with and independently apply skills and strategies when they are allowed extended practice in various settings. In short, appropriate pacing is determined by individual student success rate.

In the following sections of this chapter, a historical perspective for grouping and pacing for reading instruction will be developed and practical suggestions for implementation will be suggested.

## BACKGROUND

For many years now, elementary students have been divided into groups for reading instruction (Hiebert, 1983; Pikulski & Kirsch, 1979). Otto, Wolf, and Eldridge (1984) describe the history of this practice:

> Between 1920 and 1935 the practice of forming three groups for reading instruction—generally students who are achieving below,

at, and above grade level—was introduced and almost universally adopted in the nation's classrooms. The three-group plan remained dominant into the 1950's, when alternative plans for targeting instruction—for example, individualized instruction, open classrooms with learning centers for reading, and a variety of schemes for team teaching or cross-class grouping—began to be more widely used. While the alternative plans continue to be refined, adopted, and adapted, the three-group plan continues as a mainstay for managing reading instruction in many schools. [p. 801]

The rationale underlying the three-group plan is that instruction is facilitated when students are placed in smaller groups. Research investigating the influence of small-group instruction on achievement has been diverse in subjects, methods, and, to a large degree, results. In summarizing the research on this topic, however, Rosenshine and Stevens (1984) state, "Students show more engagement and higher achievement gains when they are placed in groups for instruction" (p. 752).

Research noting the positive effects of grouping on achievement has generally been interpreted as an endorsement for homogeneous grouping, that is, grouping students of similar ability. Within any classroom, there may be great diversity in the reading strengths and weaknesses students exhibit. Ekwall and Shanker (1985) note that "the normal range of reading ability in elementary classrooms extends from 2.5 years at the second grade level . . . to 7 years at the sixth grade level. . . . Thus, it is obviously not possible for teachers to meet students' needs without some sort of ability grouping" (p. 73).

The arguments for homogeneous grouping for reading instruction are appealing. Forming groups of students who are more alike than different facilitates teachers' efforts to deliver instruction that meets students' needs. Such grouping practices also allow students to experience learning with others of similar reading strengths and weaknesses (Otto et al., 1984). Students with average or above-average reading ability will be challenged by group members possessing similar characteristics. In the same sense, lower-ability students will not be frustrated by trying to deal with materials and instructional procedures appropriate for more able readers.

Like most issues of significance, there are also negative aspects of homogeneous grouping. Critics note that grouping students on some common characteristic, often ability, does not prevent grouped students from differing on other characteristics such as interests or group skills (Otto et al., 1984). Others note that instructional grouping seldom changes, once it has been established. Because of this stability of reader group membership, grouping may constitute a stable social fact that follows students throughout their school careers (Austin & Morrison, 1963; Hiebert, 1983; Shake, 1986; Weinstein, 1976). Weinstein (1986) notes that students are aware of their reading instructional placement relative to peers. She suggests that this awareness, in combination with differential teacher expectations and treatment, may contribute to a self-fulfilling prophecy for students who are grouped for reading instruction, particularly for those students in the lower-ability groups.

Furthermore, it has been suggested that the instructional group to which students are assigned determines, at least partially, the pace of instruction they will receive and the learning progress they will make. Allington (1984) measured the total number of words read (orally and silently) by good and poor reader groups in 600 reading group sessions conducted at grades one, three, and five. At all grade levels, good readers were found to read more words in context than were poor readers, although the differences narrowed as grade levels increased. That is, while at grade one good readers read nearly three times as many words as poor readers, good readers at grade five read only about 40 percent more words than poor readers.

Barr (1975) comments, "By knowing a child's reading group, we also know whether it will be paced faster or slower than other groups in the class" (p. 495). Generally, pacing refers to the rate at which new material is introduced during instruction. It has been indicated that pacing is interrelated with grouping practices, and therefore it is difficult to separate completely the two central issues of this chapter. It is important, then, to keep in mind the background on grouping for reading instruction when reading about pacing.

It has been found that, although the time allocated to reading groups of differing abilities does not differ significantly, the manner in which these groups are taught varies. Pacing is one way in which instruction is differentiated across reader groups. Barr (1973–1974), for example, used the number of new words introduced to students as a measure of pacing and found above-average, average, and poor readers to be differentially paced. More specifically, poorer readers were paced slowly and, therefore, learned fewer new words than members of the average and above-average reader groups in differentially paced classrooms. In classrooms where the instructional pace was homogeneous across reader groups, the rate of word learning was slightly slower for the poor readers than for the average readers in differentially paced classes. Barr (1975) proposes that teachers who differentially pace reading instruction across reader groups tend to be influenced by expectations for students and the instructional pace set by colleagues. She suggests that, while the decision to form reading groups is planned, the pacing decisions themselves are reactive in nature and based on teachers' perceptions formulated during instruction.

Carroll's (1963) model of school learning indicates that the degree of learning is a function of the time actually spent in learning, divided by the time needed to learn. Echoing Carroll's model, Allington (1983) and Barr (1982) suggest that, in order to narrow the achievement differences between good and poor readers, poor readers should be allocated more instructional time. They base this suggestion on their observations of classroom reading instruction, which indicate that poorer readers are instructed at a slower pace and spend comparably less time reading in connected text during the time allocated for instruction.

While studies such as the ones previously discussed provide us with information regarding how pacing occurs in our classrooms, they do not tell us how it *should* occur. This is not meant as a criticism of such research, since it would be impossible to set pacing criteria that would accommodate all learners in every possible reading instructional situation. Allington (1984) notes that, while quicker pacing usually results in more content being covered, this content is not necessarily mastered. Similarly, Rosenshine (1979) suggests that we are ignorant as to how much content needs to be covered or mastered in order for an average student to make average progress. While it would be difficult to give a blanket endorsement to any supposedly ideal pace for reading instruction, we do recognize that instruction that progresses too slowly or too rapidly may prevent students from learning at their optimal level.

The research data gathered in the Beginning Teacher Evaluation Study give us some clues as to the appropriate pacing of instruction. In this study Fisher and associates (1980) developed a measure of student classroom learning called "Academic Learning Time" (ALT). As they define it,

> Time spent by a student engaged on a task that s/he can perform with high success and that is directly relevant to an academic outcome constitutes a measure of student classroom learning. We refer to time spent under these conditions as Academic Learning Time (ALT). The basic components of ALT are allocated time, student engagement, and student high success (balanced with some medium success). The ALT model states that the accumulation of Academic Learning Time will lead to gains in achievement. [p. 10]

To summarize the previous discussion, both grouping and pacing are factors that influence how students learn to read. As has been pointed out, ability grouping for reading instruction is common practice in our schools, and its historical roots lead us to believe that this practice will continue, particularly when basal readers are the primary instructional materials employed. We know that appropriate instructional pacing will be facilitated when students are placed in reading groups with reading materials that allow moderate to high levels of success. However, we have evidence that indicates that traditional ability-grouping practices may be detrimental to students' progress and self-perceptions. Furthermore, it has been estimated that between 50 percent (Guthrie, 1980) and 60 percent (Ekwall & Shanker, 1985) of our elementary students are working with inappropriate reading instructional materials. Such a situation occurs as a result of improper grouping and/or pacing practices, or misuse or inadequate supply of materials.

It appears that grouping and pacing for reading instruction are issues that must receive attention if students are to learn to read and to love reading. Grouping and pacing should be the result of conscious teacher decision making based on a thorough knowledge of students' instructional needs and the demands of the reading materials. In the sections that follow, I will make suggestions that I hope will facilitate such teacher decision making.

Recommended procedures for grouping and pacing will be presented separately. With respect to grouping, the suggestions are intended to provide teachers with a framework that avoids some of the negative aspects of grouping previously mentioned and promotes the positive ones. Additional reasons for these practices will be provided under each recommended procedure. As to pacing of reading instruction, the recommended procedures are largely suggestions, or possibilities, which may or may not be appropriate in a given instructional situation.

## RECOMMENDED PROCEDURES FOR GROUPING

### Criteria for Forming Reading Groups

We recommend that teachers begin reading instruction on the first day of the school year but use the first few weeks to gather important information which will inform their grouping decisions. In the interim, teachers may elect to follow the previous teachers' grouping recommendations, telling students that these are trial groups and it is likely that group membership will change several times throughout the school year. An alternative would involve having the students engage in strictly independent reading activities during the period of time in which teachers are gathering information. The following is a list of useful types of grouping information that teachers could gather; it should not, however, be considered exhaustive:

1. The number of reading groups you can realistically accommodate in your instructional schedule
2. Student reading scores from the most recently administered standardized test
3. The last basal level each student completed successfully
4. An instructional reading level for each student from the basal informal reading inventory
5. Previous teachers' recommendations
6. Observations about students' independent work habits
7. Observations about students' ability to work in groups
8. Students' reading interests
9. Students' hobbies
10. Students' tendency to read at home

There are several viewpoints on the criteria teachers should use in forming reading groups. Representing an extremely practical perspective, Leu and Kinzer (1987) note that, before deciding on reader group membership, teachers need to decide how many reading groups they can accommodate. They suggested three factors that teachers should consider in making this decision:

1. The amount of previous experience students have had with small group instruction
2. Their own previous experience with small-group instruction
3. The amount of supplemental reading materials available for use by teachers and students

The first factor is important because, if students are used to small-group instruction, they may be more able to work independently and require less continuous direct supervision. With respect to the second factor, Leu and Kinzer (1987) suggest that, if small-group instruction is a new procedure for a teacher, he or she may wish to begin the year with fewer groups and gradually form additional ones as the task of managing small-group instruction becomes more famil-iar. Third, if the supply of materials prohibits the teacher from differ-entiating reading instruction by placing students in groups with mate-rials appropriate to their reading ability levels, he or she may need to adjust the number of groups upward or downward, to accommodate students' instructional needs in other ways.

Once the number of groups has been decided upon, teachers need to make decisions regarding the group in which each student should be placed. Duffy and Roehler (1986) suggest that the for-mation of reading groups is one of the most crucial and difficult tasks facing teachers. With respect to the criteria upon which groups should be formed, they propose that, "as with all dilemmas, there is no 'right' answer; instead, teachers use what data are available to make the best decisions possible and, when additional data be-come available, remain flexible enough to modify the decisions" (p. 140).

Research investigating the criteria employed when reading groups are formed has indicated that teachers rely heavily on reading achievement indices (Borko, Shavelson, & Stern, 1981). It has been noted, however, that when teachers are asked to make grouping decisions about students they instruct daily, they also rely on such information sources as previous teachers' recommendations, basal tests, group skills, and general classroom behavior (Shake, 1983, 1986). Similarly, it has been found that teachers who rely heavily on standardized indices of reading achievement, when deciding group placements for above-average and poor readers, attend to additional sources of information when placing borderline or average readers (Borko & Niles, 1983; Haller & Waterman, 1985).

I recommend, therefore, that teachers gather and consider the various types of information listed at the beginning of this section when forming reading groups.

Once teachers have gathered information and formed reading instructional groups, their task is by no means done. Leu and Kinzer (1987) stress that group placements, particularly at the beginning of the school year, should be considered tentative. They further propose that initial group placements should be conservative and that stu-dents should be moved to higher-level groups if subsequent perfor-mance warrants such a move. They stress, and I concur, that flexibil-ity in grouping decisions is extremely important. Duffy and Roehler (1986) also stress the need for teachers to gather information regard-ing students' reading strengths and weaknesses throughout the school year: "It is this willingness to continually collect fresh data as the basis of instructional decision making that is one of the principal characteristics of professional teachers" (p. 157).

Stating that one of the most common misuses of basal materials is improper pupil placement and inappropriate grouping, Ekwall and Shanker (1985) echo several of the concerns just mentioned. They suggest several reasons for inappropriate placement and grouping of students:

1. Use of inappropriate procedures for gathering data on students
2. Unwillingness or inability to form enough groups to meet students' needs
3. Unawareness of the criteria for placing students according to their performance level (minimum 95-percent word recognition accuracy and 75-percent comprehension accuracy)
4. Adherence by teachers and/or administrators to grade-level designations of texts, rather than to criteria regarding probable student success (i.e., instructional level)

I reiterate that, during the first few weeks of school, teachers should (1) decide on how many reading groups they can accommodate in their instructional schedule and (2) attempt to gather several types of information on each student. I cannot overemphasize the notion that placement should be based on multiple sources of information, gathered both formally and informally. Once the groups are formed, the notion should be kept in mind that students should be moved upward or downward if initial placements seem inappropriate based on daily performance.

### Flexible Grouping

One way to counteract the negative aspects of homogeneous grouping is to employ flexible grouping for reading instruction. There exist three interpretations of flexible grouping; I will present all three and make my recommendations.

From one perspective, flexible grouping centers primarily on the purpose and duration of reader group membership. Operating from this perspective, Unsworth (1984) suggests the following principles:

1. There are no permanent groups.
2. Groups are periodically created, modified, or disbanded to meet new needs as they arise.

3. At times there is only one group, consisting of all students.
4. Groups vary in size from two or three to nine or ten, depending on the group's purpose.
5. Group membership is not fixed; it varies according to needs and purposes. [p. 301]

Although this form of flexible grouping may be an effective means of eradicating the negative aspects of traditional reading ability groupings, we do not recommend it as a preferred format when basal reading series are being used. Because most basal series introduce skills and strategies in a sequential fashion and presuppose that students will receive both direct and guided instruction, regularly moving students around in groups could prove counterproductive to their learning. Ekwall and Shanker (1985) note three major criticisms of this first perspective on flexible grouping. First, they suggest that such procedures make it difficult for teachers to monitor and document students' progress. Second, because time schedules and group composition will vary frequently, they note that management and discipline problems may become more acute. Third, there will be an increase in the amount of preparation teachers must make and the number of groups they must instruct, while the length of the school day and, therefore, the total amount of time that can be allocated to reading instruction remain static. They suggest that fractionating teachers' time in this manner may have a negative impact on the quality of instruction the teachers are able to deliver.

The second and third perspectives on flexible grouping involve supplementing traditional grouping patterns with other arrangements, rather than supplanting traditional reading groups altogether. For many teachers, they may provide a more realistic alternative.

The second interpretation of flexible grouping is one offered by Blair (1984), who notes that one characteristic of effective teachers of reading is the way that they incorporate whole-class, small-group, and individualized instruction into their daily schedules. When such a mixed format is employed, teachers may form relatively stable reading ability groups. To counteract the negative aspects of homogeneous groups, however, whole-class instruction is employed periodically to allow students of various abilities to interact and learn from each other. Sustained silent reading and story sharing are good uses of whole-class instruction for reading. Obviously, whole-class instruction in other curricular areas provides for interaction among students as well. Similarly, individualized instruction, even if used for only a few minutes daily, allows teachers to determine and accommodate the instructional needs of all students (see chapter 5 for additional suggestions).

Recently we have seen a more moderate perspective taken in relation to flexible grouping. This third interpretation appears to counteract both the criticisms of flexible grouping mentioned previously and the disadvantages of using strictly homogeneous groups. Duffy and Roehler (1986) suggest that two types of reading groups should be formed in our classrooms: traditional reading groups focused on reading ability level and collaborative groups. "Collaborative groups are temporary and heterogeneous groups in which three or four children of different reading abilities work together on a particular project" (p. 134). They suggest that collaborative groups be formed on such criteria as students' interests, interpersonal skills, or current social relationships. Information useful in forming collaborative groups can be gathered from

1. Interest inventories completed by students
2. Observations of students' interpersonal patterns in various settings (e.g., in class, on the playground, in the lunchroom)
3. A sociogram based on students' choices of the three or four classmates they would most like and dislike working with

(Other suggestions for collecting data are given in the appendix to this chapter.) Such groups are often termed cooperative groups, since all the group's members, regardless of reading ability level, contribute to the completed group product or activity. When both types of groups are used, achievement goals can be met through ability groups, while attitude goals can be addressed with collaborative groups.

If teachers collect the information about students' reading abilities, interests, hobbies, independent work, and group skills mentioned in the previous section, they will be able to form both traditional reading ability groups and collaborative groups. This arrangement seems desirable for teachers who wish to avoid strictly homogeneous grouping, while at the same time minimize instructional preparation, discipline and management problems, and problems related to monitoring student progress.

## Schedule for Group Meetings

Blair (1984) notes that "useful time" is one of the characteristics of effective reading instruction. "Useful time" generally refers to the amount of time students spend actively engaged in reading and reading-related activities. One aspect to address is the order in which the teacher meets with the reading groups. This is important because, if reading groups consistently meet in the same order, the same group(s) may be shorted on instructional time every day. Some teachers might argue that consistently meeting with reading groups in the same order facilitates smooth activity flow in the classroom; in other words, students quickly learn the classroom routine, can accurately predict which activities will follow each other, and can determine what role they will play in each of the activities.

I believe that students can easily learn a rotational schedule and that it would prevent a situation in which the same group is consistently the last to receive teacher-led instruction and therefore is possibly the recipient of less instructional time. The first sample rotational schedule, shown in Table 2.1, is based on the three-group plan and a total time allocation of 75 minutes. The second sample schedule, shown in Table 2.2, is based on a total time allocation of 90 minutes and depicts a schedule for meeting with four reading groups during that time.

## RECOMMENDED PROCEDURES FOR PACING

If students are to make progress in acquiring and improving reading skills and strategies, they must have high amounts of Academic Learning Time (ALT). As previously mentioned, in order to insure high ALT, students must be placed with materials with which they can be successful. This is important to mention, since it has been documented that many of our elementary students are presently using materials that are too difficult for them to read with more than miniscule success. The initial reading ability diagnosis completed at the beginning of the school year should result in students being

**Table 2.1**   Rotational Schedule for a Three-Group Plan

|               | Monday | Tuesday | Wednesday | Thursday | Friday |
|---------------|--------|---------|-----------|----------|--------|
| 9:00 - 9:25   | High   | Poor    | Avg.      | High     | Poor   |
| 9:25 - 9:50   | Avg.   | High    | Poor      | Avg.     | High   |
| 9:50 - 10:15  | Poor   | Avg.    | High      | Poor     | Avg.   |

**Table 2.2**  Rotational Schedule for a Four-Group Plan

|                | Monday | Tuesday | Wednesday | Thursday | Friday |
|----------------|--------|---------|-----------|----------|--------|
| 9:00 -  9:22   | Poor   | Avg. 2  | Avg. 1    | High     | Poor   |
| 9:22 -  9:44   | Avg. 2 | Avg. 1  | High      | Poor     | Avg. 2 |
| 9:44 - 10:06   | Avg. 1 | High    | Poor      | Avg. 2   | Avg. 1 |
| 10:06 - 10:30  | High   | Poor    | Avg. 2    | Avg. 1   | High   |

placed with materials which they can read independently or instructionally. Although developed over 40 years ago, Betts's (1946) criteria are still the most widely used for determining the levels at which students read independently, instructionally, and frustrationally.

1. Independent: at least 99-percent word recognition accuracy, and at least 90-percent comprehension accuracy; student has little or no difficulty reading this level material alone.
2. Instructional: at least 95-percent word recognition accuracy and 75-percent comprehension accuracy; student needs some teacher-led instruction when reading material at this level.
3. Frustrational: word recognition accuracy less than 90 percent, and comprehension accuracy less than 50 percent; student finds this level material too difficult, even with direct teacher instruction.

Once students' instructional reading levels have been established, continuous diagnosis, particularly of the informal nature, is needed so that teachers can keep a constant check on their students' reading strengths and weaknesses. Students' reading abilities do not remain static; what is an appropriate placement at the beginning of the school year may become inappropriate as the year progresses and the students meet more difficult reading material. It is within this realm that the pacing of instruction becomes particularly important. Some students may need to move through material at a slower pace than others, in order to perform with moderate to high rates of success (Allington, 1983; Barr, 1982). Some students will need more practice than others on specific reading skills and strategies, in order to feel comfortable using them. If students do not receive ample practice, they may attain only partial learning and have no strategies they can employ independently, with success, or generalize to other reading situations. Vernon (1958) terms this lack of understanding "cognitive confusion." We suggest that instruction that moves at a too rapid pace may contribute to cognitive confusion, since it may prevent students from mastering any of the concepts taught. Similarly, instruction that moves too slowly fails to challenge students, and may cause them to lose their love for reading, even lose all interest in it, or fail to reach their full potential.

Research has shown that instruction that moves at too slow or too rapid a pace is detrimental to student learning. The problem remains, however, that we have no definitive criteria for determining the appropriate pace of reading instruction. Some publishers make suggestions for pacing at each level of the basal series, but these must be taken strictly as guidelines to be adjusted upward or downward as individual teachers deem appropriate. What little we do know about pacing leads us to conclude that pacing decisions are best left to individual teachers who instruct students on a daily basis.

### Provisions for Remedial Reading

Just as improper pacing may contribute to cognitive confusion, so may incongruence in instruction. It has been found that poor readers who receive remedial reading instruction often experience an incongruence between the classroom and the remedial setting, in both methods and materials (Allington & Shake, 1986; Allington, Stuetzel, Shake, & LaMarche, 1986). It has been argued further that, if remedial reading programs are to help poor readers achieve greater success in reading, they should serve one of two functions: (1) an a priori or preinstructional function or (2) a post hoc or reinforcement function (Allington & Shake, 1986). It seems safe to say that remedial teachers cannot provide instruction that either introduces or reinforces the classroom reading curriculum if they do not know what that curriculum contains. Both classroom and remedial teachers report concern regarding the lack of time for communication about programs and target students (Allington & Shake, 1986; Johnston, Allington, & Afflerbach, 1985). It is important to overcome this, since coordination of classroom and remedial reading curricula may reduce cognitive confusion and provide poor readers with the additional practice and instruction needed to become better readers. To achieve this congruence, I suggest that a record sheet, such as shown in Figure 2.1, travel with each child receiving remedial instruc-

**Figure 2.1** Student Record Sheet

Student Name _____  Homeroom Teacher _____
Week of _____  Grade _____

| | Classroom Program | Remedial Program |
|---|---|---|
| MONDAY | | |
| TUESDAY | | |
| WEDNESDAY | | |
| THURSDAY | | |
| FRIDAY | | |

Homeroom Teacher Comments: _____
_____
_____

Remedial Teacher Comments: _____
_____
_____

tion. This record sheet would keep both the classroom and remedial teachers informed as to the methods and materials being employed in each setting. For example, teachers should record the name of the materials, the pages read and whether the reading was oral or silent, the nature of worksheets completed, and if appropriate, the particular reading skill or strategy stressed during the class period.

**Provisions for All Readers**

It was suggested in the section of this chapter on procedures for grouping that teachers occasionally must place students in inappropriate reading ability groups because it would be impossible for them to schedule instructional time for additional ability groups. It was also noted that, even when students are grouped homogeneously in terms of reading ability, they will vary relative to specific reading strengths and weaknesses. Teachers need to make adjustments in reading lessons based on their perceptions of how well students understand and apply the skills, strategies, and concepts presented. In addition to this constant monitoring, I suggest incorporating the following cooperative learning strategies into your reading program.

*Paired Reading.*   In this activity, two students of differing reading abilities are paired for oral reading. They may belong to the same classroom or two different classrooms, although younger, better readers should never be paired with older, poorer readers. When the two students are paired, each reads orally from an appropriate-level text. While one student is reading, the other follows along. In this way, the more able reader is allowed to read materials at an appropriate level of difficulty, while the poorer reader is being exposed to new vocabulary. Tierney, Readence, and Dishner (1985, p. 308) summarized the benefits of this strategy: "The more competent reader gains prestige from becoming a 'teacher'; the less fluent reader profits from the relaxed atmosphere of the situation and gains confidence in reading through working with a more knowledgeable reader."

*Inquiry Reading.*   This activity, described by Searfoss and Readence (1985), allows students to investigate independently a topic of their interest. There are four steps to inquiry reading. First, students identify a topic they wish to learn more about. Second, students must formulate research questions related to this topic of their choice. These questions must be answerable in a convincing way and should be ones that will lead to about a month-long inquiry. Third, students must locate resources that will provide information on their topic, and they should include reading materials, traditional reference materials, audiovisual aids, human resources, and so forth. Fourth, students must share the results of their inquiry, preferably with other students as well as the teacher. The sharing of results can take many forms, such as a demonstration, written report, or oral report. Inquiry reading would present an ideal activity framework for collaborative reading groups as well as individual student work.

## Provisions for Gifted Readers

If a given student is reading at a level well above the highest reading group designation, we suggest that teachers allow her or him to read with the highest reading group, for peer interactional purposes. In addition, however, gifted readers should be allowed and encouraged to read independently materials that they find interesting and challenging. One activity that may prove beneficial for gifted readers is story sharing. Many elementary students enjoy having a story read to them. Most often, it is a teacher who does this story sharing. I suggest that this may be a beneficial activity in which gifted readers could participate. It would be better, however, for gifted readers to share stories with students in lower grade levels, because consistently placing a student in a position normally held by the teacher can cause peer relation problems for that student.

Teachers should help gifted readers select a story or book that would be appropriate in content and interest for students in the grade level at which it will be read. In addition, the teacher should contact other teachers and set up the schedule for story sharing. If there are several gifted readers in one classroom, the teacher should form a rotational schedule so that all targeted students have the opportunity to participate in this activity with relative frequency.

## SUMMARY

Several issues surrounding the grouping of students for reading instruction and the pacing of that instruction have been discussed in this chapter. While ability grouping is recommended, there are advantages and disadvantages involved in its use. Teachers should base grouping decisions on several sources of information, and these decisions should be considered tentative, pending additional information gathered through continuous diagnostic procedures conducted during the school year (see chapter appendix). Teachers also should form collaborative groups, in which students of various reading abilities work together on a group project. Forming this second type of group may lessen the negative impact of using strictly homogeneous grouping for reading instruction. In addition, a rotating order should be used in meeting reading groups, to avoid continually shorting the same students on instructional time.

Too slow or too rapid an instructional pace is detrimental to student learning. Proper pacing is related to the reading group in which students are placed and the rate of success students are able to experience when reading. Pacing is more likely to be appropriate when students are placed in reading materials at their instructional level and when the skills and strategies presented match the reading strengths and weaknesses of the students. Because appropriate pacing depends on students' instructional needs, no set pacing criteria can be recommended. Instead, as with grouping, teachers must make pacing decisions based on information gathered through daily observations of and interaction with students (see chapter appendix).

The following list summarizes the suggestions made in this chapter:

1. Based on your (and your students') previous experience with small-group instruction and the amount of supplemental reading materials available, decide on the number of reading groups you can accommodate in your instructional schedule.
2. Get students reading on the first day of school.
3. During the first few weeks, gather information, both formally and informally, that will allow you to form reading groups.
4. Place students in groups reading materials at their instructional level.
5. Stress to the students that reading group membership will change several times throughout the school year.
6. Form collaborative groups in which students of different abilities work together on a project.
7. Provide opportunities for whole-class, small-group, and individualized instruction during reading and other curricular areas.
8. Form a rotational schedule to vary the order in which reader groups are met with on a day-to-day basis.
9. Continue to gather information on students' reading strengths and weaknesses throughout the school year. Make changes in reading group placement and pacing based on these observations.
10. Through consultation with the remedial teacher, set up a report form that will travel with each of your students receiving remedial reading instruction. This form should serve the

purpose of informing both you and the remedial teacher of the instructional emphasis in both settings.

11. Allow students additional opportunities for reading outside of their reading group. Activities such as paired reading, inquiry reading, and story sharing will both challenge gifted readers and provide extra reading practice for less able students.

12. Be aware that students know their reading placement relative to peers. Counteract the competitiveness of this situation by initiating positive interactions among all students.

## APPENDIX:
## ADDITIONAL INSTRUCTIONAL ACTIVITIES

At the beginning of the school year, make a chart for each of your students that includes the information in the following list. Once the information is recorded, form both traditional reading groups based on ability/achievement and collaborative groups based on interests, group skills, hobbies, and so forth. Make sure to include students of various reading abilities in each of the collaborative groups.

1. Student's name
2. Instructional reading level (from basal IRI)
3. Reading scores from the most recently administered standardized test
4. Last basal level text successfully completed
5. Ability to work in groups
6. Ability to work independently
7. Reading interests
8. Other interests
9. Hobbies

Observe your practices with your reading groups for five consecutive days, then answer the following questions.

CONTENT COVERAGE
1. What is the average number of words read daily in connected text during reading instruction by your
   above-average readers? _____
       average readers? _____
   below-average readers? _____
2. What is the average number of pages read daily during reading instruction by your above-average readers? _____
                   average readers? _____
               below-average readers? _____
3. What is the average number of stories read each week during reading group by your
   above-average readers? _____
       average readers? _____
   below-average readers? _____

4. What is the average number of new words introduced per story to your above-average readers? _____
   average readers? _____
   below-average readers? _____
5. What is the average number of reading workbook/worksheet pages completed daily by your above-average readers? _____
   average readers? _____
   below-average readers? _____

Are the foregoing numbers for each reader group comparable? If not, which of the following suggestions would be most appropriate in your particular teaching situation?

   1. Meet for a longer period of time with the group that has been moving at the slowest pace.
   2. Allow the more slowly paced group to engage in repeated readings.
   3. Have each student in the more slowly paced group read to an aide or parent volunteer several times weekly.
   4. Other _____

SUCCESS RATE
1. Can your above-average readers read orally with approximately 95-percent word recognition accuracy? _____
   average readers? _____
   below-average readers? _____
2. Can your above-average readers answer comprehension questions about what they have read with approximately
   75-percent accuracy? _____
   average readers? _____
   below-average readers? _____
3. Do your above-average readers exhibit mastery of the reading skills and strategies previously taught? _____
   average readers? _____
   below-average readers? _____
4. Are your above-average readers able to comprehend successfully when reading independently? _____
   average readers? _____
   below-average readers? _____

Are any of your students exhibiting reading performance (word recognition and/or comprehension) that falls in the frustrational range?

If so, which of the following would be most appropriate in your teaching situation?

1. Change the reading group placement of these students.
2. Remove these students from their present reading group and work with them individually.
3. Send the students to another classroom for reading instruction.
4. Keep the students in their present reading group, but provide additional reading practice and/or instruction at some other time during the day.
5. Refer the students for Chapter I or another remedial reading program.
6. Other _____

Are any students exhibiting reading performance (word recognition and/or comprehension) that is considerably above the highest group placement in your classroom? If so, which of the following instructional activities would be most appropriate in your teaching situation?

1. Form another reading group and place these students in a higher-level text.
2. Remove the students from their present reading groups and provide them with individual instruction.
3. Send the students to another classroom for reading instruction.
4. Keep the students in the highest reading group but provide them with additional enrichment activities (i.e., paired reading, inquiry reading) at some other time during the school day.
5. Other _____

Do any students exhibit particular difficulty in reading independently, as compared to their performance when in a reading group? If so, which of the following instructional activities might you employ to promote independent reading ability?

1. Sustained silent reading
2. Buddy reading or paired reading
3. At-home reading program
4. Other _____

# REFERENCES

Allington, R. L. (1983). The reading instruction provided readers of differing abilities. *Elementary School Journal, 83,* 548–559.

Allington, R. L. (1984). Content coverage and contextual reading in reading groups. *Journal of Reading Behavior, 16,* 85–96.

Allington, R. L., & Shake, M. (1986). Remedial reading: Achieving curricular congruence in classroom and clinic. *The Reading Teacher, 39,* 648–654.

Allington, R. L., Stuetzel, H., Shake, M., & LaMarche, S. (1986). What is remedial reading? A descriptive study. *Reading Research and Instruction, 26,* 15–30.

Austin, M., & Morrison, C. (1963). *The first R: The Harvard report on reading in elementary schools.* New York: Macmillan.

Barr, R. (1973–1974). Instructional pace differences and their effect on reading acquisition. *Reading Research Quarterly, 9,* 526–554.

Barr, R. (1975). How children are taught to read: Grouping and pacing. *School Review, 83,* 479–498.

Barr, R. (1982). Classroom reading instruction from a sociological perspective. *Journal of Reading Behavior, 14,* 375–389.

Betts, E. A. (1946). *Foundations of reading instruction.* New York: American Book Company.

Blair, T. (1984). Teacher effectiveness: The know-how to improve student learning. *The Reading Teacher, 38,* 138–142.

Borko, H., & Niles, J. (1983). Teachers' cognitive processes in the formation of reading groups. In J. A. Niles & L. A. Harris (Eds.), *Searches for meaning in reading/language processing and instruction* (*Thirty-second yearbook of the National Reading Conference*) (pp. 282–288). Rochester, NY: The National Reading Conference.

Borko, H., Shavelson, R., & Stern, P. (1981). Teachers' decisions in the planning of reading instruction. *Reading Research Quarterly, 16,* 449–466.

Carroll, J. B. (1963). A model of school learning. *Teachers College Record, 64,* 723–733.

Duffy, G. G., & Roehler, L. (1986). *Improving classroom reading instruction: A decision-making approach.* New York: Random House.

Ekwall, E., & Shanker, J. (1985). *Teaching reading in the elementary school.* Columbus, OH: Charles E. Merrill.

Fisher, C., Berliner, D., Filby, N., Marliave, R., Cahen, L., & Dishaw, M. (1980). Teaching behaviors, academic learning time, and student achievement: An overview. In C. Denham & A. Lieberman (Eds.), *Time to learn* (pp. 7–32). Washington, DC: National Institute of Education.

Guthrie, J. (1980). Research reviews: Time in reading programs. *The Reading Teacher, 33,* 500–502.

Haller, E., & Waterman, M. (1985). The criteria of reading group assignments. *The Reading Teacher, 38,* 772–781.

Hiebert, E. H. (1983). An examination of ability grouping for reading instruction. *Reading Research Quarterly, 18,* 231–255.

Johnston, P., Allington, R., & Afflerbach, P. (1985). The congruence of classroom and remedial reading instruction. *Elementary School Journal, 84,* 465–477.

Leu, D., & Kinzer, C. (1987). *Effective reading instruction in the elementary grades.* Columbus, OH: Charles E. Merrill.

Otto, W., Wolf, A., & Eldridge, R. (1984). Managing instruction. In P. D. Pearson (Ed.), *Handbook of reading research* (pp. 799–828). New York: Longman.

Pikulski, J., & Kirsch, I. (1979). Organization for instruction. In R. Calfee & P. Drum (Eds.), *Teaching reading in compensatory classes* (pp. 72–86). Newark, DE: International Reading Association.

Rosenshine, B. (1979). Content, time, and direct instruction. In P. Peterson & H. Walberg (Eds.), *Research on teaching: Concepts, findings, and implications* (pp. 28–56). Berkeley, CA: McCutchan.

Rosenshine, B., & Stevens, R. (1984). Classroom instruction in reading. In P. D. Pearson (Ed.), *Handbook of reading research* (pp. 745–798). New York: Longman.

Searfoss, L. W., & Readence, J. E. (1985). *Helping children learn to read.* Englewood Cliffs, NJ: Prentice-Hall.

Shake, M. (1983, December). *Teachers' instructional philosophies: Beliefs about reading instruction and reader group needs.* Paper presented to the National Reading Conference, Austin, TX.

Shake, M. (1986). Bases for grouping decisions. In J. A. Niles & R. Lalik (Eds.), *Solving problems in literacy: Learners, teachers, and researchers (Thirty-fifth yearbook of the National Reading Conference)* (pp. 171–177). Rochester, NY: National Reading Conference.

Tierney, R., Readence, J., & Dishner, E. (1985). *Reading strategies and practices: A compendium* (2nd ed.). Boston, MA: Allyn & Bacon.

Unsworth, L. (1984). Meeting individual needs through flexible within-class grouping of pupils. *The Reading Teacher, 38,* 298–304.

Vernon, M. (1958). *Backwardness in reading.* New York: Cambridge University Press.

Weinstein, R. (1976). Reading group membership in first grade: Teacher behaviors and pupil experiences over time. *Journal of Educational Psychology, 68,* 103–116.

Weinstein, R. (1986). Teaching reading: Children's awareness of teacher expectations. In T. E. Raphael (Ed.), *The contexts of school-based literacy* (pp. 233–252). New York: Random House.

## RECOMMENDED READINGS

Allington, R. L. (1977). If they don't read much, how they ever gonna get good? *Journal of Reading, 21*, (1) 57–61.

Allington, R. L. (1980). Poor readers don't get to read much in reading group. *Language Arts, 57*, 872–876.

Denham, C., & Lieberman, A. (Eds.). (1980). *Time to learn.* Washington, DC: National Institute of Education.

Eder, D. (1981). Ability grouping as a self-fulfilling prophecy: A micro-analysis of teacher-student interactions. *Sociology of Education, 54*, 151–162.

Grant, L., & Rothenberg, J. (1986). The social enhancement of ability differences: Teacher-student interactions in first- and second-grade reading groups. *Elementary School Journal, 87*, (1) 29–49.

Leinhardt, G., Zigmond, N., & Cooley, W. (1981). Reading instruction and its effects. *American Educational Research Journal, 18*, 343–361.

Peterson, P., Wilkinson, L. C., & Hallinan, M. (Eds.). (1984). *The social context of instruction: Group organization and group process.* New York: Academic Press.

Pink, W., & Leibert, R. (1986). Reading instruction in the elementary school: A proposal for reform. *Elementary School Journal, 87*, 51–67.

Chapter 3

# *Integrating Seatwork with the Basal Lesson*

JUDITH A. SCHEU
DIANE K. TANNER
KATHRYN H. AU

Elementary students may spend up to 70 percent of their reading instruction time doing seatwork assignments (Fisher et al., 1978), considerably more time than they spend in teacher-led lessons. Because of this, it is important for teachers to think about how seatwork assignments can best be used to promote students' learning to read. Teachers should consider

1. How seatwork assignments fit with the overall goals of the classroom reading program
2. How to coordinate seatwork assignments with teacher-led lessons
3. How to make the purposes of seatwork assignments clear to students

We begin this chapter by discussing research that focuses on the seatwork materials typically used for reading instruction, as well as research related to the use of these materials by teachers and students in classrooms. We then present examples showing how the recommendations and implications of this research can be applied to enhance students' learning from work they complete independently.

## BACKGROUND RESEARCH

Basal workbooks and duplicated work sheets are probably the most common types of seatwork used as part of the classroom reading program. Teachers often assign students several workbook pages or work sheets to complete each day. The question is, how beneficial to students' learning to read is the routine assignment of so many practice pages? *Becoming a Nation of Readers* (Anderson, Hiebert, Scott, & Wilkinson, 1985), the report of a national commission, is highly critical of work sheet tasks, pointing out that many require only a "perfunctory level of reading" and often provide drill on skills of little value in learning to read. Cunningham (1984) believes that work sheets would be of more value if they focused on helping students (1) to access background knowledge and set purposes for reading, (2) to follow the structure of the story, and (3) to become increasingly independent in the use of comprehension strategies. In general, existing work sheets do not deal with these and other important aspects of reading comprehension.

Yet, in spite of the materials' numerous shortcomings, the demand for them seems insatiable. The national commission's report (Anderson et al., 1985) recommends that "workbook and skill sheet tasks should be pared to the minimum that will actually contribute to growth in reading" (p. 76), and that children should spend more time reading independently as well as engaged in more extended writing opportunities.

Research conducted by Osborn (1981) pinpointed the weaknesses in typical basal seatwork materials. She suggests that workbooks have the appearance of being designed separately from the rest of the reading program—of being afterthoughts. Workbook pages usually focus on the practice of subskills (such as short vowels or compound words) and are seldom related to the selection in the students' reader. To correct these weaknesses, Osborn recommends that workbooks be better integrated with the rest of the basal program. If workbook pages are related to the selections in the students' reader, they can be used to maintain skills taught in the teacher-led lesson. Osborn also detected weaknesses in the design of many workbook pages and worksheets. Directions are sometimes unclear. Often, workbooks have confusing formats or use many different formats. These design problems lead students to devote most of their attention to understanding what to do and how to do it. As a result, they end up paying little attention to the reading skills they are supposed to be practicing.

Based on her findings, Osborn (1981) drew up a set of guidelines for designing and evaluating workbook and work sheet tasks. A slightly adapted version of these guidelines is presented in Figure 3.1. Teachers may use them for evaluating commercial workbooks and

**Figure 3.1**   Selected Guidelines for Developing Work Sheets

1. The layout of the pages should combine attractiveness with utility.

2. Instructions to the students should be clear, unambiguous, and easy to follow. Brevity is a virtue.

3. Most student response modes should be consistent from task to task.

4. Student response modes should be the closest possible to reading and writing.

5. When appropriate, tasks should be accompanied by brief explanations of purpose.

6. There should be a finite number of task forms.

7. Workbook tasks should contain enough content so that there is a chance students doing the task will learn something and not simply be exposed to something.

8. The instructional design of individual tasks and of task sequences should be carefully planned.

   a. As students become more competent in using a particular skill, their practice tasks should become increasingly more complex.
   b. Individual tasks should be doable by students.
   c. Responses should indicate whether or not students understood the task.

9. The skills being practiced should relate to the main reading.

*Source:* Adapted from Osborn, J. (1981). *The purposes, uses and contents of workbooks and some guidelines for teachers and publishers* (Reading Education Report No. 27). Urbana, IL: Center for the Study of Reading, University of Illinois, pp. 100–101. Used with permission.

work sheets, as well as for adapting existing materials. The adaptation process can be very time-consuming, however, and in our experience teachers' energies are often better spent in the development of new practice materials.

When new practice materials are being developed, Osborn (1981) recommends that they be put through a tryout procedure whereby students are observed while using the materials. When flaws are detected, the materials are revised and retested until the problems are resolved. For example, suppose the observer discovered that the directions were too difficult for many students to understand. The rections would be rewritten, and the observer would check to see that they were then understandable to students.

Using Osborn's (1981) design guidelines and tryout procedure, Scheu, Tanner, and Au (1986) developed several work sheet formats for the practice of comprehension skills. Each format went through several cycles of tryout and revision, based on direct observations of second-grade students working with it. Scheu et al. found these formats to be effective in focusing students' attention on the comprehension skills to be practiced. The formats can be used with most basal stories (for this reason, they are referred to as "open formats") and are readily adapted for use with older students. Examples of these open formats are presented later in this chapter, when we present two case histories of reading instruction.

Other research has focused on the way in which seatwork usually is presented and performed in classrooms. Anderson (1981) found that teachers and instructional conditions have a strong influence on students' responses to their seatwork. Anderson discovered that, when teachers talked about seatwork assignments, they usually spoke of procedures for completing them (the "how to") or gave reminders of consequences about finishing: "Don't waste time. Hurry and get done so you can go to recess." Teachers rarely discussed with students the purposes of their assignments or how completing seatwork would help students to become better readers. Not surprisingly, Anderson's observations and interviews in first-grade classrooms revealed that most students think the only reason for doing work sheets is to get them done. When asked why their teacher had given them particular assignments, students responded,

"This is just our work."

"Well, when it's done I get to take it home."

Anderson recommended that teachers balance their messages about procedures and consequences with information about the reading-related reasons for independent activities.

To be able to discuss the purposes of seatwork with students, teachers need to have well-thought-out instructional goals. In other words, they should first have made decisions about lessons and seatwork based on their students' needs in learning to read. One difficulty, pointed out by Shannon (1983), is that the use of basal programs appears to be associated with teachers' abandoning their role as instructional decision makers. When they use basal programs, they sometimes become overly reliant on the teacher's manual. Durkin (1974) found that teachers were often unable to explain the purposes for the instructional materials they used. When asked, "Why are you teaching that?" they answered, "That's what the manual said to do." She suggested that, instead of putting blind trust in the basal manual, teachers assume a more active role in deciding what is to be taught, how it will be taught, and to whom it will be taught.

## DEVELOPING AN INTEGRATED MODEL

What can teachers do to avoid the problems described in the research and make seatwork more beneficial to students' learning to read? The general model we recommend calls for teachers to act as decision makers who consider both their students' needs as developing readers and the qualities of the selection to be read. They will design and assign seatwork tasks based on the kinds of independent practice students need to understand that selection in particular and to become more proficient readers in general. In this model, seatwork is seen as an integral part of the classroom reading program because of the opportunities it provides for students to apply skills on their own, to reflect upon the text, and to make discoveries. Activities are thoroughly integrated with the teacher-led reading lessons, because they give students the chance to work independently with the concepts and skills needed for a thorough understanding of the selection. Teachers explain and have students discuss the purposes of seatwork assignments. Finally, seatwork assignments just completed often serve as the basis for starting the day's discussion of the selection.

In this chapter we will be describing only those seatwork activities that reinforce the comprehension emphasis of the reading lesson. We see these activities as only one part of students' daily seatwork assignments in reading, which should be balanced with other independent activities, such as recreational reading (see chapter 10 in this volume), journal and other writing activities (see chapter 8), and research projects (see chapter 9). We believe that many students can benefit from practice in word identification skills; however, it should generally be embedded in reading and writing activities students find meaningful. Practice of skills in isolation should be kept to a minimum, and, if teachers assign basal workbook pages or work sheets, they should do so in a highly selective manner. As mentioned earlier, teachers will want to evaluate basal practice materials in terms of the Osborn (1981) guidelines, while keeping in mind their own major goals for students' learning.

To make our model for integrating seatwork with reading lessons clearer, we next present examples of lessons and assignments actually given in a second-grade and a fifth-grade classroom. These examples show how two teachers planned and taught lessons and provided appropriate comprehension-oriented seatwork based on particular basal reader selections. In these examples we highlight the following beliefs:

1. Planning of teacher-led lessons and seatwork assignments should be ongoing and responsive to students' needs.
2. Lessons and seatwork should be closely linked to one another.
3. Teachers should take the time to make certain that students understand the reasons for doing seatwork.

## INTEGRATED SEATWORK IN SECOND GRADE

### Overall Planning

Ms. T., a second-grade teacher, previews the story in a student copy of a basal reader, to begin preparation for her instruction. The story, *The Secret Hiding Place* (Bennett, 1978), may be summarized as follows:

> Little Hippo is cared for by the overprotective Big Charles and the other hippos. He wishes to be alone once in a while, especially after he notices that all of the other animals in the jungle have their own hiding places. When Big Charles announces a game of hide-and-seek, Little Hippo seizes the opportunity to run off by himself. After several attempts he finally finds a hiding place that satisfies him.

Ms. T. recognizes that the story is typical in structure, in that it presents a problem, the attempts to deal with the problem, and a resolution. Because her students have read other stories with this structure, Ms. T. expects them to use knowledge of these elements (problem, attempts, resolution) to comprehend this new story. Next she thinks about possible central themes in the story. She decides that the theme, "solitude is good sometimes," is one likely to be meaningful to the children. After viewing the story in this holistic way, Ms. T. begins forming her goals and plans for daily instruction.

## Day 1

*Planning for Day 1.*    Ms. T. decides to begin the lesson by activating her students' background knowledge of the word *jungle*, through a writing activity to be assigned as seatwork. In order to alert students to the link between the seatwork assignment and the story they will be reading, she will tell them that they are expected to share their writing during their small-group reading lesson. She thinks a focus on the word *jungle* should help students understand the story's setting, a point of concern because the illustrations are somewhat abstract. When Ms. T. meets with this reading group, she will elicit the students' ideas about the jungle and assist them in constructing a chart that organizes their contributions. She predicts that her students will probably include in their writing the names of jungle plants and animals and their habitats. By using a chart, Ms. T. expects to set the stage for classifying information about specific animals and their hiding places, information important to understanding the story. Ms. T. will save this visual display so that it can be developed further as the story lessons proceed.

*Reading Group Lesson.*    During their seatwork time, Ms. T. asks students in the reading group to "write what you know about a jungle." When they meet with Ms. T. for their reading lesson, students share ideas they have written. Ms. T. begins the visual display, shown in Figure 3.2. She writes students' contributions on chart paper, helping students decide where in the structure their ideas should be placed. Michael reads what he has written: "The jungle is filled with wild animals like lions and tigers and snakes and hippos." Jennifer contributes, "In the jungle there's lots of trees, bushes, vines, and thorns."

## Day 2

*Assessment and Planning.*    Based on her students' writing and discussion of the word *jungle*, Ms. T. concludes that their background knowledge is adequate for understanding the story and that they should be able to interpret the jungle pictures. She also believes that the use of specific story vocabulary during the discussion will facilitate the decoding of those words when her students encounter them in silent reading of the story. Specific story vocabulary includes the names of the jungle animals and words such as *cave, river,* and *dark.*

On the second day, Ms. T. decides that she will ask the children to make predictions about the story they will be reading. She believes

**Figure 3.2** Visual Display for Day 1 of *The Secret Hiding Place*

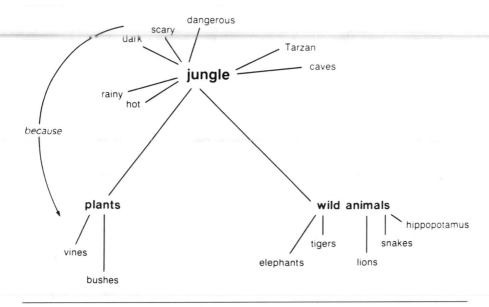

that such questioning will help them see reasons for the first day's activities, focus them on the story's setting, and aid their interpretation of the pictures. Ms. T. will guide her students in the reading and discussion of the first three story pages, to identify the main character and his problem.

Ms. T. decides to prepare a work sheet using an open format for a paragraph cloze task, as shown in Figure 3.3. In the paragraph cloze task, which occupies the upper half of the page, students are required to fill in the blanks with words chosen from the word bank located at the top of the page. The completed paragraph is a summary of the day's reading. When filling in the blanks, students review important story vocabulary. On the bottom half of the page, students answer questions which focus on critical story elements. Because there are several compound words in the passage, Ms. T. includes a review of that skill in item 4. As she assigns the activity, Ms. T. will lead her students to understand the relationship of the activity to that day's reading lesson.

*Reading Group Lesson.* Ms. T. posts the visual display created the day before. She asks, "Why do you think we talked about the

**Figure 3.3**  Work Sheet for Day 2 of *The Secret Hiding Place*

---

Name _____     The Secret Hiding Place

Vocabulary                              pages 7-9

| wish around watch | while want | *Word Bank* morning | cross took | walk care talk |
|---|---|---|---|---|

Directions: Fill in the blanks using words from the <u>Word Bank</u>.

___One_____ Little Hippo felt_____.
"I don't want any breakfast," he said. "I_____
the other hippos wouldn't _____ everything
I do. I wish I could be by myself once in
a_____." All the hippos went along when
Big Charles_____ Little Hippo for his
morning_____. We will take_____ of
you," said Big Charles. But Little Hippo
didn't_____ all the hippos to come. He _____
wanted to look_____ by himself.

Directions: Think about the above story as you answer these questions.

1. How did Little Hippo feel one morning?

_____

2. What did he wish?

_____

3. What is Little Hippo's problem?

_____

4. Look in the story above. Circle all
   the compound words.

94

jungle yesterday?" After the students have discussed their ideas, Matthew concludes, "We were getting our brain ready for our new story." Matthew's thought is confirmed as the students open their books and see the colorful jungle pictures. They read the title, *The Secret Hiding Place*. Ms. T. instructs the children to "read the first three pages silently to see what that title might have to do with a jungle story." After the students have read silently, she asks, "Did you find out anything about the title?" Discussion focuses on identification of the characters and their relationship to Little Hippo. The students suggest that the other hippos "watching Little Hippo all the time" is a problem and that Little Hippo might want a hiding place.

Ms. T. gives the students the work sheet with the paragraph cloze task and questions (Figure 3.3), designed to review the day's reading. She asks, "How will you do this sheet?" The students are already familiar with this format and have often spoken with Ms. T. before about the proper procedures for completing this and other work sheet tasks. Together the students are able to explain the procedure of choosing words from the word bank to complete the sentences. Russell warns, "Be sure they make sense." Allison tells the others, "Cross out the words after you use them." To remind her students of the relationship between the practice activity and the story, Ms. T. then asks, "Where do you think these sentences came from, and why are you doing this work?" "From our story," they chorus. Matthew says, "These are the hardest words from our story." "Yes," answers Ms. T. "On this work sheet you'll be reviewing the story and practicing its more difficult words."

## Day 3

*Assessment and Planning.* Ms. T. assesses both the small-group discussion of the story and the seatwork completed by the children. As she evaluates each child's work sheet, her predictions that the prereading activities would aid students in decoding new vocabulary are confirmed. Students' answers to the question about Little Hippo's problem demonstrate their understanding. For example, students have written that "he doesn't want to be watched" and "he wishes that [he could] walk by himself." Ms. T. is confident that her students are on their way to understanding both the content and structure of the story.

Now that the students have identified the problem in the story, Ms. T. believes they will be able to use their knowledge of story structure to predict that problem-solving attempts and a resolution will follow. She will ask students to read the next three pages, to identify Little Hippo's first attempt to deal with his problem. After discussion of his attempt, students will read three more pages, to see if his attempt was successful.

At this point in the story, other jungle animals and their hiding places are described, so Ms. T. plans for the group to expand the visual display created on day 1. Because the information about animals and their hiding places is important to the story's development, Ms. T. will reinforce these ideas through an independent seatwork activity. She chooses an open format for the practice of classification and prepares the work sheet shown in Figure 3.4.

*Reading Group Lesson.* Ms. T. reinforces the connection between the day 3 lesson and the children's seatwork assignment for day 2 by asking, "What is Little Hippo's problem?" The students read their answers, including, "He doesn't want to be watched all the time" and "He wishes he could walk by himself." Seeing that all students have understood the problem in the story, Ms. T. asks, "What might happen next in our story?" Students predict that Little Hippo might try to solve his problem. "Maybe he will," says Ms. T. "Yesterday we talked about Little Hippo's problem. If Little Hippo tries to solve his problem, what part of the story will that be?" "The trying part," answers Jennifer. "Yes," Ms. T. replies. "We call the 'trying part' the 'attempt.'"

The students read the next three pages to check their prediction. They find that Little Hippo did try to escape from the overprotective hippos by running away into the jungle. "Did running away solve Little Hippo's problem?" Ms. T. asks. This question sets the purpose for the children's silent reading of the next three pages. After reading, the group discusses Little Hippo's attempts to find a place of his own. During his search, he encountered many jungle animals in their hiding places. Ms. T. leads her students to add this new information to the visual display, as shown in Figure 3.5. Then she distributes the classification work sheet, the day's story-related seatwork assignment. "How do you think you will use this sheet?" she asks the children. Together the students conclude that they will use the work sheet and the expanded visual display to help them group and match the animals with their hiding places. Then they go off to work independently.

## Day 4

*Assessment and Planning.* Judging from the students' accurate predictions and thoughtful responses in working through the story,

**Figure 3.4**  Work Sheet for Day 3 of *The Secret Hiding Place*

Name _____      The Secret Hiding
Classification                                Place
Directions: Group words from the BANK under each title below.

<u>Jungle Animals</u>                    <u>Hiding Places</u>

_____          _____

_____          _____

_____          _____

_____          _____

_____          _____

_____          _____

*******************************************************************
Think about the story as you answer these questions:

1. How did Little Hippo try to solve his problem?

_____

2. Where could a hippo hide?

_____

3. Color a picture of the jungle on the back.

_____

Tanner/Scheu  Kamehameha Schools 1984

**Figure 3.5**   Expanded Visual Display for Day 3 of
*The Secret Hiding Place*

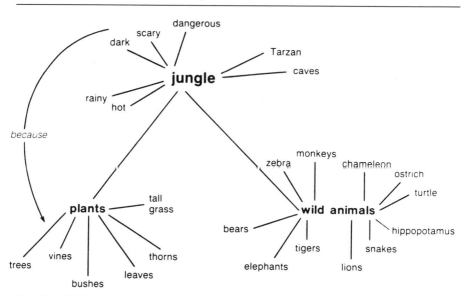

Ms. T. feels that they are demonstrating a growing command of reading comprehension skills. She is pleased with their predictions about how the story will develop, based on knowledge of story structure. As she evaluates the completed classification work sheets, she notes that the students are dealing successfully with the vocabulary. Their written answers to the question, "Where could a hippo hide?" include "behind the grass," "in the water," and "in a cave." Students' responses reveal their involvement with and understanding of the story.

Ms. T. makes plans to conclude reading of the story. She wants to be sure that her students can use the story's events to infer the theme, and that they have the opportunity to draw relationships between the theme and their own life experiences. She also wants them to recognize the place of the resolution within the story's structure. She wants the questions she asks during the discussion to lead to these goals. Because of the importance of these concepts, Ms. T. will also include a seatwork activity designed to practice and reinforce them. She selects an open format for a sequencing work sheet, shown in Figure 3.6. The work sheet presents five sentences that restate the problem, describe attempts to deal with the problem, and restate the

**Figure 3.6**   Work Sheet for Day 4 of *The Secret Hiding Place*

Name_____          The Secret Hiding Place

Sequencing                                      _____

Directions:  Read these sentences.

Little Hippo tried to hide like the other jungle animals.
Little Hippo wished the hippos wouldn't watch everything he did.
Little Hippo can be alone on the top of the hill.
Little Hippo hid in the lion's cave.
Little Hippo ran away from the hippos.

Directions:  Write the sentences as they happened in the story.

1. _____

2. _____

3. _____

4. _____

5. _____

Directions:  Think about the sentences as you answer these questions.

1. What was Little Hippo's problem?

_____

2. How did he solve his problem?

_____

3. Write about times when you like to be alone.

Tanner/Scheu  Kamehameha Schools  1984

resolution, in scrambled order. At the bottom she includes questions that will require the students to reflect on the story's theme and its relationship to their own lives. Ms. T. also plans to have the students reread the entire story on their own. Giving students the chance to read the text without interruption should help them gain an appreciation of the story as a whole, as well as develop reading fluency.

Ms. T. has contingency plans in mind, in the event that students run into difficulty. For example, if students seem to have little background knowledge about jungles, she will read them a trade book on the topic. If students have trouble with the vocabulary, she will spend more time in discussion of the visual display and include troublesome vocabulary in the next day's seatwork assignment. Rather than locking herself into a set course, Ms. T. uses thoughtful planning that will allow her to be responsive to her students' needs.

*Reading Lesson.* "I think we're going to get to the solving part of the story today," says Michael. The rest of the group members agree, and this expectation guides their silent reading of the remainder of the story. Ms. T. asks, "Were you right? Was Little Hippo's problem solved?" Then she asks, "Do you think Little Hippo will use his hiding place? When?" Her questions lead her students to consider the theme, "solitude is good sometimes." Students reflect on the theme's relationship to their own lives when Ms. T. asks, "What about you? Do you ever like to be alone?" Students share their own experiences, stating that sometimes they go "in my bed," "in my room," or "outside" to be by themselves. They talk about why they might want to be alone sometimes, but conclude that they usually like to be "by my family." Ms. T. prepares her students for their sequencing assignment by reviewing the story's main ideas within the structure of problem, attempts, and resolution. Then when they are given their work sheets, the children say, "We know what to do. Put the sentences in the order from our story. Then answer the questions."

## Day 5

*Assessment and Planning.* Thinking through the group's discussion, Ms. T. knows that her students have gained an understanding of the story's theme and have had an opportunity to consider it in terms of their own lives. Her students' sequencing work sheets confirm that they have understood the major story events. She finds particularly interesting their responses to the third item, "Write about times when you like to be alone."

Ms. T. decides on an additional reading and writing activity to reinforce the theme of the story and to encourage independent application of important concepts and reading comprehension skills. She chooses a trade book, *My Secret Hiding Place* (Greydanus, 1980), for the children to read independently as a seatwork activity. She also prepares two questions for them to answer in writing:

1. Why do you think I gave you this book today?
2. Little Hippo thought it was good to be alone once in a while. Write what you think about that.

*Reading Lesson.*   First, Ms. T. leads her students in a short discussion about the book, *My Secret Hiding Place* (Greydanus, 1980). Then she asks them to share their answers to the first question. As a group, they compare and contrast the characters, the settings, and the main ideas. Students are able to summarize: "The *story* is about a little hippo who lives in the jungle and wants to find a place to be alone once in a while. The *book* is about a girl who lives at home and has a place to be away from her family sometimes." Russell's answer to the second question reflects the consensus of the group: "I think it was good to be alone once in a while but not too long."

## Overall Assessment

Ms. T. feels that the sequence of lessons and seatwork assignments for the story, *The Secret Hiding Place*, was quite successful. By integrating meaningful practice activities with small-group discussion lessons, she has had opportunities to work toward goals for the children's development as readers, to evaluate the success of the activities in leading toward these goals, and to formulate new goals for the children's learning. The cyclical planning process she uses is appropriate for reading teachers at all grade levels:

1. Set goals for student learning.
2. Attempt to achieve the goals through small-group discussion and integrated independent activities.
3. Assess the effectiveness of discussion and seatwork.
4. Set new goals.

The lessons described in this section are appropriate when teacher and students are working together on stories at the students' instructional level, where considerable teacher guidance is required for students to understand the story fully. Students may also be assigned to read easier material independently. A whole story may be read at once, without breaks for guided discussion. Students may be asked to complete independent teacher assignments like those just described, provided that they are already familiar with the formats. The instructional cycle for a less challenging story would be much shorter than the five-day one outlined here, although the teacher should plan the cycle to follow much the same process.

A major consideration in reading instruction is that students be led to focus on the general process or strategies used during reading. With the approach recommended here, it is easy for teachers to point out to students how comprehension processes important in one story are also important in others. For example, after several weeks students may have completed sequencing work sheets based on more than one story. At this point the teacher may discuss with students how understanding the sequence of events is generally useful when reading stories. Because work sheets are consistently related to the story and use familiar formats, students are more likely to see connections across stories and to recognize opportunities for the application of comprehension skills and strategies.

In the next section, a fifth-grade teacher's planning is described. This example will highlight how the capabilities of older children allow for longer, more open-ended reading and writing assignments. The teacher still monitors the students' work and provides daily instruction, but the students' greater proficiency as readers and writers is taken into account in both lessons and teacher assignments.

## INTEGRATED SEATWORK IN FIFTH GRADE

### Overall Planning

Ms. O., our fifth-grade teacher, previews *The Dun Horse* (Grinnell, 1983), the story she has selected for one of her reading groups. The story may be summarized as follows:

> *The Dun Horse* is a Pawnee legend about a poor boy and his grandmother, who are tribal outcasts. They acquire a magical horse who helps the boy in hunts and battles. The dun horse tests the boy's loyalty, and the boy fails. When he is given a

second chance, the boy is found worthy and earns an elevated status in the tribe.

Because her students have just completed a social studies unit on American Indians and the West, Ms. O. knows they have some background knowledge that will help them to understand the story. Next she considers possible themes in the story and decides that several may be salient to the children. She predicts that students might infer the themes of "obedience," "not being greedy," and "kindness to all in spite of outward appearances."

Ms. O. decides that her students will read most of the story independently and will meet daily to discuss their assignments. She divides the story into three sections, each of which will give her students opportunities to predict and validate their predictions. She prepares a study guide with several seatwork assignments based on the reading, including tasks calling for students to make links between this story and their prior knowledge, to predict and validate their predictions, and to summarize key story events.

## Reading Group Lessons and Seatwork Assignments

*Day 1.* To begin work with *The Dun Horse*, Ms. O. asks students to complete the first assignment in their study guide. "Look up information and record interesting facts about the Pawnee." The students must choose from classroom reference materials to complete this assignment.

They come to their day 1 lesson with their study guides. Combining the dictionary's definition of *dun* with their information about the Pawnee, the students predict that they are going to begin reading an Indian horse story. Ms. O. asks them to read the first two pages to confirm their prediction and to identify the setting, characters, and problem. After discussion of these points, she directs the students' attention to another study guide assignment: "Predict what you think will happen next in the story." Students understand that they are to write their answers as seatwork.

*Day 2.* The students share their written predictions. For example, Nicole predicts, "What I think will happen next in the story is the little boy is going to be a hero and all the people in the village are going to like him, and him and the grandmother are going to be really rich and famous." Keeping their predictions in mind, students independently read the next part of the story. After reading the assigned pages, they complete their next study guide assignment: "Record what actually happens in the story." Nicole writes, "What actually happened in the story is he is going to get the cow and he is going to kill it and he is going to win. All the people in the village are going to like him and he will marry the daughter."

*Day 3.* Students finish reading the story and complete the next task in their study guides: "Make a comic strip to illustrate the story's events. Make sure each event is in the proper sequence." This activity requires these fifth graders to generate their own interpretation of the story's problem, main events, and resolution. They find the task highly motivating. Their well-detailed pictures include such captions as

> BOY:   Look, a horse. Let's put our pack on it.
> CHIEF:   Whoever gets the calf marries my daughter.

In the reading lesson that follows, discussion focuses on the story's main elements and the relationship of these elements to the theme. Julie has written:

> The lesson I learned from this story is if you really love someone and you promise to obey them, do what they say. And if someone is poor and they have not so nice things, don't tease them about it.

Trevor has included the idea "not to be selfish," while Keith has written about how "you should never brag."

## Overall Assessment

Ms. O. has found that her fifth-grade students were able to draw from their past literary experiences to predict that, in this legend, the outcast would become a hero and triumph over his adversities. She recognizes that her students' prior knowledge about American Indians also helped them to understand the story. In evaluating their daily seatwork assignments, she is pleased with the development of the students' comprehension skills. Students have made appropriate predictions, and their written validations reveal careful reading. Ms. O. understands that the ease with which her students can express and sequence the story's main ideas on their own shows a rather sophisticated ability. She recognizes that they have been guided through the grades to reach their present level of proficiency. While Ms. O. herself identified several possible themes when she planned the lesson, she notes that most of her students were able to generate appropriate themes of their own. The knowledge she has gained about these learners during lessons based on *The Dun Horse* will guide her in planning the students' next set of lessons.

## CONCLUSION

Seatwork will be effective in promoting students' learning to read only if it is designed to support the overall goals of the classroom reading program. Seatwork must be seen as part of teachers' ongoing planning of reading instruction and assessment of students' progress. In our second- and fifth-grade examples, teachers determine the comprehension goals for each story and provide seatwork that reinforces these goals. Seatwork is tied to daily reading lessons, and students understand its reading-related purposes and the proper procedures for completing it. Through completing well-designed assignments, they gain independence in the application of important aspects of reading ability. Well-designed seatwork requires students to engage in extended reading and writing and focus on skills of real value in learning to read. When work sheets are used, their formats are clear, not confusing. Finally, to encourage students' growth as readers further, seatwork will always be balanced with extensive opportunities for students to engage in recreational reading and writing.

## REFERENCES

Anderson, L. M. (1981). *Student responses to seatwork: Implications for the study of students' cognitive processing* (Research Series No. 102). East Lansing, MI: Institute for Research on Teaching, Michigan State University.

Anderson, R. C., Hiebert, E., Scott, J., & Wilkinson, I. (1985). *Becoming a nation of readers: The report of the Commission on Reading.* Washington, DC: National Institute of Education.

Bennett, R. (1978). The secret hiding place. In W. Durr, J. LePere, B. Niehaus, & B. York (Eds.), *Sunburst,* Level 7 (pp. 7–22). Atlanta: Houghton-Mifflin.

Cunningham, P. (1984). What would make workbooks worthwhile? In R. C.

Anderson, J. Osborn, & R. J. Tierney (Eds.), *Learning to read in American schools* (pp. 113–120). Hillsdale, NJ: Lawrence Erlbaum.

Durkin, D. (1974). Some questions about questionable instructional materials. *Reading Teacher, 27,* 13–15.

Fisher, C., Filby, N., Marliave, R., Cahen, L., Dishaw, M., Moore, M. J., & Berliner, D. (1978). *Teaching behaviors, academic learning time and student achievement: Final report of Phase III-B, Beginning Teacher Evaluation Study.* San Francisco: Far West Laboratory for Educational Research and Development.

Greydanus, R. (1980). *My secret hiding place.* Mahwah, NJ: Troll Associates.

Grinnell, G. B. (1983). The dun horse. In B. Weiss, L. Stever, S. Cruikshank, & L. Hunt (Eds.), *Freedom's Ground,* Level 14 (pp. 364–373). New York: Holt, Rinehart and Winston.

Osborn, J. (1981). *The purposes, uses, and contents of workbooks and some guidelines for teachers and publishers* (Reading Education Report No. 27). Urbana, IL: Center for the Study of Reading, University of Illinois.

Scheu, J., Tanner, D., & Au, K. H. (1986). Designing seatwork to improve students' reading comprehension ability. *Reading Teacher, 40,* 18–25.

Shannon, P. (1983). The use of commercial reading materials in American schools. *Reading Research Quarterly, 19* (1), 68–85.

## RECOMMENDED READINGS

Rupley, W. H., & Blair, T. R. (1987). Assignment and supervision of reading seatwork: Looking in on 12 primary teachers. *Reading Teacher, 40,* 391–393.

Scheu, J., Tanner, D., & Au, K. H. (1986). Designing seatwork to improve students' reading comprehension ability. *Reading Teacher, 40,* 18–25.

# PART II

# Evaluation
# and
# Individualization

Chapter 4

# Student Evaluation
# and Basal Instruction

MARJORIE Y. LIPSON
KAREN K. WIXSON

In this chapter we examine three purposes for engaging in assessment in basal programs. First, we discuss placement as a traditional focus of basal assessment. Second, we discuss using the basal lesson as a means of formative or diagnostic evaluation of student performance and instructional effectiveness. Finally, summative evaluation in terms of mastery is examined as we describe alternative means of evaluating student learning and performance.

We argue in this chapter that the appropriate role of evaluation in basal instruction is to inform instruction (Wixson & Lipson, 1986). The purpose in evaluating either students' performance or the instructional effort should be to find ways to facilitate student learning. In addition to traditional types of evaluation (e.g., skills mastery tests and comprehension questioning), we describe assessment strategies and instruments that can be used for ongoing assessment of the student in interaction with the basal lesson.

## BACKGROUND

Assessment within a basal reading program typically includes several types of evaluation procedures. First, most basal series employ some type of informal reading inventory (IRI) to determine students' appropriate level of placement within the series. These types of tests typically have word lists, to assess word recognition, and short reading selections followed by questions, to assess oral reading and comprehension. Although many educators have raised questions about IRIs as assessment tools, they can provide teachers with a "best guess" estimate of where to begin instruction in a series.

Placement decisions, however, should be tempered by an awareness of the limitations and problems associated with all such instruments. For example, today's basals do not control content and vocabulary to the extent that basals did when IRIs were first introduced as a method of placement. Passages taken from a single level in a current basal differ greatly, and students' performance is likely to vary according to the passages selected for use on the IRI. Therefore, it is difficult, if not impossible, to determine if a student's performance is representative of how she or he is likely to perform on various selections in her or his reader. Other problems associated with placement inventories will be discussed somewhat later. For now, it is important to know that IRIs provide only the most general guidance for placing students, merely suggesting a starting point, and must be supplemented with continuous teacher observation and judgment.

The second type of evaluation procedure found in basals is the periodic end-of-level or end-of-unit tests used to assess students' mastery of skills that have been taught. These instruments are criterion-referenced tests that have been designed to compare students' performance to some preestablished criterion or standard. As such, they are meant to determine whether and how well a student has learned what has been taught. They are not designed to compare a student's performance to the achievement of other students, although they are frequently used as accountability measures, somewhat like standardized achievement tests.

In general, the mastery tests provided in basal reading programs evaluate students' mastery of the "scope and sequence" of skills within the series itself. The periodic administration of skills mastery tests also provides for continuous assessment of individual and/or class performance throughout the year. A major problem with these measures, however, is that they frequently assess skills in isolation, on a series of discrete subtests. In addition, they presume that the order of skill acquisition is invariable; that students must master a specific skill before proceeding to other skills and/or materials. Neither this assumption nor the assumption that reading skill can be evaluated in discrete parts is warranted, given current knowledge about the reading process (Mason, Osborn, & Rosenshine, 1977).

The third type of basal assessment is the questions designed to evaluate students' understanding of the reading selections. Indeed, student responses to the questions posed during reading are the only real measure of comprehension that most teachers have available to them. This is particularly interesting when contrasted with the more formal measures used to assess skill mastery, because the difference in emphasis placed on the assessment of various components of a basal reading program almost certainly influences the emphasis that is placed on instruction of these same components.

Most basals use a classification scheme to label the comprehension questions they provide. These schemes are typically based on one of several well-known taxonomies (e.g., Barrett, 1972; Bloom, 1956). However, there is little evidence that these taxonomies represent real differences in comprehension skills or in the level of difficulty of different questions. In addition, many basal questions require memory rather than understanding or divert students' attention from important to unimportant information.

The questions students are asked influence both the products they produce and the manner in which they process information. Thus, the comprehension that is revealed through questioning is, at least in part, a function of the questions that have been asked (Raphael, Winograd, & Pearson, 1980; Wixson, 1983, 1984). Although questioning can be a potent form of assessment, the techniques employed must be carefully considered. As we have seen, this is also true of basal assessment procedures for placement and mastery.

## RATIONALE

Effective assessment in reading should be consistent with what we know about the reading process, and with what and how we teach. The most serious problem with current reading assessments in general, and basal assessments in particular, is that they do not adequately reflect either of these concerns. The newest basal series incorporate many instructional innovations based on current views of reading that have emerged from research during the past fifteen years. However, this research has had little impact on our assessments, which remain virtually the same as they were in the 1920s (Farr & Carey, 1986; Johnston, 1984). It is clear that there is a mismatch between what we know about the reading process and how we typically test reading (Valencia & Pearson, 1987).

What do we know about reading that is not reflected in basal assessments? First, as described in the introduction to this book, we know that reading is a holistic, constructive process that varies as a function of the interaction among reader, text, and task factors.

Current basal assessments treat reading as an aggregate of isolated skills and, furthermore, imply that reading is a static process, that students can be evaluated under one set of conditions and that this performance will be representative of their performance under all conditions. For example, placement tests evaluate students on passages that are much shorter than those students are expected to read in their classroom texts. In addition, these tests do not take into account differences in genre or coherence. Similarly, skills mastery tests evaluate a skill such as main-idea identification under highly restricted conditions (e.g., short, unfamiliar, informational passages with initial topic sentences) that do not reflect the complexity and variety of factors that are likely to influence students' ability under "real" reading conditions.

A second thing we know about reading that is not accounted for in basal assessments is that students' background knowledge of the topics about which they are reading; their knowledge about the purposes, goals, and strategies of reading; and their attitudes and motivation toward reading affect their reading performance. Teachers need to understand that reading ability may vary depending on the amount and type of prior knowledge students possess (Lipson, 1984). More important, they will need to use their understanding of students' prior knowledge to make differential decisions about basal instruction.

There are several dangers in the situation where instruction and assessment are based on different views of reading. A primary concern is that advances in instructional methods and materials are undermined because inappropriate assessment continues to drive instruction (Valencia & Pearson, 1987). As noted in *Becoming a Nation of Readers* (Anderson, Hiebert, Scott, & Wilkinson, 1985),

> If schools are to be held accountable for performance for reading test scores, the tests must be broad-gauged measures that reflect the ultimate goals of instruction as closely as possible. Otherwise, the energies of teachers and students may be misdirected. They may concentrate on peripheral skills that are easily tested and readily learned. Holding a reading teacher accountable for scores on a test of, say, dividing words into syllables is like holding a basketball coach accountable for the percentage of shots players make during the pre-game warm up. [p. 100]

There is also danger in the fact that teachers and administrators have come to trust test data over their own good judgment. Teachers must come to trust that assessment within the instructional reading program is a continuous process necessary to making decisions that increase the "goodness" of the match between each child and the materials and methods of instruction. The goal of assessment should be to find the conditions that "call forth learning" (Hunt, 1965); to determine the conditions under which children *can* and *will* learn (Wixson & Lipson, 1986).

It appears that we need to consider a completely different relationship between instruction and assessment, one that is based on our current understanding of reading. Present knowledge suggests that we need to develop assessment procedures to evaluate reading in ways that are more relevant to the holistic, terminal goals of reading instruction, and that we need to assess directly the factors that are known to influence reading, rather than to ignore them or attempt to create situations where they do not matter. Basal assessments need to be viewed from the larger perspective of the purpose for the test or procedure and the type of information that is necessary for achieving that purpose. There are three main purposes for basal assessment, and they form the basis for the three types of evaluation described in the remaining sections of this chapter: *placement, formative* (diagnostic), and *summative* (achievement or mastery) evaluation.

## PLACEMENT EVALUATION

As described previously, placement evaluation is common in current basals and is designed to provide the teacher with enough information to begin instruction. We open this section of the chapter with a plea that you exercise caution. Current research clearly suggests that reading ability is not static, that students' performance is likely to vary under different reading situations. As we have already noted, however, the existing placement tests can provide you with a "best-guess" notion of where to place students in basal reading materials *for the purposes of getting started.* In order to enhance the utility of these first global measures, we would suggest that you supplement your placement procedures with additional information about your students' understanding of the reading process.

### Knowledge About Reading

Children create their own theories of reading, based on the types of instructional activities or recreational opportunities they have encountered. When student theories of reading are inaccurate, or their image of their own competence is askew, learning can be difficult. Note the responses of three young readers to the question, Do you have trouble in reading?

> MICHAEL (age 13):   I must, my Mom's making me come here [to a reading clinic].
>
> JANE (age 11):   Yes, when I read, the stuff just seems to go out of my head. [A probe suggests that "stuff" means "ideas."]
>
> SARA (age 7):   Yes, I read too softly.

Note that Michael estimates his reading difficulty only in terms of someone else's appraisal—he takes little or no responsibility. Sara, on the other hand, estimates reading competence using a criterion appropriate only for public performance. Such definitions can cause problems because students often fail to see the reason for instructional activities. Only Jane provides a response that suggests she may grasp the nature and demands of real reading and has recognized a serious limitation in her own ability.

Increasingly, researchers and educators have begun to realize that explicit knowledge of reading facilitates the ability to control one's reading actions (often called metacognitive skills). Several instruments have recently demonstrated that it is possible to gather useful assessment information about children's perceptions of reading goals and tasks. For example, Paris and his associates (Paris, Cross, & Lipson, 1984; Paris & Jacobs, 1984) have developed the Index of Reading Awareness, which is helpful because it may be used as a screening tool for an entire class. Questions such as the following (Paris & Jacobs, 1984, p. 2092) are included on this test of metacognitive awareness:

1. What is the hardest part about reading for you?
   a. Sounding out the words.
   b. When you don't understand the story.
   c. Nothing is hard about reading for you.
2. Why do you go back and read things over again?
   a. Because it's good practice.
   b. Because you didn't understand it.
   c. Because you forgot some words.

The Index of Reading Awareness uses a multiple-choice format, but there is no reason why you could not use open-ended questions if you believe that your students are capable of writing their responses.

In Figure 4.1, you will find another assessment instrument, the Reading Comprehension Interview (RCI), designed for individual administration (Wixson, Bosky, Yochum, & Alvermann, 1984). The RCI is designed to assess "(1) the student's perception of the goal/purpose of reading activities in the context of different reading materials; (2) the child's understanding of different reading task requirements, both in terms of the task demands and the teacher's criteria for evaluation; and (3) the strategies that the reader reports using when engaging in various reading tasks, such as answering questions and remembering information" (p. 347). This is an especially appropriate instrument because, as you can see from the sample forms, you will glean information about your students' perceptions of reading within *and* beyond the basal. Students' knowledge of reading and the purposes of instruction can influence their performance in different reading settings; therefore, it is important to keep these influences in mind when you are making placement decisions.

### Deciding on Basal Placement

From the foregoing, you can see that placement decisions are not likely to be definitive, nor even very accurate. Therefore, you need to be aware of the factors associated with placement testing that affect performance in ways that make it difficult to predict how students will perform on other passages within a particular level of the series:

- Selections (e.g., length, familiarity, type, coherence)
- Task conditions (e.g., number and nature of the comprehension questions)
- Test administration and scoring (oral versus silent reading; what miscues are scored as errors)

To temper the problems associated with these instruments, teachers must ask the question, Are the testing materials and procedures representative of, and comparable to, the basal materials and procedures used during instruction? As Wood (1988) notes, what is needed is a structured approach to determine how an individual handles the reading of actual textbook material under conditions that simulate the classroom situation. Given the problems associated with existing placement inventories, a teacher may find it just as useful to sit down with a student, armed with a series of levels of the basal to be used and a willingness to listen. The teacher might then ask the child to read (orally or silently) several brief portions of each text and

**Figure 4.1** Reading Comprehension Interview

Name:                                                          Date:
Classroom teacher:                    Reading level:          Grade:

*Directions:* Introduce the procedure by explaining that you are interested in finding out what children think about various reading activities. Tell the student that he or she will be asked questions about his/her reading, that there are no right or wrong answers, and that you are only interested in knowing what s/he should say so and you will go on to the next one.

General probes such as "Can you tell me more about that?" or "Anything else?" may be used. Keep in mind that the interview is an informal diagnostic measure and you should feel free to probe to elicit useful information.

1. What hobbies or interests do you have that you like to read about?
2. a. How often do you read in school?
   b. How often do you read at home?
3. What school subjects do you like to read about?

*Introduce reading and social studies books.*
*Directions:* For this section use the child's classroom basal reader and a content area textbook (social studies, science, etc.). Place these texts in front of the student. Ask each questions twice, once with reference to the basal reader and once with reference to the content area textbook. Randomly vary the order of presentation (basal, content). As each question is asked, open the appropriate text in front of the student to help provide a point of reference for the question.

4. What is the most important reason for reading this kind of material?
   Why does your teacher want you to read this book?
5. a. Who's the best reader you know in _____?
   b. What does he/she do that makes him/her such a good reader?
6. a. How good are you at reading this kind of material?
   b. How do you know?
7. What do you have to do to get a good grade in _____ in your class?

8. a. If the teacher told you to remember the information in this story/chapter, what would be the best way to do this?
   b. Have you ever tried _____ ?

9. a. If your teacher told you to find the answers to the questions in this book what would be the best way to do this? Why?
   b. Have you ever tried _____ ?

10. a. What is the hardest part about answering questions like the ones in this book?
    b. Does that make you do anything differently?

*Introduce at least two comprehension worksheets.*

*Directions:* Present the worksheets to the child and ask questions 11 and 12. Ask the child to complete portions of each worksheet. Then ask questions 13 and 14. Next, show the child a worksheet designed to simulate the work of another child. Then ask question 15.

11. Why would your teacher want you to do worksheets like these (for what purpose)?

12. What would your teacher say you must do to get a good mark on worksheets like these? (What does your teacher look for?)

*Ask the child to complete portions of at least two worksheets.*

13. Did you do this one differently from the way you did that one? How or in what way?

14. Did you have to work harder on one of these worksheets than the other? (Does one make you think more?)

*Present the simulate worksheet.*

15. a. *Look over this worksheet.* If you were the teacher, what kind of mark would you give the worksheet? Why?
    b. If you were the teacher, what would you ask this person to do differently next time?

Source: Wixson, K. K., Bosky, A. B., Yochum, M. N., & Alvermann, D. E. (1984). An interview for assessing students' perceptions of classroom reading tasks. Reading Teacher, 37, 354-359. Reprinted with permission of Karen Wixson and the International Reading Association.

talk about what has been read. Although this technique is hardly controlled, it may result in decisions as fine-grained as can be expected at this stage of the assessment process.

Despite the problems associated with current placement inventories, we believe that teachers nevertheless need a starting point, even for conducting more sophisticated types of assessment. Basal-linked IRIS, coupled with information about students' knowledge of the reading process, can provide a quick initial assessment.

## FORMATIVE EVALUATION

Formative evaluation provides for ongoing student assessment during instruction. This level of assessment includes the questioning traditionally found in basals but is expanded to include all phases of the basal lesson—prereading, guided reading, and postreading. The types of information that should be gathered at this level of assessment include students' background knowledge of the reading selection, their knowledge of the purposes and strategies relevant for reading a particular selection, their ability to apply their skills and strategies to the reading selection, and their comprehension and learning of the reading selection.

We would like to suggest strongly that the bulk of assessment in reading can and should be done continuously and in conjunction with the daily instructional program. These continuous assessments may be designed to refine placement decisions made earlier, but more often they will be used to make decisions about how to adapt and refine instruction (see chapter 5).

### Prior Knowledge

As you have seen, students may vary substantially in the amount and type of prior knowledge they possess. It should also be clear that this variation in prior knowledge can and does produce variation in reading performance. Thus, it will be important to evaluate your students' prior knowledge throughout your instructional exchanges and to estimate the influence of prior knowledge differences on comprehension. Before we describe how to assess prior knowledge, we need to consider briefly the issue of what to assess. Because the time available to both teachers and students is limited, we need to be certain that we are assessing information that is important for understanding the present reading selection.

Some basal series present all selections in units organized around central themes. For example, Scott-Foresman's 1987 edition of their American Tradition Series presents all instruction in three-week blocks, using topics such as "Day and Night" or "Birds" as conceptual organizers. Of course, it is appropriate to conduct prior knowledge assessments at the beginning of these units. Caution should be exercised, however, since these "themes" may be only loosely related to the reading selections and may actually divert students' attention from the portions of text most critical to comprehension. For example, in a recent suggestion for enhancing instruction, Cooper (1986) provides a selection about a little owl. The obvious inclination is to evaluate students' prior knowledge about owls. The story, however, revolves around an owl's concern that no one remembers his birthday. When the owl returns home, he discovers that a surprise birthday party awaits him. Along the way, he finds a new friend and is able to enjoy his birthday even more because it is shared. In situations like this, prior knowledge about the apparent topic (owls) is less critical than is knowledge about how to read this type of text (a fantasy about friends with cause-and-effect relationships throughout). The story can be enjoyed and understood if children know about birthdays and surprise parties, even if they know very little about owls.

Thus, you can see that assessing prior knowledge requires you to understand exactly what background will be critical to understanding the particular text the children will be reading. Some stories can be fully understood without a great deal of specific prior factual knowledge. What they may require is knowledge about human relationships and/or some specific reading knowledge or skill.

There are a variety of ways to assess prior knowledge. Holmes and Roser (1987) identify and compare five techniques that can be used during instruction: free recall, word association, structured questions, recognition, and unstructured discussion. These are easily adaptable to any basal instructional program, requiring only observant teachers who understand their purpose in gathering such information.

When using free recall, the teacher simply asks students, "Tell me everything you know about _____." Assessing prior knowledge through *word association* requires that the teacher select several key words and ask children what comes to mind when they hear each one. A similar technique involves *recognition*, in which the teacher prepares several statements or key terms beforehand. Then students are asked to select the words, phrases, or sentences they believe are related to the key terms or would be present in a particular selection.

As an alternative, teachers can use *structured questions* to assess prior knowledge. In this case, questions are posed, and answered, before the reading, to determine how much and what students know *prior* to reading. Finally, teachers can use *unstructured discussion.* This is most like what is traditionally done in basal instruction, since students freely generate their own ideas about a topic, with no focusing from the teacher. However, Holmes & Roser (1987) conclude that this approach may not be worth the effort, since it is the least effective and efficient procedure of the five.

The special value of the work of Holmes & Roser (1987) is that they have actually collected data to determine the utility and efficiency of these assessment strategies. In a recent paper, however, Valencia et al. (1987) suggest that different procedures actually provide different types of information. Thus, prior knowledge measures may not all be assessing the same aspects of existing information. In short, we may need to use multiple measures of prior knowledge, something that is most easily accomplished by a skilled classroom teacher during actual instruction.

One procedure that has been well researched and is easily incorporated into instruction is a word-association procedure developed by Langer (1982, 1984). Called the Prereading Plan, or PREP, it is designed to assess both the quality and quantity of students' prior knowledge. Because it can be used for assessment purposes at the time of instruction, PREP is a particularly effective strategy. The general procedure is as follows:

1. Review materials and list two to four key concepts.
2. Use these questions as the basis for a discussion:
   a. What comes to mind when you hear/read _____? (Write the students' responses on the board.)
   b. What made you think of _____?
   c. Given our discussion, can you add any new ideas about _____?
3. Students arrange the ideas listed on board into some sensible order.
4. Evaluate student responses as follows:
   a. *Much prior knowledge*—precise definitions, analogies, conceptual links among concepts.
   b. *Some prior knowledge*—examples and characteristics, but no connections or relations.
   c. *Little prior knowledge*—sound-alikes or look-alikes, associated experiences, little or no meaning relations.

Langer suggests that you compile this information for each group of students as you work together by creating a matrix, with students' names down one side and the three categories (Much, Some, Little) across the top. Although it is not explicitly called for, teachers can use the technique to make decisions about grouping and pacing (see chapter 2) or about appropriate instructional adaptations (see chapter 5).

## Metacognitive Knowledge

Our previous discussion of metacognitive interviews focused on general knowledge about reading; however, students need to use this knowledge in actual reading settings. Thus, you may wish to question students about their knowledge of the specific reader, text, and instructional factors before, during, and after their reading of a particular selection (Wixson, Peters, Weber, & Roeber, 1987).

Questions to ask before a student reads a selection might investigate the purposes and goals for reading a particular selection and how understanding the nature of the task(s) they must complete during and/or after reading influences the way they read. Other questions may evaluate students' awareness that experience, knowledge, and interests influence their reading. Questions about the type of text to be read and where it might be found outside of reading instruction are appropriate, as are questions about students' awareness of the skills they have that will enable them to complete a particular reading activity successfully. The following are some suggestions:

1. What type of text is this?
2. How can you tell?
3. Where else would you find a text like this?
4. Have you ever read a text like this before?
5. What do you know about the topic of this text?
6. How will your existing knowledge/experience affect your reading?
7. Is there anything special about the way you read this type of text?
8. How will you use this information after you've read (i.e., what's the task)?
9. How will you read so that you can complete these tasks?

Questions you may want to ask during and after reading focus on the organization of the text as a whole and of different sections of the text, as well as on various other features such as the author's use of linguistic devices (e.g., connective ties, referential terms), literary devices (e.g., figurative language, imagery, flashback), and adjunct aids (e.g., illustrations, charts, italics, headings, and subheadings). Questions asked during reading may also focus on the strategies that are appropriate for undertaking a particular reading activity. Examples include:

1. How did the author organize this section? Why?
2. Why did the author use *(linguistic device)* to organize this section?
3. What clues are there to the author's organization?
4. Why did the author start this section with *(e.g., however)*?
5. What does the author mean by *(e.g., metaphor)*?
6. What techniques does the author use to tell us _____?
7. What is the purpose of the illustration/chart/figure on page ____?
8. How did you know you had made a mistake and needed to go back?
9. How did you figure out the word you missed?

Those questions asked during reading may typically be asked after as well; however, three questions are probably best posed after reading:

1. How did what you knew before reading make a difference in reading this text?
2. How did you figure out the answer to the question on page ____?
3. How does the story check out against the prediction we made in the beginning?

A similar but more open-ended procedure involves using "think-alouds" throughout the actual reading of text (Lipson, Bigler, Poth, & Wickizer, 1987). During think-alouds, students are stopped periodically as they read aloud from text and asked to talk about what they were *doing* and *thinking* as they read that portion of text. Although there may be problems using this procedure with young or less verbal students (Afflerbach & Johnston, 1984), we have gathered useful information about students' metacognitive awareness using this approach. For example, some students respond with statements like, "Oh, I don't usually *think* while I read" or, "I wasn't thinking, I was too scared." Others give responses like, "I was thinking about how this is just like what we've been studying in social studies" or, "I was trying to see how this information fit with the part up there [previous text]." Such comments can reveal both the existence and absence of strategies and approaches useful for effective reading.

The advantage of asking metacognitive questions within the context of the basal lesson is that you are learning about students' knowledge of particular reading situations in a manner that permits immediate intervention. Once again, as we clarify the connections between assessment and instruction, we create a more integrated approach, one that respects their interdependence.

## Comprehension

As you consider assessment of comprehension, you must try to keep in mind that there are really two issues involved. First, we are interested in students' comprehension of a specific selection. Second, and more important, we are concerned about assessing students' growing comprehension *ability* (Johnston, 1985). Thus, as we describe ways of expanding your assessment repertoire in the area of comprehension, we will be focusing on procedures that tell you not only whether students have understood what they have just read but also something about whether they are acquiring the tools needed to understand other texts. Because the first of these purposes is formative and the latter is summative, we will be returning to this issue again in the next section.

*Retelling.* Readers' understanding of textual materials has traditionally been evaluated using question response scores. Indeed, the practice of answering questions is so pervasive that it is sometimes difficult for teachers to recognize that ability to answer questions is not the same thing as understanding. An alternative or complement to questioning is to evaluate students' comprehension using free recall or retelling. This allows you to determine what students understand and remember without the structure and information provided by probing (questions). You may also gather additional information, since readers often construct meaning from a passage that is not captured by their question responses. Retelling can add immeasurably to our understanding of readers' comprehension, because it allows us to get a view of the quantity, quality, and organization of information gleaned during reading.

During retelling, students' initial responses to the material should involve *free* recall of the text without the interference of the teacher.

This provides you with information about how students are constructing meaning from the text, without external influence. Because it is important to influence student response as little as possible, initial requests for retelling should be intentionally open-ended. You can initiate the retelling of text with statements or questions like

> Tell me what you have read, using your own words.
> What is the text about?
> Tell me as much information as you can about what you have just read. [Ringler & Weber, 1984]

Following the uninterrupted retelling, questions that probe readers' understanding of the text can be used to elicit further information. Probes should be based directly on the retelling, for example,

- Tell me more about what you have read.
- Tell me more about what happened.
- Tell me more about the people about whom you just read.
- Tell me more about where this happened.

If you wish to structure the retelling even more at this point, you may want to ask probe questions using elements of text structure appropriate to the type of reading selection. The following are examples of probes for thematic stories and informational selections.

STORY SELECTIONS
- What is the main problem the characters face? (problem)
- What makes it difficult for the characters to solve their problem? (conflict)
- How is the problem solved? (resolution)
- What lessons are there in the story? (theme)
- What is the main thing that happens in the story? (theme)
- What do you learn about the main characters? (characterization)
- How is the setting of the story important? (setting)
- Which event is a "turning point" in the story? (events)

INFORMATIONAL SELECTIONS
- What is the central idea of this selection? (central purpose)
- What are the main points of the subsections in this text? (major ideas)

- What details does the text provide to support the major ideas? (supporting details)
- How does the author organize the information to tell you about the central and major ideas? (structure)

Using these or similar probes, you gather information about the child's ability to recall and infer important story information. In addition, you can regularly check students' affective responses to their readings with questions like the following:

Did you learn anything from reading this?

Did you find this selection interesting?

Did you enjoy reading this?

A checklist can be employed to organize the assessment information. Ringler and Weber (1984) suggest summarizing on a chart the information you gather from either retelling or questioning. Thus you could record students' ability to recall or answer questions related to components of text (e.g., theme, character). By recording the text title and date, you can also track changes in these abilities over time.

In addition to free recall and probed retelling, you may also use structured questions (see next section). Since these impose someone else's view of what is important in the text, you should avoid using them until students have provided all possible information during retelling. In this way, you will be able to distinguish between that information generated freely, information elicited with minimal cueing, and information generated through direct cueing.

*Questioning.* As a classroom teacher, you will continue to make questioning a mainstay of your comprehension assessment. Although we believe that retelling enriches the picture, careful questioning can tell you much about students' understanding of a particular selection and about their ability to comprehend *in general.*

We noted earlier that there are problems associated with most of the taxonomies used to classify questions. As Pearson and Johnson (1978) point out, questions must be considered in relation to the probable source of the answer if we are to know what is required for a correct response. Pearson and Johnson originally devised a three-level taxonomy that captured the relationship between a question and its answer source: text-explicit questions, text-implicit questions, and scriptally-implicit (schema-based) questions. This taxonomy has been extended and used widely as an instructional tool by Raphael (1982; 1986). Her latest refinement of these question-answer relationships (QARs) includes four types in all, by dividing the last into two subtypes: These are

1. *Right-There QARs.* The answer is explicitly stated in the text and is usually easy to find. The words used to make up the question and to answer it are "right there," in the same sentence.
2. *Think-and-Search QARs.* The answer can be inferred from text information. The answer is in the story, but you need to put together different story parts to find it. Words for the question and the answer are not found in the same sentence.
3. *In-My-Head QARs.* These scriptally implicit questions—those that must be answered by referring to prior knowledge—have been divided into two types.
   a. *Author-and-You QARs.* The answer is not in the story. You need to think about what you already know, what the author tells you in the text, and how it fits together.
   b. *On-My-Own QARs.* The answer is not in the story. You can even answer the question without the story. You need to use your own experience.

Distinguishing between questions on the basis of the source of the answer is extremely important in assessment. We want to be able to characterize children's comprehension strengths and weaknesses as accurately as possible. If we are not sure what is required to answer the questions we ask, then it will be difficult to make instructional decisions about comprehension. For example, if we think the answer is right there (explicit), when in fact the answer requires connecting text information through inference, then we may incorrectly assume that students cannot locate detail information in text, while the problem is actually related to inferential ability. Therefore, you must first determine the task demands of the questions themselves.

You may also want to consider the effects of question placement, as you will get a far more comprehensive picture of students' comprehension abilities if you systematically vary the position of the questions. Most teachers regularly ask questions *after* the selection has been read. Questions in this position place a premium on student recognition of important information. However, another aspect of comprehension is students' ability to locate and recognize information, depending on their purpose. Thus you may want to ask questions *before* reading. Finally, you can ask questions *during* reading, to help you to determine whether students are making connections and integrating relevant information. By refining your questioning strategies, you can gather important instructional information.

Of course, in addition to concerns about the quality and placement of questions in general, you will be concerned about what to ask questions about. As we have already noted, you can gather more helpful information if your structured questions are crafted with some purpose in mind. Ringler and Weber (1984) provide an extremely helpful discussion of the role of questions in comprehension assessment, and we suggest you seek it out. It is important that you devise some means for mapping or outlining text, in order to determine the important elements of information and their relationships within a particular selection (see chapter 5). These maps or outlines can then serve as the basis for the formulation of structured comprehension questions. They are also useful for evaluating the importance of preexisting assessment questions and the content of students' retelling.

Although these strategies may seem time-consuming, you can see that the instructional value of assessment information is enhanced. You do not have to characterize students simply as "good comprehenders" and "poor comprehenders," but can describe quite precisely what and how they understand.

## Dynamic Assessment

An interactive view of reading has led to a new set of procedures, often referred to as "dynamic assessment." According to Cioffi and Carney (1983), dynamic assessment is an interactive teaching/learning relationship. The examiner (as teacher/observer) presents the student with a reading activity, observes the response, and then introduces modifications of the task. These modifications are really hypotheses about the teaching/learning situation. The purpose of this type of assessment is to identify the student's potential for learning under different instructional conditions or to identify factors and conditions that facilitate or inhibit learning so that a student's behavior can be changed. Dynamic assessment is an important advancement because it permits the evaluation of how a student can and will perform under different conditions. In so doing, it provides an opportunity for true integration of instruction and assessment.

One of the most versatile dynamic assessment procedures available is the individual Comprehension Profile described by Wood (1988) and shown in Figure 4.2. It can be used both as a placement procedure and as a device for continuous assessment. The profile

# Figure 4.2  Individual Comprehension Profile

Name  _Eric Matthews_          Date  _September 3_          Grade  _3_

| | Reading type | | Genre | | | | | Recall mode | | | Degree of guidance | | | Overall compr. | Comments |
|---|---|---|---|---|---|---|---|---|---|---|---|---|---|---|---|
| | Oral | Silent | Poetry | Plays | Realistic fiction | Fantasy | Nonfiction | Free recall | Probed recall | Infer, predict | Background knowl. | Preteaching vocab. | Assist during rdg. | 1 = none<br>2 = some<br>3 = most<br>4 = all | |
| Level 2₂ p. 41 | ✓ | | | | ✓ | | | | ✓ | | – | – | – | 3 | A little choppy at first, then very fluent with accurate recall |
| Level 2₂ p. 76 | ✓ | | | ✓ | | | | ✓ | ✓ | ✓ | – | – | – | 4 | Very fluent reading and retelling |
| Level 2₂ p. 168 | | ✓ | | | | | ✓ | ✓ | ✓ | ✓ | – | – | – | 4 | Needs no assistance – has control over word recognition and comprehension |
| Level 3₁ p. 101 | ✓ | | | | ✓ | | | ✓ | ✓ | | – | – | – | 2 | Some fluency problems & sketchy recall (e.g., misread "trail" for "trial," "beautiful" for "body") |
| Level 3₁ p. 96 | ✓ | | | | | ✓ | | ✓ | ✓ | ✓ | ✓ | ✓ | | 3 | With help, recall is improved; can predict and infer (e.g., Why do you think...) |
| Level 3₁ p. 66 | | ✓ | | | | | ✓ | ✓ | ✓ | ✓ | ✓ | ✓ | ✓ | 4 | Had difficulty recognizing "ambulance" – "emergency." Defined "Red Cross" & "swerved." This helped! |
| Level 3₁ p. 119 | | ✓ | | | | | ✓ | ✓ | ✓ | ✓ | ✓ | ✓ | | 4 | Tried with and without guidance. Comprehension is improved with help. |

Overall assessment  Eric's comprehension while reading silently seems better than while reading orally. Can retell in own words at level 3, but gives more detail when probed or prompted. With assistance, seems to benefit from instruction in this material.

Appropriate placement level  _3₁_

*Source:* Wood, K. D (1988). Techniques for assessing students' potential for learning. *The Reading Teacher, 41,* 440–447, Figure 2. Reprinted with permission of Karen Wood and the International Reading Association.

results from gathering information and charting it on a matrix. The information is recorded as students read from the basal, under conditions that parallel the daily expectations in the classroom. Because the matrix is teacher made, you can enter whatever conditions are relevant for your program and students. Wood, however, suggests that the following conditions be observed and recorded: type of reading, genre being read, mode of recall, and degree of guidance.

The last of these conditions, degree of guidance, is especially critical to dynamic assessment, since observation in this area can provide the most instructionally useful information. As Cioffi and Carney (1983) note,

> When a child fails to respond to a question at the literal level after reading the text silently, the lack of response itself is of limited value. The examiner must explore why the question was not answered. Possible hypotheses include: the child is unable to decode the material; the child reads the material but has difficulty remembering it; the child has inadequate prior knowledge or cannot apply that knowledge to the text. If the child has difficulty with recall the tester should determine whether the learner can recognize the right response in the text or if relating the text to his/her own experience facilitates recall. [p. 765]

Continuous observation and assessment of students' reading abilities, under a variety of conditions and with different levels of support, can provide exceptionally fine-tuned implications for instruction.

## SUMMATIVE EVALUATION

Summative evaluation is also common to basal programs, in the form of skills mastery tests designed to evaluate how well students have learned what was taught. This type of evaluation is used to establish program accountability, since instructional effectiveness is typically assessed using student performance data. There are at least two problems associated with this approach to summative evaluation. First, this view typically leads to static appraisals of student ability rather than to renewed decision making about instruction. When reading is viewed as an interactive and dynamic process, "mastery" is a relative thing. We may be able to demonstrate that students are more proficient in some tasks, under some circumstances, but progress in other areas will need to be undertaken.

The second problem with the status quo is that the current means of collecting summative data are not sensitive to certain aspects of student growth. This insensitivity of existing tests and instruments is especially disturbing because so many program decisions are made based on the results. As Valencia and Pearson (1987) note, the danger here is that instructional innovation may be abandoned because the resulting changes in student reading performance are not evident on the types of tests used to measure achievement.

What is needed is a more valid assessment of reading proficiency than that provided by existing summative assessments. According to the recommendations provided in *Becoming a Nation of Readers* (Anderson et al., 1985), a more valid assessment can be obtained by determining whether students can and will engage in a variety of reading activities such as reading unfamiliar but grade-appropriate selections with acceptable fluency and writing satisfactory summaries of them; explaining the plots and motivations of the characters in unfamiliar grade-appropriate fiction; and reading extensively from books, magazines, and newspapers during leisure time.

Clearly, many of the procedures discussed previously could be used to evaluate how well students learned what was taught; however, we would like to suggest a different way to think about summative evaluation. We are suggesting that it take place in the form of a *portfolio* (Wixson & Winograd, 1987). This portfolio would consist of many samples of student performance and a variety of types of information, including anecdotal records of student interviews, observations of students' skills and attitudes during reading, samples of student work, traditional test information, and the results of dynamic assessments. It is impossible for us, in the limited space available here, to describe all of the types of assessment procedures you might want to consider for this type of summative evaluation; therefore we will focus on interviewing and observing.

### Interviewing

Interviewing can be used to evaluate students' knowledge about reading; their perceptions of what they have learned and when and why to apply it; and their attitudes, interests, and motivation toward reading activities.

We have already described the types of interviews you might want to consider for purposes of placement, and these could be used for summative purposes as well. Obviously, however, you can talk to your students about reading and reading instruction at any time, and this talk can be extremely informative. For example, Roehler, Duffy, and Meloth (1986) have used a variety of questions following instruction to assess students' understanding and learning. The types of questions they ask are

1. What did you learn about reading today?
2. How do you do it?
3. When and why would you use it for reading?

These three questions are simple but extremely powerful because they reveal students' understanding of the procedural knowledge needed to use a new skill or strategy. In addition, the questions convey to children the need to consider *when* and *why* they would use the skill during other reading acts (Paris, Lipson, & Wixson, 1983).

## Observing

We have noted that teachers seem to have come to distrust their own daily evaluations of children's performance. We are asking that you take these evaluations seriously. You will, however, need to find ways to systematize your observations so that they are both more accessible and more meaningful.

*Oral Reading.* Assessing children's errors during oral reading is one of the most commonly suggested ways of evaluating children's reading competence. Most teachers indicate that they listen to children read out loud so that they can assess word recognition and word identification skills. This normally means that teachers make general and quite global judgments about how well children read words. However, few teachers actually try to evaluate the specific strengths and weaknesses of children as they read.

The "running record" is a method of assessment that is ideally suited to the basal reading program. "This task requires the teacher to observe and record the strategies the child uses 'on the run' while attempting to read a whole text" (Pinnell, 1985, p. 74). The technique was originally described by Clay (1979, 1985) and is based on the work of the Goodmans and their associates (Goodman, 1969, 1973; Goodman & Goodman, 1977; Goodman & Burke, 1983). Although the running record may seem complex at first, it is especially useful for the classroom teacher because no special preparation is required. As long as you can see the text being read and hear the child, you can create a running record. Thus it is possible to collect data any time you are listening to a child read aloud.

Figure 4.3 shows a sample running record, along with a key to the various teacher markings. "The subsequent analysis of the record sharpens the teacher's awareness of error behavior. Errors or 'miscues' have been described by Goodman as well as by Clay as the basis for making inferences about strategies which go on in the child's head" (Pinnell, 1987, p. 54). A teacher's summary of the small sample you have examined in Figure 4.3 might read something like this:

> David's most consistent miscues are word substitutions. These substitutions often are made using both language structure (syntax) and meaning (semantics). Thus, "Isabel *was* a kitten" is both structurally and semantically acceptable, as is, "The kitten *had* a happy *morning.*" In fact, David uses this combination of cueing systems so effectively, he actually makes one miscue in order to accommodate an earlier miscue ("her *eyes were* hurt"). What David does *not* do is monitor effectively for miscues. He makes virtually no use of rereading or self-correc-tion. He appears to prefer moving forward, even if text must be altered to conform to earlier miscues. In addition, David does not make full and effective use of the graphic and phonic information available, nor does he appear to have mastered all high-frequency sight words. Miscues in these areas (*"was,"* *"sutting"*) are tolerated, even when they result in syntactically and/or semantically unacceptable productions. Although he generally seems to "read for meaning," his comprehension is affected by word recognition.

Students' miscue patterns vary depending on a number of fac-tors (Wixson, 1979). As with any "test," miscue analysis provides a sample of behavior that may or may not be representative of the way a student interacts with different types of texts under different read-ing conditions. The best way to address the problem of variability in miscue patterns is to obtain repeated samples of a particular reader's miscues under a variety of predetermined conditions. The nature and content of the reading selections should be varied with regard to each individual reader's skills and background, in an attempt to present the reader with a range of reading tasks and materials. This can be accomplished by regularly analyzing the performance of a child in

**Figure 4.3** Sample Running Record

| TEXT | CHILD'S READING |
|---|---|
| Isabel saw a kitten. | ✓ ~~was~~/saw ✓ ✓ |
| It was on the side of the street. | ✓ ✓ ✓ ✓ ✓ ✓✓ stairs/streets |
| It was sitting under a blue car. | ✓✓ sutting/sitting ✓ ✓ ✓ ✓ |
| "Come here, little kitten," Isabel said. | ✓ ✓ ✓ ✓ ✓ ✓ |
| The kitten looked up at Isabel. | ✓ ✓ ✓ up ✓ ✓ |
| It had big yellow eyes. | ✓ ✓ a/• ✓ ✓ |
| Isabel took her from under the car. | sa-bel/Isabel ✓ ✓ ✓ ✓ ✓ |
| She saw that her leg was hurt. | ✓ was/saw ✓ ✓ eyes/leg were/was ✓ |
| "I will take care of you," Isabel said. | ✓ ✓ ✓ ✓ ✓ ✓ ✓ ✓ |
| She put her hand on the kitten's soft, | ✓ ✓ ✓ ✓ ✓ her/the ✓ ✓ |
| black fur. | ✓ ✓ |
| "You can come home with me." | ✓ ✓ ✓ ✓ ✓ ✓ |
| The kitten gave a happy meow. | ✓ ✓ had/gave ✓ ✓ morning/meow |

KEY FOR RUNNING RECORD:

| | | | |
|---|---|---|---|
| Accurate Reading | ✓✓✓ | Self-Correction | sc |
| Substitution | substitute/text word | Omission | text word |
| Appeal | A | Insertion | inserted word |
| Told | T | Repetition | ✓R |
| | | Return & Repetition | ✓✓✓✓R |

your reading group, and running records are an excellent vehicle for doing so.

*Reading Fluency.* Fluency describes how well readers preserve the author's syntax and the meaning relations in text and is reflected in the ways readers organize words, phrases, and sentences while reading. It can be an important indicator of the degree to which readers have "put the pieces together," of how well they have learned and are able to apply the various reading skills and strategies.

   Aulls (1982) has proposed a fluency scale that can be applied to students' reading of selections from 500 to 1,000 words in length. To score a fluency sample, you simply put a slash mark between each word or word group that characterizes the reader's intonation. These patterns result from pitch sequences and pauses during oral reading. The sample markings below characterize different students' ability to organize words into groups.

   1. Word-by-word: *The/brown/pony/galloped/toward/the fence./*
   2. Beyond word-by-word reading, but not consistently in phrases: *The brown pony/galloped/toward/the fence./ It was/...*
   3. Consistently in phrases: *The brown pony/galloped toward the fence./ It was/...*

After all sentences have been marked, a value of 1, 2, 3, or 4 is assigned to each sentence. Each weighted value represents a category for characterizing how each sentence was read. The values and associated categories are listed below.

   1. A value of 1 is assigned to a sentence if the majority of words in the sentence were read word by word.
   2. A value of 2 is assigned to a sentence if the majority of words were read in two-word groups, with a few read word by word.
   3. A value of 3 is assigned to a sentence if the majority of words were read in phrase groups, with some two- or three-word groups.
   4. A value of 4 is assigned to a sentence if all the words were grouped in phrases.

To obtain an overall estimate of students' word grouping during reading, the teacher adds all the values and divides the total by the total number of sentences read. Scores of 1.0 and 4.0 represent the two extremes: either not being able to group words at all, or having learned to group words consistently.

   Students in the 1.0-to-1.6 range need to become more fluent before moving on. They may need to be provided with easier materials until they have learned to group words better. Scores from 1.1 to 3.9 represent students who are acquiring word-grouping strategies. The two major categories here are the ranges 1.7 to 2.6 and 2.7 to 3.9. Those readers in the 1.7-to-2.6 category are different from those in the 2.7-to-3.9 category in their ability to get beyond two-word groups, to reading in phrase groups with relatively high frequency. This is an important shift because it seems to allow those in the 2.7-to-3.9 score range to give much more attention to the development of the more advanced strategies for processing sentence meaning (Aulls, 1982). Students in the 1.7-to-2.6 range, meanwhile, will be much more likely to be ready to refine the less complex sentence processing strategies involved in confirming or integrating word identification cues. Once the student has attained a score between 2.7 and 3.9, the teacher should begin stressing the development of more sophisticated sentence processing strategies.

Although this type of assessment may look time-consuming, it takes very little additional effort. We find that we need to tape-record students periodically, in order to do miscue analyses, and these same samples are then used to estimate fluency. The information is very useful, since it can also help you to determine what level of control students have achieved in terms of word identification. Fluency, unlike simple measures of reading rate, can help you to estimate the quickness of students' use of text cues to focus on meaning.

## A Critical Note:
## Attitudes, Effort, Interest, and Motivation

It does no good to evaluate programs and their characteristics if student outcomes continue to be measured only in traditional ways. Although most school systems use standardized achievement tests, most of these are poor matches for the types of outcomes we advocate. In addition to the assessment procedures already described, schools must consider ways of assessing attitude outcomes. These will likely include such nontraditional approaches as evaluating the amount of voluntary reading done by students (see chapter 7) or tallying the amount of actual reading done in a given classroom (Winograd & Johnston, 1987). If we value lifelong reading and learning, then we will need to assess the extent to which our students are acquiring the inclination to read.

Research in this area is critically important but has only recently been undertaken. In the near future, efforts like those in Michigan (Wixson et al., 1987) should help provide us with ways of measuring the affective dimensions of reading ability. In the meantime, teachers must come to trust and value the assessment data they have before them every day. As you strive to implement the types of instructional adaptations suggested throughout this text, you will need also to adapt and develop assessment procedures that are suitable for evaluating student ability and progress on important reading tasks/skills and in holistic ways. The best available assessment of attitude and motivation is your evaluation of your students' enthusiasm for reading.

## CONCLUSION

Educators must continue to press for assessment instruments and methodologies that provide instructionally useful and contextually valid information. The assessment efforts described in this chapter can and should provide much more specific information about how and what to teach, but they are suggestive only. Ingenious teachers will find many other ways to evaluate their students' performance for the purpose of making placement and curricular decisions. In this chapter we argued that assessment is a continuous process, lasting as long as the working relationship with the child. Each encounter with a child must be seen as an opportunity for interactive assessment. In this manner, teaching and testing become integral events. By adopting this stance, we have taken a positive step toward providing instructional programs that are responsive to the needs of all children.

## REFERENCES

Afflerbach, P., & Johnston, P. (1984). On the use of verbal reports in reading research. *Journal of Reading Behavior, 16,* 307–323.

Anderson, R. C., Hiebert, E., Scott, J., & Wilkinson, I. (1985). *Becoming a nation of readers: The report of the Commission on Reading.* Washington, DC: National Institute of Education.

Aulls, M. W. (1982). *Developing readers in today's elementary school.* Boston, MA: Allyn & Bacon.

Barrett, T. C. (1972). Taxonomy of reading comprehension, Reading 360 Monograph. Lexington, MA: Ginn & Co.

Bloom, B. (1956). *Taxonomy of educational objectives.* New York: David McKay.

Cioffi, G., & Carney, J. J. (1983). Dynamic assessment of reading disabilities. *The Reading Teacher, 36,* 764–768.

Clay, M. M. (1979). *Reading. The patterning of complex behavior.* Auckland, New Zealand: Heinemann Educational Books.

Clay, M. M. (1985). *The early detection of reading difficulties* (3rd ed.). Auckland, New Zealand: Heinemann Educational Books.

Cooper, J. D. (1986). *Improving reading comprehension.* Boston: Houghton Mifflin.

Farr, R., & Carey, R. F. (1986). *Reading: What can be measured?* (2nd ed.). Newark, DE: International Reading Association.

Goodman, K. S. (1969). Analysis of oral reading miscues: Applied psycholinguistics. *Reading Research Quarterly, 5,* 9–30.

Goodman, K. S. (1973). Miscues: Windows on the reading process. In K. S. Goodman (Ed.), *Miscue analysis: Applications to reading instruction* (pp. 57–70). Urbana, IL: ERIC Clearinghouse on Reading and Communication Skills/National Council of Teachers of English.

Goodman, K. S., & Goodman, Y. M. (1977). Learning about psycholinguistic processes by analyzing oral reading. *Harvard Educational Review, 47,* 317–333.

Goodman, Y. M., & Burke, C. L. (1983). *Reading miscue inventory.* New York: Macmillan.

Holmes, B. C., & Roser, N. L. (1987). Five ways to assess readers' prior knowledge. *The Reading Teacher, 40,* 646–649.

Hunt, J. McV. (1965). *Intelligence and experience.* New York: Ronald.

Johnston, P. (1984). Assessment in reading: The emperor has no clothes. In P. D. Pearson (Ed.), *Handbook of reading research* (pp. 147–182). New York: Longman.

Johnston, P. (1985). Teaching students to apply strategies that improve reading comprehension. *Elementary School Journal, 85,* 635–645.

Langer, J. (1982). Facilitating text processing. The elaboration of prior knowledge. In J. Langer & M. T. Smith-Burke (Eds.), *Reader meets author/bridging the gap* (pp. 149–162). Newark, DE: International Reading Association.

Langer, J. (1984). Examining background knowledge and text comprehension. *Reading Research Quarterly, 19,* 468–481.

Lipson, M. Y. (1984). Some unexpected issues to prior knowledge. *The Reading Teacher, 37,* 760–765.

Lipson, M. Y., Bigler, M., Poth, L., & Wickizer, B. (1987, December). *Instructional applications of a verbal report methodology: The effects of thinking aloud on comprehension ability.* Paper presented at the 37th annual meeting of the National Reading Conference, St. Petersburg, FL.

Mason, J., Osborn, J., & Rosenshine, B. (1977). *A consideration of skill hierarchy approaches to the teaching of reading* (Tech. Rep. No. 42). Urbana: University of Illinois, Center for the Study of Reading.

Paris, S. G., Cross, D., & Lipson, M. Y. (1984). Informed strategies for learning: A program to improve children's awareness and comprehension. *Journal of Educational Psychology, 76,* 1239–1252.

Paris, S. G., & Jacobs, J. E. (1984). The benefits of informed instruction for children's reading awareness and comprehension skills. *Child Development, 55,* 2083–2093.

Paris, S. G., Lipson, M. Y., & Wixson, K. K. (1983). Becoming a strategic reader. *Contemporary Educational Psychology, 8,* 293–316.

Pearson, P. D., & Johnson, D. (1978). *Teaching reading comprehension.* New York: Holt, Rinehart and Winston.

Pinnell, G. S. (1985). Helping teachers help children at risk: Insights from the Reading Recovery Program. *Peabody Journal of Education, 62,* 70–85.

Pinnell, G. S. (1987). Helping teachers see how readers read: Staff development through observation. *Theory into Practice, 26,* 51–58.

Raphael, T. E. (1982). Question-answering strategies for children. *The Reading Teacher, 36,* 186–190.

Raphael, T. E. (1986). Question-answer relationships, revisited. *The Reading Teacher, 39,* 516–523.

Raphael, T. E., Winograd, P., & Pearson, P. D. (1980). Strategies children use in answering questions. In M. L. Kamil & A. J. Moe (Eds.), *Perspectives in reading research and instruction: 29th Yearbook of the National Reading Conference* (pp. 56–63). Washington, DC: National Reading Conference.

Ringler, L. H., & Weber, C. K. (1984). *A language-thinking approach to reading.* San Diego: Harcourt Brace Jovanovich.

Roehler, L. R., Duffy, G. G., & Meloth, M. B. (1986). What to be direct about in direct instruction in reading: Content-only versus process-into-content. In T. E. Raphael (Ed.), *Contexts of school-based literacy* (pp. 79–96). New York: Random House.

Valencia, S., & Pearson, P. D. (1987). Reading assessment: Time for a change. *The Reading Teacher, 40,* 726–733.

Valencia, S., Stallman, A. C., Commeyras, M., Hartman, D. K., Pearson, P. D., & Greer, E. A. (1987, December). *Three methods of assessing prior knowledge: A validation study.* Paper presented at the 37th annual meeting of the National Reading Conference, St. Petersburg, FL.

Winograd, P., & Johnston, P. (1987). Some considerations for advancing the teaching of reading comprehension. *Educational Psychologist, 22,* 213–230.

Wixson, K. K. (1979). Miscue analysis: A critical review. *Journal of Reading Behavior, 11,* 163–175.

Wixson, K. K. (1983). Postreading question-answer interactions and children's learning from text. *Journal of Educational Psychology, 30,* 413–423.

Wixson, K. K. (1984). Level of importance of postquestions and children's learning from text. *American Educational Research Journal, 21,* 419–434.

Wixson, K. K., Bosky, A. B., Yochum, M. N., & Alvermann, D. E. (1984). An interview for assessing students' perceptions of classroom reading tasks. *Reading Teacher, 37,* 354–359.

Wixson, K. K., & Lipson, M. Y. (1986). Reading (dis)ability: An interactionist perspective. In T. E. Raphael (Ed.), *The contexts of literacy* (pp. 131–148). New York: Random House.

Wixson, K. K., Peters, C. W., Weber, E. M., & Roeber, E. D. (1987). New directions in statewide reading assessment. *The Reading Teacher, 40,* 749–755.

Wixson, K. K., & Winograd, P. (1987, December). *A critical analysis of end-of-level tests.* Paper presented at the 37th annual meeting of the National Reading Conference, St. Petersburg, FL.

Wood, K. D. (1988). Techniques for assessing students' potential for learning. *The Reading Teacher, 41,* 440–447.

## RECOMMENDED READINGS

Caldwell, J. (1985). A new look at the old informal reading inventory. *The Reading Teacher, 39,* 168–173.

Cioffi, G., & Carney, J. J. (1983). Dynamic assessment of reading disabilities. *The Reading Teacher, 36,* 764–768.

Clay, M. M. (1985). *The early detection of reading difficulties* (3rd ed.). Exeter, NH: Heinemann Educational Books.

Cunningham, J. (1986). How to question before, during, and after reading. In E. K. Dishner, T. W. Bean, J. E. Readence, & D. W. Moore (Eds.), *Improving classroom instruction* (pp. 215–223). Dubuque, IA: Kendall Hunt.

Henk, W. A. (1987). Reading assessment in the future: Toward precision diagnosis. *The Reading Teacher, 40,* 860–869.

Johnston, P. (1985). Understanding reading disability: A case study approach. *Harvard Educational Review, 55,* 153–177.

Ringler, L. H., & Weber, C. K. (1984). *A language-thinking approach to reading.* San Diego: Harcourt Brace Jovanovich.

Squire, J. R. (1987). The state of reading assessment. *The Reading Teacher, 40*(8), 724–832.

Chapter 5

# Individualizing Within Basal Instruction

MARJORIE Y. LIPSON

A mistake we often make in education is to plan the curriculum materials very carefully, arrange all the instructional materials wall to wall, open the doors of the school, and then find to our dismay that they've sent us the wrong kids! [Siegel, 1981, p. 58E]

Even the most well-conceived commercial program cannot respond to Siegel's rueful commentary. Only teachers can know whether their students are "right" or "wrong" for a given reading program. In this chapter, I will demonstrate some ways that teachers may individualize aspects of their instructional program in response to information gleaned during assessment of their students' knowledge and needs. It will be argued that individualization is important for all students, not simply for those students who are perceived to have reading difficulties. Specific strategies will be described for adapting instructional practices and content to respond to differences between and among all students.

## BACKGROUND

Decades of research and the daily experiences of classroom teachers have amply demonstrated the influence of individual differences on reading performance and achievement. Experience and developmental maturity, socioeconomic and cultural background, knowledge and skills, motivation and interests, among others, have all been linked to differences between students in both ease of acquisition of reading skill and ultimate achievement.

In general, studies of individual differences assume that individual variability is static; that is, we have come to accept differences between students not only as inevitable but as relatively unchanging and unchangeable. Thus, these individual differences are usually associated with judgments about inherent ability.

Educators have responded in a number of ways to the recognition that students come to school with differing experiences, interests, and skills. Over the years, there have been many attempts to adapt and adjust school reading curriculum to address individual needs. At the risk of oversimplifying the situation, these efforts can be said to fall into two large philosophical categories that have engendered different types of instructional approaches (see Huus, 1971; Otto, Wolf, & Eldridge, 1984; Paris, Wixson, & Palincsar, 1986).

L. Hunt (1971) has aptly called these two approaches to addressing individual differences "individually prescribed" and "personalized" instruction. Individually prescribed programs generally individualize students only in terms of time allowed to learn (pacing). All students are expected to complete the same sets of materials and tasks, but they may enter the series at different points and take differing amounts of time to conclude the sequence. Personalized reading programs, on the other hand, are "based on students' self-selection of materials and self-pacing of the reading experience" (Otto et al., 1984, p. 808).

Both personalized and prescribed programs typically reside outside the basal reading approach, as alternatives that supplant basal reading instruction. For a variety of reasons, both practical and philosophical, neither of these approaches to individualizing has enjoyed widespread support, although each continues to thrive in some schools and communities. For the vast majority of teachers and children, however, the basal reading program remains the primary mode of instruction and the provisions for individualizing within the basal have not been extensive. Teachers are generally left to generate their own accommodations to individual variability. As Otto & Chester (1976) note, "The concept of individual differences is easier to accept than the consequences" (p. 13). The consequences, of course, involve trying to figure out just how to address these differences instructionally.

Basal reading programs do typically suggest some ways that teachers can accommodate varying needs and abilities. Most often, these involve suggestions for grouping and pacing (see chapter 2), and most teachers attempt to follow these suggestions. Indeed, many teachers who employ a traditional three-reading-group instructional arrangement do so because they believe it will address individual differences. Similarly, virtually all major publishers of basals include provisions for pacing. These usually appear in the form of (1) additional practice materials for those who need more time to master specific skills and/or (2) suggestions and materials for re-teaching a particular component.

Although these provisions are often helpful, they do not respond to the many ways in which individual differences may influence reading performance. In particular, they usually limit teachers to believing that individualizing is only important for less able students. In the next section, I will provide a brief rationale for another view of individual differences, one that provides stronger direction for in-struction.

## RATIONALE

As we have just seen, basal reading programs typically suggest that teachers adjust instruction through grouping and pacing. Shake (in chapter 2) has noted many of the problems associated with grouping. For the purposes of this chapter, its most troublesome aspect is that students are subsequently described as merely "high," "average," or "low"; or labeled "fast" or "slow"—in all areas and on *all* tasks. In addition, this appraisal is usually seen as more or less permanent; thus, little movement occurs from group to group. The current state of affairs follows from a view of reading that equates "individual differences" with reading "problems."

### An Interactive View of Individual Differences

Recent research suggests a different possibility: that *individual differences in reading performance are unavoidable*. Although inter-est in individual differences is hardly new, research over the past two decades (see the introduction to this book) has made the importance of individual variability even more apparent. Given our current un-derstanding of the reading process, we must understand and come to expect that children in our classrooms will differ in many ways, both in terms of the products of their reading efforts and in the processing strategies they employ to arrive at those products.

The view of reading and reading ability developed throughout this text requires that individual variability be accepted as a given for *all* children. Thus, when individual differences are discussed, I distinguish this view from a deficit view of reading and reading problems. Differences are simply that—*differences*.

Those interested in individualizing instruction must now ask the questions, What differences must be accommodated in our instructional programs? What are the sources of variability? The research to date suggests that student performance and achievement are likely to be influenced by individual differences in prior knowledge, reading knowledge and skill, comprehension, and motivation and attitude. Because these factors have been discussed in other parts of this book, I will provide only a brief review here, focusing on the ways these factors influence individual performance.

As they enter school, students vary in the sheer quantity of their *knowledge of, and experiences with, the world.* In addition to frequently noted differences in overall quantity and quality of information, every child knows more about some things than others, is more skilled in some areas than others, and is capable of reading for some purposes but not others. This is called "within-child" variability. Recognizing the existence of both "between-child" and "within-child" differences in prior knowledge means that we assume that students' performance may vary from selection to selection, rather than remaining stable across all stories (Lipson & Wixson, 1986; Wixson & Lipson, 1986).

Teachers are well aware of prior-knowledge differences in terms of conceptual or "real-world" knowledge. Most are equally aware of differences in student skill. Few teachers, however, reflect on differences among students in their *knowledge about reading*. One student is not clear about why people read, while another understands both the functional and the recreational nature of reading. These differences are likely to influence their performance on classroom reading tasks. Unfortunately, far too many young readers still do not understand that reading is not "saying the words" (Canney & Winograd, 1979; Paris & Myers, 1981). During reading instructional time, students should be acquiring information about how reading works and how they can get better at it. Students should be acquiring a repertoire of strategies and an awareness of the need to use different strategies for different purposes.

In addition, students vary in their *comprehension* of textual materials. Two decades of research have demonstrated that comprehension varies as a result of many factors for all readers. For some students, the difficulty may lie in comprehending a particular text type; for others it may lie in comprehending unfamiliar content; and for still others, it may result from an inability to link ideas in text or separate important from unimportant information.

Finally, students vary in their interest in and *motivation* for reading. These differences have clear impact on their performance and motivation for learning (Wigfield & Asher, 1984). On the other hand, what appears to be limited motivation is sometimes limited awareness of task demands (Paris, Lipson, & Wixson, 1983). In these cases, instructional adaptations can improve performance.

This view of individual variability provides richer ways of looking at and adapting instruction. Since we no longer accept that performance is the result of an unchanging "ability," we can begin to seek out factors that influence reading performance in both "able" and "less able" students and find ways to respond to these factors instructionally.

## Implications for Instruction

The question before us now, of course, is, How can we accommodate these individual differences in performance? Because reading is a dynamic process, individualized efforts will likely be necessary, even after groups have been formed and pacing adapted. While individualizing may be accomplished for some children by adjusting the pace of instruction, not all individual differences will be accommodated in this manner, and there are many other ways in which reading instruction may be altered to meet varying needs.

In some cases, student differences in interest, background knowledge, and skill may require that the *content* of the reading instruction be varied. There are other responses, as well; for example, students may bring unique experiences, learning styles, and knowledge to the instructional setting, so unique that the same sequence or even the same instructional tasks may not be required of all students. Thus, it may be necessary to alter the *delivery system* to match differences in individual knowledge and style. When the delivery system of a reading program is individualized, teachers vary their approaches, techniques, strategies, and criterion tasks from one student or group of students to another.

Individualizing instruction is only necessary, of course, to the extent that we have identified variation in individual needs. Making decisions about what, when, and how to individualize depends on the knowledge base we already possess. A sound reading program will include three types of objectives: process, content, and attitude objectives (Duffy & Roehler, 1986). In order to address these objectives, teachers may make decisions about whether to alter the pace, the delivery system, or the content of instruction, depending on what previous evaluative efforts have revealed. Over twenty-five years ago, Hunt (1961) argued that effective instruction requires that we discover the situations that "call forth learning" for each child. A revised view of individual differences encourages us to find these situations.

In the remainder of this chapter, I provide suggestions for how to individualize within the basal materials. The intent is to help teachers match available strategies to student needs, not to create entirely new instructional practices.

## GENERAL GUIDELINES FOR INDIVIDUALIZATION

Before moving into the discussion of specific recommended procedures for individualization of basal instruction, there are some general points that should be kept in mind. First, given the research findings of the past decade, there can be no question that reading performance is influenced by the material that is read; moreover, all students will have difficulties comprehending *something*. As a general rule, it is helpful to select familiar materials and genres when teaching difficult skills or strategies, so your students can focus on applying and practicing newly acquired skills without undue difficulty coping with the content itself. Wherever possible, then, you will make decisions about which basal materials are suitable for which types of lessons. Of course, you can also make decisions about which selections are appropriate for your students.

Issues of appropriateness should be considered at many levels before selections are taught. For example, Bruce (1984) compared stories in basal readers with those in trade books and concluded that the basal reader stories were actually more difficult and less interesting because their plots offered less intrigue, the characters were less well defined, and the goals and motives were unclear. Most existing basal readers have been written to conform to one or another of the readability formula guidelines, which typically use only word and sentence length as indicators of text difficulty. Recent research suggests that such formulas fall far short of the mark in estimating "comprehensibility," since they do not consider such factors as coherence or the influence of prior knowledge (Davison & Kantor, 1982). "The conclusion of these studies is that commercial materials must be improved in order to facilitate students' reading and teachers' instruction" (Paris et al., 1986, p. 113).

Although most commercial publishers are making strides toward remedying this situation, all materials should be evaluated carefully for their comprehensibility. Some students who are experiencing difficulty in the basal may be able to read other selections with greater ease because of their familiarity, predictable pattern, or well-defined structure.

In addition, there are several ways to improve your instruction which require nothing more than awareness of the factors that influence reading performance (see the introduction to this book). Thus, the procedures presented in the following sections are hallmarks for good instruction and should probably be incorporated in the everyday practice of reading instruction.

Effective instructional techniques share several common characteristics. First, these procedures provide for "informed instruction" (Brown, Campione, & Day, 1981) in which children are provided not only with information about how to do a task but also with some information about the value and usefulness of a skill or strategy. Next, sound instruction should provide a "self-control" component in which the students are taught how to regulate their learning themselves. Both of these components can be accomplished most successfully if you or a competent child peer "models" the task for the children. Learning will be enhanced if you provide for careful "direct explanation." Finally, you must plan for a gradual release of responsibility, insuring that your students can perform the strategy or skill when needed during real reading (Pearson & Gallagher, 1983).

Throughout the remainder of this chapter, I suggest ways that you can provide differential support to insure learning and comprehension among your students. This supported instruction is often called "scaffolding":

> Scaffolding has been described as instructional assistance that enables someone to solve a problem, carry out a task, or achieve a goal that the person could not accomplish alone (Wood, Bruner, & Ross, 1976). The metaphor of a scaffold calls attention to a support system that is both temporary and adjustable. . . . From this point of view, the instructional problem is to choose the best way in which teachers can assist students to move from one level of competence to the next so that, in time, students will be able to apply problem-solving strategies independently and judiciously [Paris et al., 1986, p. 109]

Roehler and Duffy (1984) suggest steps to follow in achieving this, which may be helpful for planning instruction of the type we have just described:

1. Think about skills as mental processes that students use when they encounter problems that interfere with comprehension during reading. As such, students need to be consciously aware of the situation in which the skill is useful and the thinking one goes through in applying the skill as a means of overcoming the barrier to comprehension difficulties.
2. Think of teaching as the explanation you provide to the students about what the skill is, what its value is, and the secret to using it successfully when encountering problems of meaning in real text.
3. Think of the traditional materials of instruction as things that are used after your direct explanation of the skill. The workbook page, work sheet, or instructional game can be used after explanation, to give pupils an opportunity to practice the skill in a controlled situation. Then the basal text story can be used to show students how the skill works in real, connected text. [p. 278]

We would add an additional item:

4. Think about what level of support you need to provide to ensure that your students will be able to learn what you are teaching. You should expect that efficient use of learned skills and knowledge will take considerable time and that your level of support should diminish as students become more adept.

In most basal readers, the content, method, and tasks are dictated by the instructional framework used to teach each unit. As was discussed in chapter 1, this framework, or Directed Reading Activity (DRA), is roughly divided into three parts: prereading, during-reading, and postreading activities. Teachers have a great deal of flexibility in adapting this framework, and experienced teachers frequently exercise their own good judgment about how to teach a particular reading selection and/or skill. This may involve something as simple as skipping a work sheet because students don't need it or something as elaborate as planning and developing substitute materials. In the following sections, you will find specific strategies for accommodating individual differences in various aspects of reading.

I will be using one basal reading selection throughout the remainder of the chapter, in order to illustrate specific recommended procedures for accommodating individual differences. You may want to take a moment right now to read it; it is *The Big Bad Wolf?* (Luther, 1986/1987), which is located in the appendix to this chapter (see pages 168–170).

## ACCOMMODATING DIFFERENCES IN
## READING KNOWLEDGE AND SKILL

For students who are less knowledgeable, or less able, teachers typically teach smaller pieces and take more time to teach the isolated component parts of reading. This is troublesome for several reasons. First, this generally means that less knowledgeable or less able students get the most fragmented type of skills instruction and less time actually to practice reading (Allington, 1977, 1983). In the sections to follow, I will suggest several ways to provide instructional support (scaffolding) that will allow these students to cope with longer, coherent segments of text.

The practice of isolating component skills instruction is trouble some for another reason. One of the things that seems to distinguish able from less able learners is the ease with which they transfer learning from one context to another (Flavell, 1977; Paris & Lindauer, 1982). Able readers may be able to take advantage of instruction that is less focused and more diffuse. These students may be able to discuss several competing skills in a two- or three-day lesson sequence and learn to apply them with relative ease. Less able students, however, may not be able to figure out just what is important or why they are practicing these different skills. This means that they are less likely to use these skills or strategies in other reading situations. The problem, then, lies with the delivery system.

One way of altering the delivery system is suggested by Cureton and Eldridge (1984). For less able readers, they recommend selecting only *one* skill to be taught with each story. They suggest that you use your own good judgment and knowledge of your readers to select the most useful skill for that selection. Although you may not want to teach just one skill, you certainly should think in terms of prioritizing the ones you do teach and making the key objective clear to the students as you focus their attention. For example, the teacher's manual accompanying *The Big Bad Wolf?* has listed objectives for each of the strands in the basal: comprehension, vocabulary-language, study-life, and communication skills. In each case, the objectives for the strand are a good match for the selection (making generalizations, recognizing punctuation clues [quotation marks], using a dictionary, and writing a report). Because the suggested skills are all reasonable for this text, you will need to make decisions about which is most important for *your* students at *this* time.

Selecting the appropriate skills to be taught is not an easy task, but it is important to limit the number of skills you teach to poor readers, since it is more desirable to have poor readers acquire a few skills than it is for them to have little or no proficiency in many different skills. Also, do not be concerned that the child will never be exposed to a skill you temporarily skip. Basal readers are designed to provide repeated exposure to many skills. [Cureton & Eldridge, 1984, p. 249]

There are times, of course, when differences in reading knowledge and skill are so great that genuine alteration of the task content will be necessary. You can obviously vary the length of assignments. This suggestion is largely an adaptation for pace, since students reading selections in smaller chunks are obviously not likely to move as rapidly through printed material as those reading longer portions.

Although you may need to use this approach in the beginning, every effort should be made to provide other accommodations so that students can deal with as much print as possible. In these cases, for example, instruction might include "task slicing" (Readence & Moore, 1980), in which minor changes in task assignment allow students to respond individually. "Slicing refers to reexamining the tasks required of students in text assignments and then recasting them to ease their demands" (p. 112). The authors go on to describe several ways that tasks can be adapted, depending on a reader's skill and knowledge.

*Limit the Scope of the Information Search.* As Readence and Moore (1980) note, an exhaustive information search, requiring students to recall and understand *all* of a selection, places high demands on skill and knowledge. Readers can often cope with difficult text as long as they are not held accountable for all the ideas, concepts, or events. To limit the scope of the information search,

The number of concepts for which students are responsible can be varied by adding or deleting the number of assigned tasks on their study guides or end-of-chapter questions. Some students may be responsible for 15 concepts while others may deal with only five. These concepts may or may not be exclusive of each other. Whatever the case, whole-class discussion should follow the directed reading so that all students are exposed to the desired information. [p. 113]

When you adapt the scope of the information search, you do not alter the amount of material to be read, only the degree to which students are expected to understand the material.

The power of this type of slicing is that it helps to focus students' attention on important information and, for those who need it, limits their focus so that they do not have to make as many judgments about what is important and what should be learned.

*Create an Information Index.*   This is simply another way of focusing children's attention and helping them locate information in text. For quite competent readers, questions at the end of a selection pose little problem. For others, however, this challenge is too great. You can help students by interspersing questions throughout the selection. Indeed, the "guided reading questions" present in most basals provide this type of task slicing. Some students will not need these at all; others will need these and more. Readence and Moore (1980) suggest keying questions to "the page, section, paragraph and/or sentence where one can find information on which answers may be based. The degree of question interspersing and information indexing may be varied according to the importance of the concept reflected in the questions, the level of thinking required, and students' reading ability" (p. 114).

*Vary the Response Mode.*   The practice of asking questions has become so pervasive that many teachers equate comprehension with ability to answer questions. As was noted in chapter 4, however, there are many means of assessing comprehension. You can alter in many ways the types of responses you expect. You might make far more extensive use of retelling as a means of responding to a reading selection. This adaptation requires absolutely no special preparation on your part, unless you wish to elicit a retelling about certain components of the text.

Similarly, Readence and Moore (1980) suggest many other ways of slicing the response mode that require little additional preparation. You can produce fill-in-the-blank or cloze passages, pulling directly from the selection. Less able readers can use the text to help. With a little more effort, you can create "mazes," which are cloze passages that offer several choices for each blank space. The authors suggest several "recognition" tasks as well. The available research suggests that readers of all abilities are more successful with recognition tasks than they are with tasks that require construction of a response (Williams, Taylor, & Ganger, 1981; Wong, Wong, & LeMare, 1982).

The familiar true-false tests are one such technique, although rarely used during basal reading instruction. Similarly, a task borrowed from research called "sentence verification" can provide the thoughtful teacher with many rich possibilities. This simply involves changing a question into a statement, to which the student must react. Thus, you might ask students to verify which of the following paired sentences was supported by the text of the story on wolves:

1. Dr. Mech tracks wolves by hiking through the woods, following transmitter noise.
2. Dr. Mech flies far above the wolves, tracking them with the transmitter.

The advantage to this task is that it requires students to defend their verification, leading to far richer discussions than most question-and-answer formats.

Finally, you can vary the response mode (task) in more discrete ways. Instead of asking "diffuse" questions (e.g., Why are people afraid of wolves?), you can ask for more specific responses (e.g., List two children's books that have wolves in them; and, Describe the wolves in these stories). In this way, children can be led more carefully toward the inferences required to understand the material being read.

As noted earlier, content may need to be altered if students are having trouble acquiring skills and strategies. Allowing them to read less difficult or more familiar text will permit a cleaner focus on the application and practice of newly emerging skills. In addition, do not overlook the possibility of moving the students to more *difficult* materials. Sufficient student motivation and interest can overcome a certain lack of skill. At least some students will acquire the requisite knowledge and ability in the process of reading fairly difficult text. This appears to be particularly true of very young students, who seem to acquire some so-called "prerequisite" skills as they read and learn to read (Ehri, 1979).

## ACCOMMODATING DIFFERENCES IN PRIOR KNOWLEDGE

During the prereading phase of basal instruction there are many strategies designed to accommodate differences in prior knowledge. The classic DRA calls for both building background and developing vocabulary. Indeed, one way to elicit and/or build background knowledge before reading is to teach relevant vocabulary (Beck & McKeown, 1983; Beck, Perfetti, & McKeown, 1982; Wixson, 1986). Vocabulary instruction designed to activate and build background knowledge, however, must consist of much more than is typically offered in basal teacher's manuals. A list of new words, even new words presented in context, followed by workbook page exercises, neither ensures that children learn those words nor that they have associated appropriate concepts with them (Anderson & Freebody, 1981). In addition, in most teacher's manuals the new vocabulary words are selected because they are likely to cause decoding problems, not because they build a conceptual base for reading the selection.

Adaptations should be used as you see the need. For example, the teacher's manual for *The Big Bad Wolf?* suggests the following new vocabulary: *methods, improved, transmitter, sturdy, mates.* In a separate section, this manual does quite an acceptable job of providing relevant background. But, for a student with really marginal knowledge of either wolves or the study of animal behavior, this may not be enough. In recent years, several vocabulary strategies have been developed, and some are ideally suited for activating and developing prior knowledge (e.g., Carr & Wixson, 1986). They provide for varying degrees of teacher support so you can decide which is appropriate.

*Word Wonder.* Spiegel (1981) designed the "Word Wonder" strategy for use with students who may have difficulty with the concepts of a particular selection. You name the topic or main idea of the story to be read, then ask the children to generate words they think will be present in such a selection. If prior knowledge is very limited or inaccurate, you can provide a list of words and ask students which words they think will appear in the passage. Thus, for *The Big Bad Wolf?* you might say, "Today we are going to read a selection about a scientist who studies wolves to find out about how they behave and how they live. What words do you think you will find in this passage?"

In a more structured form of Word Wonder, you might provide such words as *mean, evil, sly, gentle, greedy, smart, dangerous, pack, loner, hunter, family, rank, habitat, territory, extinct, kiss, mates, transmitter,* and *zoo.* As students discuss the meanings of these words, you can elaborate on just those words for which students have inadequate meaning associations. "Word Wonder fulfills the vocabulary step of the DRA, but in a diagnostic manner. Vocabulary words are pretaught only when necessary. Similarly, background is assessed as the children offer or react to the words and is filled in as necessary" (Spiegel, 1981, p. 919). If children make incorrect selections, you can also be alert to possible misconceptions and the likelihood that these may interfere with comprehension (Lipson, 1984).

*List-Group-Label.* According to Tierney, Readence, & Dishner (1985), "List-Group-Label" (L-G-L) is a technique for encouraging students to improve their vocabulary and categorization skills and to organize their verbal concepts, as well as for aiding them in remembering and reinforcing new vocabulary. This procedure is easy to use in a basal reading group and can be especially helpful when members of the group differ in the amounts of prior knowledge they have about a topic. Students with relatively more prior knowledge can help to shape the lists and the groupings in ways that will be informative to less knowledgeable readers. With very young or less able students, you may need to model the entire process before asking students to participate.

The three steps of the L-G-L activity proceed as follows:

1. The teacher writes a one- or two-word topic on the board that will be used to generate the *list* of words. Students are asked to brainstorm all words related to the topic. For our sample text, the topic would likely be "wolves."
2. In the next step, *grouping*, students generate sublists from the large list, so that all the words in each sublist have something in common.
3. Finally, they *label* each sublist and share it with the group, providing a rationale for the grouping.

In Figure 5.1 you will see a sample of an L-G-L activity for *The Big Bad Wolf?*, including the groupings and labels that emerged in the prereading stage.

If students possess a great many preconceptions, L-G-L can also be a particularly effective postreading activity. For example, the groupings and lists in Figure 5.1 could later form the basis of an excellent postreading activity, with students generating *new* lists and labels. The two lists might even be compared and a final L-G-L activity conducted using the labels *misconceptions* and *facts*.

*Expectation Outline.* Spiegel (1981) designed this strategy to help students read unfamiliar material, and therefore it can be helpful any time students encounter such texts. In order to create an expectation

**Figure 5.1**   Sample List-Group Label Activity (Topic: "Wolves")

---

**STEP 1:  GENERATING A LIST (the original)**

| | |
|---|---|
| grey wolf | howl |
| mean | packs |
| tricky | wild |
| clever | dangerous |
| timber wolf | woods |
| Little Red Riding Hood | dogs |
| big nose | hunt |
| sharp teeth | eat chickens |

**STEP 2:  GROUPING AND LABELING**

<u>What They Look Like</u>                         <u>How They Survive</u>

    big nose                                          mean
    sharp teeth                                       clever
    dogs                                              tricky
                              wild
<u>How They Live</u>                                  dangerous
                                    hunt
    woods                                             eat chickens
    packs

<u>Types of Wolves</u>

    grey wolf
    timber wolf
    Little Red Riding Hood wolf

---

outline, the teacher asks students what questions about, for example, wolves they think will be answered in the selection they are going to read. After students have asked as many questions as they can, the questions are grouped and the children are asked to make up a heading or title for the questions. For example, the label *hunting* might be given to the following questions: What do wolves eat? How do wolves catch their prey? Why do wolves attack people? Why do wolves travel in packs? When this phase is accomplished, the children read the story to find answers to their questions. Finally, they read portions of the text that verify the facts.

Spiegel (1981) suggests that unanswered questions be posted so that children are encouraged to read beyond the basal to find additional information. In addition, children might be encouraged to check other sources for answers to questions that surprised them (that is, to verify information about which they had misconceptions).

When prior knowledge is extremely limited, you may choose to use a prediction guide (Nichols, 1983), a close relative of the expectation outline. A sample prediction guide is shown in Figure 5.2. Limited prior knowledge can prevent students from identifying important and unimportant information. These guides provide support in this area and will be most useful when you yourself have prepared a set of prediction statements beforehand.

Before reading, students check off (in column A) those predictions they think will occur. After reading, students turn to column B. They place a check next to those statements that were supported in the text, a zero next to those statements that were refuted by the text, and a question mark next to those statements not addressed or answered in the text.

Both expectation outlines and prediction guides have the advantage of activating students' prior knowledge in such a way as to raise questions about the veracity of their knowledge base. Helping students to realize that they already have some ideas about the topic to

**Figure 5.2** Sample Prediction Guide (*The Big Bad Wolf?*)

Directions:  In column A, check those statements you think are true, concerning wolves and the study of wolves.  Don't put anything in column B yet.

A       B

1. Wolves are smart animals.
2. Wolves are easy to track.
3. Wolves can be tracked by airplane.
4. Wolves can be tracked by using a radio transmitter.
5. Wolves hunt and kill for no reason.
6. Wolf packs are small, family units.
7. Wolves are gentle, loving parents.
8. Wolf packs roam around, never forming a home base.
9. Wolves are vicious and dangerous to humans.
10. Wolves are in danger of becoming extinct.

Source:  Adapted from J.N. Nichols, "Using prediction to increase content area interest and understanding." Journal of Reading, 27, 1983, 225–228.  Used with permission.

be considered is an important component in individualizing instruction. In addition, however, students must be encouraged to pay attention as they read, monitoring their predictions to determine the fit between new text information and their prior knowledge.

## ACCOMMODATING DIFFERENCES IN COMPREHENSION

Differences in comprehension will need to be accommodated in a number of ways. For some students, the difficulty may lie in comprehending a particular text; for others, it may be a generalized comprehension problem. Thus, differences here may require adaptations in content, methods, and tasks.

There are many instructional strategies available to you—strategies designed to vary the level of instructional support that is offered to readers before, during, and after reading. As you did with prior knowledge, you can provide instructional support for comprehension before reading by using vocabulary. However, vocabulary instruction designed to enhance comprehension must be carefully crafted, with an eye toward words that are critical for understanding the material to be read (Wixson, 1986).

As with all prereading activities, teacher preparation is important. First, you must select *key* words from the material to be read. These should be words that will present trouble to students as they read and will also be necessary or important for understanding the text. The "new vocabulary" in many basals is selected primarily because of decoding difficulty. Ability to pronounce new words is obviously important, but not all words that are difficult to pronounce are necessarily important for understanding the selection.

Even when students understand each word, they may have trouble comprehending the text. Many children simply do not understand how the ideas in text are related to each other. Visual maps of reading selections can prove especially useful to you. Available research suggests that "maps improve children's reading comprehension by showing them not only how vocabulary words are related to each other in some conceptual hierarchy, but also how the ideas in texts are organized in associative ways" (Sinatra, Stahl-Gemake, & Berg, 1984, p. 22).

*Semantic Mapping.*   Semantic mapping allows for individual response to group tasks and is, therefore, an ideal way to individualize within basal groups. This technique can be executed in several ways, depending on your students and your instructional objectives. It can be used in much the same way as L-G-L, with you supplying key words that are then grouped in a semantic map (McNeil, 1987). It can also be used to help students focus on important aspects of the selection, thus setting a purpose for reading (Spiegel, 1981). To do this, you set up several key questions or categories and ask the students to respond with information from their existing knowledge base. Together, you create a prereading semantic map (see Figure 5.3). These topics or questions can then guide students' reading. After the selection has been read, the group creates a postreading semantic map, embellishing and correcting as necessary (see Figure 5.4).

*Fanning.* This is a strategy similar to mapping, developed by Swaby (1984). As can be seen in Figure 5.5, it draws its name from the fanlike shapes that are made. Students create a fan by using three levels of questions to guide their reading: text-explicit, text-implicit, and personal or extending questions. Factual information is arrayed at the top, and more inferential information is extended off the bottom. One appealing feature of fanning is its natural connection to the question taxonomy developed by Pearson and Johnson (1978) and used by Raphael (1986) to teach children about question-answer relationships (QARs; see chapter 4). Thus, you might simultaneously use QAR instruction and the visual support of fans for those students who need that much support. For very difficult expository text, most

**Figure 5.3** Prereading Semantic Map (*The Big Bad Wolf?*)

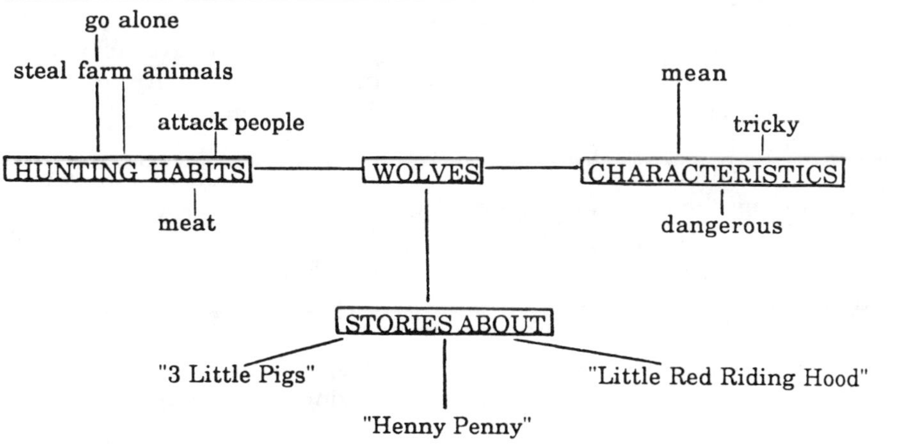

**Figure 5.4**   Postreading Semantic Map (*The Big Bad Wolf?*)

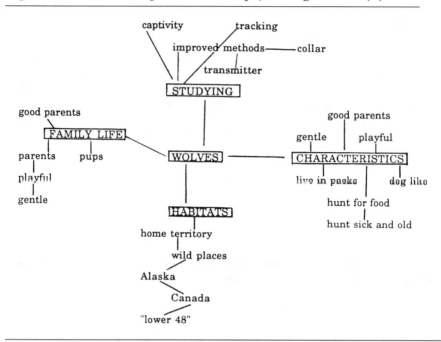

students could benefit from the combination of approaches. The fan can also serve as an accessible study aid for content-area reading.

*Story Maps.*   The underlying relationships among characters, events, and settings in a given story are revealed through story maps (Pearson, 1985; Reutzel, 1985). They provide, for narrative selections, the same types of support as semantic maps and fans do for informational text. The story map in Figure 5.6 shows the underlying relationships for the familiar story of "Jack and the Bean Stalk." As you can see, a good map will help children to see the relationships between and among the events in a story. This particular map focuses on the story's problem-solution structure; however, since not all stories have this structure, other formats would obviously need to be created for them.

For all three types of visual displays, you may accommodate variation in comprehension ability by altering the degree of prereading and during-reading support that is provided. For example, stu-

**Figure 5.5** Sample Fanning Activity (*The Big Bad Wolf?*)

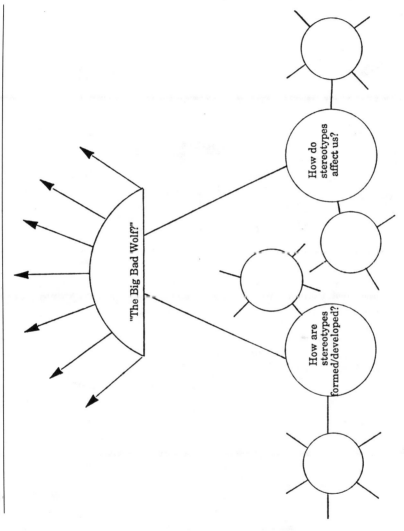

Source: Based on Barbara Swaby, "Fan out Your Facts on the Board." The Reading Teacher, May 1984, p. 915. Used with permission of Barbara Swaby and the International Reading Association.

**Figure 5.6** Sample Story Map (*Jack and the Bean Stalk*)

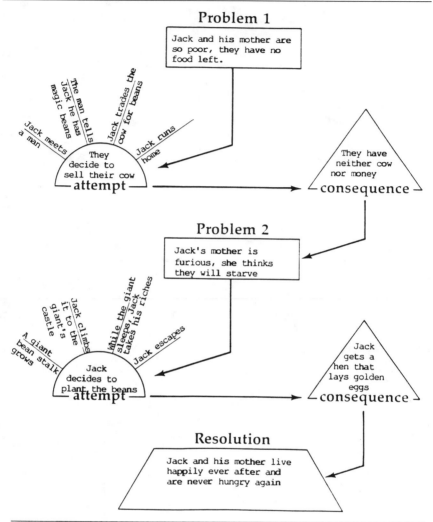

Source: Marjorie Lipson, Instructor's Resource Book for Reading Instruction Today, Scott Foresman & Company, 1986, Story Map, p. 58. Used with permission.

dents can be provided with a blank but fully structured story map so that their task is to read for the purpose of completing the network. For some children, this will provide the right degree of support. For others, who have comprehension abilities that are even less well developed or who are reading especially difficult text, you can fill in portions of the map, leaving only a few blanks to be completed. The same strategy is possible for fans and semantic maps. I have used each successfully, adapting for individual needs by leaving only the inferential portions blank or by leaving only the text-based information for the child to complete.

The point of these examples is not to provide an exhaustive list of comprehension support activities. Rather, my aim is to suggest to you that there are many ways to scaffold instruction so that you provide additional supports for readers who need them. These supports should be faded as soon as possible (Pearson, 1985). We neither expect nor desire that students fill out a visual grid for each selection they read. Once they have internalized the overarching structures that help them to understand difficult or unfamiliar text, these should be replaced by more typical response modes, such as discussion and product creation. Finally, these supports are designed for use during direct instruction segments only. They should not be coupled with voluntary reading selections unless, of course, the students self-select these activities.

## PUTTING IT ALL TOGETHER

Because teachers need to find manageable instructional arrangements, individual differences in most classrooms will still be addressed within the framework of groups (see chapter 2). Although differences in reading knowledge and skill are most often the basis for forming these reading subgroups, there are other grouping arrangements that can be used effectively to individualize instruction.

### Making Reading Public

For teachers using a basal reading program, one of the most promising ways to individualize involves whole-class instruction, or "making reading public" (Paris, 1986). Public discussions help children to express their ideas and thereby, enhance the likelihood that these ideas will be transferred to other settings. In addition, of course, discussions can provide diagnostic information. "Conversations in classrooms also help to 'make reading public' so that students can learn from one another. As they assert, defend and question their ideas about their own reading and studying skills, they are being persuaded about the value of effective strategies" (Paris, 1986, p. 120).

Obviously public discussions of reading can be useful in small groups; however, by making reading public, you can also provide for whole-class instruction on process or content objectives, while individualizing instruction in only the application phase of lessons. Thus, all students can receive a lesson related to a particular skill and then read a selection at their own reading level (and in their own reading group), in order to apply the skill or strategy. There is evidence that this type of public discussion of reading can be an effective adjunct to any existing program (Palincsar & Brown, 1984; Paris, Cross, & Lipson, 1984).

Organizing instruction around a theme can permit whole-group instruction in a particular skill or strategy, with each child reading (or applying the skill) in different reading material. There are presently several well-organized basal programs that make such efforts easier to attempt. Many new editions have organized the selections around fairly global themes, such as *friends* or *surprises*. A thoughtful reading of the selections is needed, to see if you can use different selections to accomplish your ends. A more direct route, especially in terms of reading knowledge and skill accommodation, involves examining the scope-and-sequence charts to find particular skills that are common across all your groupings. Then you might attempt to teach all groups the same thing at the same time, allowing students to apply their newly acquired skill in different materials.

*The Big Bad Wolf?* provides a good example of the potential here. The publisher of the materials has identified an important skill (generalization) that is well matched to the demands of the selection. This section is prefaced with this note: "This lesson teaches students that generalizations are general rules or ideas. Generalizations can be incorrect. They can also be true, when based on enough facts or particular instances" (Cassidy, Roettger, & Wixson, *Turn a Corner Teacher's Edition*, 1987, p. 404). This skill is significant and slow to develop. Therefore, all students are likely to benefit from public discussion of the topic. In this case, individual skill differences are less important than opportunities to practice the skill with meaningful materials, after it has been appropriately taught.

*The Big Bad Wolf?* requires readers to make generalizations *and* to examine preexisting generalizations. Other texts can be used to accomplish the same ends, however, so you might teach a whole-class lesson on generalization, using several brief samples and linking the discussion to issues in the students' experience. Then, students who would normally read *The Big Bad Wolf?* would do so, while students in other reading groups would read selections from their own basals that targeted the same skill.

In Figure 5.7 you will find a model that demonstrates just how the various individualizing efforts might come together under this type of plan. For each group, you will see a number of activities listed. You would select the one or more options you felt represented the best response for your students. As you can see, it is also possible for

**Figure 5.7** Sample Plan for Individualizing Within the Basal

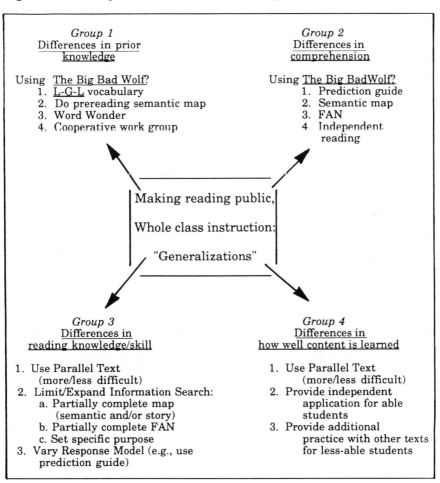

*Group 1*
Differences in prior
knowledge

Using The Big Bad Wolf?
 1. L-G-L vocabulary
 2. Do prereading semantic map
 3. Word Wonder
 4. Cooperative work group

*Group 2*
Differences in
comprehension

Using The Big Bad Wolf?
 1. Prediction guide
 2. Semantic map
 3. FAN
 4. Independent
    reading

Making reading public,

Whole class instruction:

"Generalizations"

*Group 3*
Differences in
reading knowledge/skill

1. Use Parallel Text
   (more/less difficult)
2. Limit/Expand Information Search:
   a. Partially complete map
      (semantic and/or story)
   b. Partially complete FAN
   c. Set specific purpose
3. Vary Response Model (e.g., use
   prediction guide)

*Group 4*
Differences in
how well content is learned

1. Use Parallel Text
   (more/less difficult)
2. Provide independent
   application for able
   students
3. Provide additional
   practice with other texts
   for less-able students

students to rotate through the plan. For example, you might start out the students who have differences in reading knowledge and skill with the adaptations suggested for group 3. These same students, however, might also benefit from the type of activities listed for group 1. In this case, you would start by using a parallel (less challenging) text but then also provide prereading vocabulary work. Of course, it is also possible that these students (or others) would benefit from activities listed for groups 2 and 4. This is obviously just one way of organizing and individualizing instruction. Your efforts may involve as little as adapting one small aspect of instruction or be as ambitious as the entire figure suggests.

### Cooperative Work Groups

Another alternative involves cooperative work groups, in which students with differing knowledge bases are intentionally placed together (see chapter 2). The group works *together* to read and understand selections. The advantage of this arrangement is that students can provide support for each other; therefore it is a natural accompaniment to the types of individualizing I have just discussed. Uttero (1988) provides a detailed plan for accomplishing effective cooperative group work. She suggests that reading work be done in three stages:

1. Connection: students activate and generate prior knowledge related to the text.
2. Guided independent reading: students work together to read and understand the text.
3. Follow-up: students summarize or apply the text information to new contexts.

Many teachers find that they can do cooperative work groups part of the time. Thus, the traditional grouping arrangements are maintained for some portions of the week (e.g., three days), and with cooperative work groups employed for the remaining time. Research suggests that students of all abilities can benefit from these arrangements (Dansereau, 1987).

## DIFFERENCES IN MOTIVATION AND ATTITUDE

Individuals also vary in terms of their motivation for reading and their need for practice. Some students find reading gratifying and therefore read widely outside of school. Others do very little reading and come to view skilled reading as flawless word calling requiring completion of a number of discrete tasks. In this chapter, I have largely addressed issues related to individual differences in the areas of process and content. Attitude outcomes are equally important, legitimate concerns for all teachers, and most students will need reading experiences that go beyond the basal if they are to become independent, voluntary readers. In chapter 7, Lesley Morrow provides a wealth of ideas for extending your reading program so that these outcomes can be appropriately addressed. Basal instruction alone cannot address such attitude outcomes.

However, "it is important for reading educators to recognize how self-regard and motivation are influenced by instructional practices. Johnston and Winograd (1985) suggest that passive failure can be prevented if educators modify instruction to fit individual students" (Paris et al., 1986, p. 117). We should hardly be surprised if students who find reading tasks extremely difficult are not motivated to engage in those tasks. These students will need our best adaptive instruction to provide the support they need to read, understand, and learn from texts. Similarly, we should not be surprised if able students, if they find their texts unchallenging or the tasks meaningless, choose not to read or fail to acquire sophisticated strategies for doing so.

We must find ways to make sensible decisions for our students, using state-of-the-art information to guide us in our task.

> We will be recognizing that true individualization has never meant that instruction is delivered individually, only that progress is monitored individually, and that what may be best for a given individual is not another worksheet but maybe a live body present to provide the guidance and feedback it will take to bring him or her to an independent level of performance. [Pearson, 1985, p. 11]

## SUMMARY

In this chapter I have described a number of strategies for adapting materials, methods, and tasks for the purpose of meeting individual needs. Individual differences among students may occur in terms of prior knowledge, reading knowledge and skill, comprehension, and motivation and attitude. I have argued that these differences do not necessarily constitute deficits but rather that they result from the normal variability that occurs because of the dynamic way that humans read.

Throughout the chapter, I have tried to suggest ways that teachers can provide instructional support for all their students while maintaining the basic framework and materials of the basal reading program. These have included prior knowledge/vocabulary strategies like Word Wonder and List-Group-Label and strategies designed to support comprehension, such as semantic mapping and story mapping. I have also discussed ways of engaging in task slicing, which alters the content and task demands of reading assignments in order to address individual differences.

The following appendix (pages 167–169) contains a basal reading selection, *The Big Bad Wolf?* (Luther, 1986/1987), which was used, above, to illustrate specific recommended procedures for individualizing within basal instruction.

Photos: Laurence Pringle, W. Nyack, NY & Photo Researchers, NY, NY. Used with permission.

# The BIG BAD WOLF?

by SALLIE LUTHER

"Who's afraid of the big bad wolf, the big bad wolf, the big bad wolf?" In fairy tales and rhymes, the wolf is always the bad guy. In this selection, you will see what David Mech thinks of wolves. Then maybe you will change your tune about them!

How did David Mech become interested in wolves? What is the biggest fear people have about wolves that Dr. Mech wants to prove is not necessary?

David Mech (his name rhymes with "peach") is a real-life scientist. He works for the U.S. Fish and Wildlife Service. And he probably knows more about wolves than anybody else. That's why some people call him "The Wolfman."

"I guess I was always interested in wolves," says Dr. Mech. "As a young boy, I used to catch animals for their fur. But I could never catch wolves. They were just too smart!

"Later on, in college, I decided to make studying wolves my work. Nobody knew much about them back then. I started out on Isle Royale in Michigan, just hiking through the woods and looking for the wolves. I walked over 1500 miles—and I saw only three wolves.

I decided there had to be a better way!" So he found one.

A few scientists were just starting to track animals from airplanes. Dr. Mech studied their tracking methods. Then to make the tracking easier, he improved on them. He came up with a sturdy leather collar that could be clamped around a wolf's neck. Built into each collar was a very small *radio transmitter*. Each battery-operated collar transmitted, or sent out, beeps.

"Now I can just fly around overhead," says Dr. Mech, "tune in my radio receiver, and pick up the beeps of whatever wolf is around."

Using his radio-tracking method, Dr. Mech started learning a lot about wolves. He found that wolves hunt only for food. And they often go hungry. "A wolf pack that makes one kill in ten tries is lucky," says Dr. Mech. "They may go as long as two weeks between meals.

"There are only about two to eight wolves in most packs. They hunt mostly for deer or moose. And the ones caught are almost always the old, the very young, the sick or the injured."

Dr. Mech discovered that a wolf pack is always a family. A male and female are

often the "bosses." When their pups grow up, they often stay with their parents as pack members. New pups are cared for by all the adults in the pack. And the wolves are gentle, loving, and playful with the pups.

"Every wolf in a pack has a *rank*, or place," explains Dr. Mech. "If a wolf with low rank doesn't like its place, it may leave. Some become lone wolves. Others find mates and start their own packs."

Dr. Mech has learned a lot by watching captive wolves, too. The captives taught him that wolves in a pack seldom fight among themselves. But they are quick to fight with strange wolves.

"Each pack has its home territory," he says, "and will

fight to defend it."

Dr. Mech learned that wolves act very much like dogs. "In fact, dogs and wolves are very closely related," the scientist explains. "Pack members act toward each other much as your pet dog acts toward you. For instance, when two pack members have been apart for a while, they rush together,

licking each other's faces and wagging their tails like crazy. It's just the way your dog might act when you come home from school!

"Once I raised a wolf pup we named Lightning. When we let her in each morning, she would race upstairs, jump on my children's beds, and cover their faces with wet wolf kisses!"

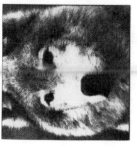

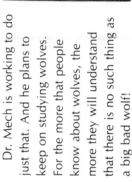

But if wolves are so much like dogs, why are so many people so afraid of them?

"Partly because of all those fairy tales we read," says Dr. Mech. "*The Three Little Pigs, Little Red Riding Hood, Peter and the Wolf*—in all of them the wolf really comes off as the bad guy."

But wolves don't huff and puff and blow houses down. And even if you went around in a red riding hood, wolves wouldn't gobble you up.

"There has not been one single case of a healthy wolf attacking a human in North America!" Dr. Mech says firmly. "I've been studying wolves—been right out there in the forest with them—for about 25 years. And I've never felt I was in even the slightest danger!"

But there is some danger—not to people but to the wolves, and to the wolves' survival. "There are plenty of timber wolves in Alaska and Canada," says Dr. Mech, "more than enough to keep the species around for a long time. But there are only about 1200 wolves left in the 'lower 48' states. Most of these are in Minnesota."

Can these few wolves be kept from becoming extinct? Dr. Mech isn't sure, but he has learned one thing. "It doesn't matter how much time and money you put into protecting each individual wolf. If wolf *habitat* disappears . . . if people take over the wild places wolves need to survive, you can kiss the wolf goodby. Save their habitat and you save the wolf! It's simple!"

Dr. Mech is working to do just that. And he plans to keep on studying wolves. For the more that people know about wolves, the more they will understand that there is no such thing as a big bad wolf!

## CHECK FOR UNDERSTANDING

1. How did David Mech become interested in wolves?
2. What makes up a wolf pack?
3. Why might a wolf leave a pack?
4. How do wolf pack members who have been apart act when they see each other again?
5. What is the biggest fear people have about wolves that Dr. Mech wanted to prove was not necessary?

## WRITE ABOUT *"The Big Bad Wolf?"*

What do you think would happen if a puppy dog were added to a litter of wolf pups? Would the pup grow up and live easily with the wolves? Would it have any problems? Write a paragraph telling what you think it would be like.

## REFERENCES

Allington, R. L. (1977). If they don't read much how they ever gonna get good? *The Journal of Reading, 21*, 57–61.

Allington, R. L. (1983). The reading instruction provided readers of differing reading abilities. *Elementary School Journal, 83*, 548–558.

Anderson, R. C., & Freebody, P. (1981). Vocabulary knowledge. In J. T. Guthrie (Ed.), *Comprehension and teaching: Research reviews.* Newark, DE: International Reading Association.

Beck, I., & McKeown, M. G. (1983). Learning words well—A program to enhance vocabulary and comprehension. *The Reading Teacher, 36,* 622–625.

Beck, I., Perfetti, C., & McKeown, M. G. (1982). Effects of long-term vocabulary instruction on lexical access and reading comprehension. *Journal of Educational Psychology, 74*, 506–521.

Brown, A. L., Campione, J. C., & Day, J. D. (1981). Learning to learn: On training students to learn from texts. *Educational Researcher, 10*(2), 14–21.

Bruce, B. (1984). A new point of view on children's stories. In R. C. Anderson, J. Osborn, & R. J. Tierney (Eds.), *Learning to read in American schools* (pp. 153–174). Hillsdale, NJ: Lawrence Erlbaum.

Canney, G., & Winograd, P. (1979). *Schemata for reading and reading comprehension performance* (Tech. Rep. No. 120). Urbana: University of Illinois, Center for the Study of Reading. (ERIC Document Reproduction Service No. ED 169 520).

Carr, E., & Wixson, K. K. (1986). Guidelines for evaluating vocabulary instruction. *Journal of Reading, 29*, 588–595.

Cassidy, J., Roettger, D., & Wixson, K. (1987). *Turn a corner, teacher's edition.* (Scribner Reading Series—Teacher's Edition). New York: Scribner Educational Publisher.

Cureton, D. B., & Eldridge, R. G. (1984). Teaching poor readers in the regular classroom. In J. Bauman & D. Johnson (Eds.), *Reading instruction and the beginning teacher* (pp. 244–261). Minneapolis: Burgess.

Dansereau, D. F. (1987). Transfer from cooperative to individual studying. *Journal of Reading, 30*, 614–619.

Davison, A., & Kantor, R. N. (1982). On the failure of readability formulas to define readable tests: A case study from adaptations. *Reading Research Quarterly, 17*, 187–209.

Duffy, G. G., & Roehler, L. R. (1986). *Improving classroom reading instruction: A decision making approach.* New York: Random House.

Ehri, L. (1979). Linguistic insight: Threshold of reading acquisition. In T. G. Waller & G. E. MacKinnon (Eds.), *Reading research: Advances in theory and practice* (Vol. 1) (pp. 63–114). New York: Academic Press.

Flavell, J. H. (1977). *Cognitive development.* Englewood Cliffs, NJ: Prentice-Hall.

Freedman, G., & Reynolds, E. G. (1980). Enriching basal reader lessons with semantic webbing. *The Reading Teacher, 33,* 677–684.

Hunt, J. McV. (1961). *Intelligence and experience.* New York: Ronald.

Hunt, L. C. (1971). Updating the individual approach to reading. In H. K. Smith (Ed.), *Meeting individual needs in reading* (pp. 43–51). Newark, DE: International Reading Association.

Huus, H. (1971). Reading and the individual. In H. K. Smith (Ed.), *Meeting individual needs in reading.* Newark, DE: International Reading Association.

Johnston, P. H., & Winograd, P. N. (1985). Passive failure in reading. *Journal of Reading Behavior, 17,* 279–301.

Langer, J. (1981). From theory to practice: A prereading plan. *Journal of Reading, 25,* 152–156.

Lipson, M. Y. (1984). Some unexpected issues in prior knowledge and comprehension. *The Reading Teacher, 34,* 760–765.

Lipson, M. Y. (1986). *Instructor's resource book to accompany Reading instruction for today, by M. Mason and K. Au.* Glenview, IL: Scott, Foresman.

Lipson, M. Y., & Wixson, K. K. (1986). Reading disability research: An interactionist perspective. *Review of Educational Research, 56,* 111–136.

Luther, S. (1986/1987). The wolfman. *Ranger Rick.* Washington, DC: National Wildlife Association. Adapted and reprinted as The big bad wolf? in *Turn a corner,* pp. 329–337. New York: Scribner Educational Publishers.

McNeil, J. D. (1987). *Reading comprehension: New directions for classroom practice.* Glenview, IL: Scott Foresman.

Nichols, J. N. (1983). Using prediction to increase content area interest and understanding. *Journal of Reading, 27,* 225–228.

Otto, W., & Chester, R. D. (1976). *Objectives-based reading.* Reading, MA: Addison-Wesley.

Otto, W., Wolf, A., & Eldridge, R. G. (1984). Managing instruction. In P. D. Pearson, R. Barr, M. L. Kamil, & P. Mosenthal (Eds.), *Handbook of reading research* (pp. 799–828). New York: Longman.

Palincsar, A. S., & Brown, A. L. (1984). Reciprocal teaching of comprehension fostering and monitoring activities. *Cognition and Instruction, 1,* 117–175.

Paris, S. G. (1986). Teaching children to guide their reading and learning. In T. E. Raphael (Ed.), *Contexts of school based literacy* (pp. 115–130). New York: Random House.

Paris, S. G., Cross, D. R., & Lipson, M. Y. (1984). Informed strategies for learning: A program to improve children's reading awareness and comprehension. *Journal of Educational Psychology, 76,* 1239–1252.

Paris, S. G., & Lindauer, B. K. (1982). The development of cognitive skills in childhood. In B. Wolman (Ed.), *Handbook of developmental psychology* (pp. 333–349). Englewood Cliffs, NJ: Prentice-Hall.

Paris, S. G., Lipson, M. Y., & Wixson, K. (1983). Becoming a strategic reader. *Contemporary Educational Psychology, 8,* 293–316.

Paris, S. G., & Myers, M. (1981). Comprehension monitoring, memory and study strategies of good and poor readers. *Journal of Reading Behavior, 13,* 5–22.

Paris, S. G., Wixson, K. K., & Palincsar, A. S. (1986). Instructional approaches to reading comprehension. In E. Rothkopf (Ed.), *Review of research in education* (pp. 91–128). Washington, DC: American Educational Research Association.

Pearson, P. D. (1985). *Changing the face of comprehension instruction* (Ginn Occasional Papers No. 21). Columbus, OH: Ginn.

Pearson, P. D., & Gallagher, M. (1983). The instruction of reading comprehension. *Contemporary Educational Psychology, 81,* 317–344.

Pearson, P. D., & Johnson, D. D. (1978). *Teaching reading comprehension.* New York: Holt, Rinehart and Winston.

Raphael, T. E. (1986). Question-answer relationships, revisited. *The Reading Teacher, 39,* 516–523.

Readence, J. R., & Moore, D. (1980). Differentiating text assignments in content areas: Slicing the task. *Reading Horizons, 20,* 112–117.

Reutzel, D. R. (1985). Story maps improve comprehension. *The Reading Teacher, 38,* 400–404.

Roehler, L. R., & Duffy, G. G. (1984). Direct explanation of comprehension processes. In G. G. Duffy, L. R. Roehler, & J. Mason (Eds.), *Comprehension instruction: Perspectives and suggestions* (pp. 265–280). New York: Longman.

Siegel, B. L. (1981, February–March). That ought to be enough. *Today's Education,* pp. 58E–59E.

Sinatra, R. C., Stahl-Gemake, J., & Berg, D. N. (1984). Improving reading comprehension of disabled readers through semantic mapping. *The Reading Teacher, 38,* 22–29.

Spiegel, D. L. (1981). Six alternatives to the directed reading activity. *The Reading Teacher, 34,* 914–920.

Swaby, B. (1984). FAN your ideas. *The Reading Teacher, 37,* 914–916.

Tierney, R. J., Readence, J. E., & Dishner, E. K. (1985). *Reading strategies and practices: A compendium.* (2nd ed.). Boston: Allyn & Bacon.

Uttero, D. A. (1988). Activating comprehension through cooperative learning. *The Reading Teacher, 41,* 390–395.

Wigfield, A., & Asher, S. (1984). Social and motivational influences on reading. In P. D. Pearson, R. Barr, M. L. Kamil, & P. Mosenthal (Eds.), *Handbook of reading research* (pp. 423–452). New York: Longman.

Williams, J. P., Taylor, M. B., & Ganger, S. (1981). Text variations at the level of individual sentence and the comprehension of simple exposition paragraphs. *Journal of Educational Psychology, 76,* 1065–1075.

Wixson, K. K. (1986). Vocabulary instruction and children's comprehension of basal stories. *Reading Research Quarterly, 21,* 317–329.

Wixson, K. K., & Lipson, M. Y. (1986). Reading (dis)ability: An interactionist perspective. In T. E. Raphael (Ed.), *The contexts of school-based literacy* (pp. 131–148). New York: Random House.

Wong, B. Y. L., Wong, R., & LeMare, L. (1982). The effects of knowledge of criterion tasks on comprehension and recall in normally achieving and learning disabled children. *Journal of Educational Research, 76,* 119–126.

Wood, D. J., Bruner, J. S., & Ross, G. (1976). The role of tutoring in problem solving. *Journal of Child Psychology and Psychiatry, 17,* 89–100.

## RECOMMENDED READINGS

Cooper, J. D. (1986). *Improving reading comprehension.* Boston: Houghton Mifflin.

Fowler, G. L. (1982). Developing comprehension skills in primary students through the use of story frames. *The Reading Teacher, 36,* 172–179.

Winograd, P. P., & Greenlee, M. (1986). Children need a balanced reading program. *Educational Leadership, 43*(7), 16–21.

# PART III

# Expanding Basal Instruction

Chapter 6

# Beyond the Basal
# in Beginning Reading

CONNIE A. BRIDGE

Young children will learn to read more easily and successfully when they understand the functions of print, when the materials for initial reading instruction are meaningful and predictable, and when the teacher employs an instructional approach that proceeds from the whole to its parts and enables children to relate skill instruction to a meaningful piece of text.

If teachers rely solely on the materials provided in the basal reading series, children may find it difficult to discover the purposes and pleasures that print serves in our daily lives. Thus my recommendations will focus on ways that teachers can extend basal reader instruction and create a literate environment in which children use and enjoy many types of print for many purposes.

## BACKGROUND AND RATIONALE

*Webster's Dictionary* defines *basal* as "bottom; part of a thing on which it rests; foundation; support; starting place." The terms *foundation* and *starting place* describe the appropriate role of the basal reading series in the total reading program. A basal reading series was never meant to provide a complete reading program but only a foundation or starting place. This is true at all levels but has particular implications for beginning reading programs, as children in the early stages of literacy acquisition have some needs that are unique to the lives of young children.

It is at this early stage of literacy development that children must develop an understanding of the purposes and pleasures of print, if they are to seek hungrily after literacy. Unfortunately, many youngsters arrive at school with little or no notion about why people read and write. If they have not seen their parents reading and writing in the course of their daily lives, and if their parents have not read aloud to them, children may see no need to learn to read and write. They have neither experienced the joys of hearing a good story nor seen how print helps one use a recipe to fix a favorite dish, locate a special program in the TV guide, or follow instructions to put together a new barbecue grill. If children's early exposures to reading are limited to the readiness workbooks, preprimers, and primers of a basal series, they will find it difficult to discover the two major functions of reading: experiencing pleasure and obtaining information.

The early reading materials of basal programs have been the focus of a great deal of scrutiny and criticism. Researchers have studied the characteristics of traditional beginning reading materials and have concluded that many of these materials have several problems. First, the inappropriate use of readability formulas has resulted in the application of strict vocabulary and sentence-length controls to early reading selections. Thus, children are often asked to read selections that are primarily a group of short, contrived sentences designed to repeat a few high-frequency words (Brennan, Bridge, & Winograd, 1986; Sampson, Briggs, & Sampson, 1986; Simons & Ammon, 1987) and do not match the syntactic complexity of the children's own spoken language. Furthermore, these sentences may comprise little more than a list of statements about a character or setting; that is, they do not have plots that unfold in natural ways and they lack the elements of conflict, surprise, and suspense found in well-written children's literature (Brewer & Lichtenstein, 1980; & Bruce & Rubin, 1981). Children find such selections uninteresting and hard to comprehend because the selections fail to match their expectations for natural language and well-formed stories.

Not only does the nature of early reading selections create problems for beginning readers, but also the sequence and nature of instruction can make learning to read more difficult. Many researchers and theorists agree that reading skill instruction should relate to a meaningful selection and should proceed from whole-to-part (Botel & Seaver, 1984; Gibson & Levin, 1975; Holdaway, 1979). Children initially learn oral language in meaningful, contextualized situations in which they listen to and participate in whole conversations. So, too, they can learn written language in the same manner, if they are exposed to meaningful materials in situations in which the functions of print are obvious.

Most beginning reading instruction, however, utilizes a part-to-whole approach in which children are first taught letter names, then letter-sound correspondences. They are then taught a few words, which are subsequently presented in sentences. When they are finally allowed to read connected discourse it is presented in the form of selections made up of short, contrived sentences that are strung together in order to give them practice in reading a limited number of previously introduced vocabulary words.

This part-to-whole sequence of instruction can prove confusing. Children arrive at school expecting to learn to read. Parents and older siblings have told them they will learn to read when they go to school, and they believe it. Yet they are often disappointed and/or confused when they aren't given a book until several weeks into first grade and when the instruction they are given in the name of reading consists only of letter recognition exercises, auditory discrimination training, matching shapes, color recognition, and other typical "readiness" activities.

The lucky children who have been read aloud to extensively are merely disappointed because they were expecting to learn to read stories like the ones they have listened to as they snuggled next to a loving parent or grandparent. But they can usually cope because they are familiar with the pleasures of print and with the way printed language sounds. However, the less fortunate children who lack prior experience with the pleasures of books and with the look and sound of printed language will be confused about the nature and purposes of reading. Isolated letters and sounds will have no meaning to them, as they have no context or background to which they can relate these abstract bits of information. These so-called "reading" lessons become an end in themselves rather than a means through which children can gain access to the pleasures and purposes of print.

What can we do in beginning reading programs to enrich and extend the instruction suggested in basal reader series, so as to avoid this disappointment and frustration? In the following sections, you will find suggestions for creating a literate environment by selecting and using meaningful, predictable materials; relating skill instruction in decoding, vocabulary, and comprehension to meaningful contexts; and building fluency through practice.

## CREATING A LITERATE ENVIRONMENT

### Reading Center

First the teacher must create an environment in which children are surrounded by books and print. A quiet corner of the room should be reserved as a reading center. In it the teacher should have many books displayed attractively and comfortable places for children to browse and to curl up with the book of their choice. Even if the school has a well-stocked central library, a classroom library is a necessity. It may consist of a relatively small, permanent collection of some of the children's favorite books and a rotating collection of books checked out by the teacher from the central library. These books may extend the theme of a basal selection or unit or of a content-area unit. They should include several books by the same author, especially authors whose stories appear in the basals and whose stories the teacher has read aloud to the children. In chapter 7 of this book, Morrow has provided more complete guidelines for setting up a classroom library, as well as suggestions for ways of integrating literature into the reading program.

### Reading Aloud to Students

In a literate classroom environment, the teachers are readers themselves and they model their love of reading in many ways. The best way for teachers to model a love of reading and books is to read aloud daily from good children's literature. Teachers should share their favorite children's books by reading them aloud in an interesting, expressive way that shows children that the teacher enjoys books and wants to share this joy. Devoting precious classroom time to reading aloud demonstrates the value that is placed on reading.

Research supports daily reading aloud as a component of effective reading programs. In a review of the literature on reading aloud, McCormick (1977) found that reading achievement test scores in vocabulary and comprehension increased significantly for children whose teachers read aloud daily from recommended children's books. She found, further, that read-aloud programs are especially beneficial for young children and low achievers. Studies by Durkin (1966) in the United States and by Clark (1976) in Scotland, of preschool children who learned to read on their own, revealed that all of these children had a supportive adult who read aloud to them frequently and who answered their questions about print. McCracken and McCracken (1986) have labeled this method of learning to read the "lap technique," because these children learned to read while seated on the lap of a loving parent, grandparent, or other adult, who read aloud to them from favorite books.

As teachers, we need to simulate the lap technique as closely as possible. Even though we cannot literally hold our students on our laps, we can do so figuratively by creating a warm, supportive climate while reading aloud. The following suggestions will help make classroom read-aloud sessions more like parent/child read-aloud sessions:

1. Have a special location in the classroom for reading aloud. A carpeted area is best, so that the children can gather close around you on the floor. Sit on a low chair so that the book is elevated enough for the children to see the illustrations but so you are still close to their level.
2. Show the front cover and read the title and the author's name. Ask the children to predict what they think might happen in a book with this title. If the author is one whose books you've read aloud before, remind the children of the other book and ask them to think about how the books are alike, noting especially the characters and illustrations.
3. Read aloud with expression, stopping at natural breaking points in the story to have the children check and, if necessary, revise their predictions.
4. If the author uses an especially descriptive word or describes a character, scene, or event in an exceptionally vivid way, stop to discuss it with the children. Have them close their eyes and try to visualize the scene, event, or character.
5. If there is a repetitive line or phrase in the book, invite the children to join in and read along with you on the repetitive part.
6. At the end of the story, ask the children if they ever had an experience like the one in the book. Let them discuss similar experiences they have had.

Read-aloud sessions should occur daily in primary classrooms. The books selected for reading aloud should be about characters and events with which young children can identify (Cohen, 1968). Books with predictable events and repetitive lines should also be read aloud frequently. In a study of teacher behaviors that enhance reading aloud, Lamme (1976) found that the teachers who were rated as most effective were those who involved the children during story reading, by chorally reading refrains or predicting what would happen next, by pointing out words and pictures in the book, by making frequent eye contact with the children, and by reading with expression. In other words, when teachers share books with children in much the same way that parents do, the read-aloud session is enhanced.

### Shared Book Experience with Big Books

Oversized books, often called "big books," are ideal for reading aloud to groups of children, as they make it possible for every child to see the illustrations and the print, and to follow along as the teacher reads (McCracken & McCracken, 1986; Slaughter, 1983). Holdaway (1979) describes procedures that he and his colleagues used with five- and six year olds in New Zealand, employing multiple rereadings of big books:

1. Gather together a small group of children, usually eight to ten, and read aloud the story or poem. The main goal of the first reading is for enjoyment, so that the children can learn that one of the major purposes for reading is to enjoy a good story.
2. Before starting to read, show the cover of the book, read the title of the selection, draw the children's attention to the cover illustration, and then ask them to predict what might happen in the story. The prereading discussion also helps the children learn concepts about print and books, such as title, author, illustrator, page, and beginning.
3. After the prereading discussion and eliciting predictions, read the story straight through with enthusiasm, so that the emphasis is on getting a sense of the meaning of the story.
4. Then discuss with the children what happened in the story and compare the happenings to their predictions.
5. In subsequent lessons, read the book aloud again, asking the children to join in when they can, and have them retell the story with and without reference to the illustrations in the book. Classic tales, such as *The Three Billy Goats Gruff* (Galdone, 1963), *Goldilocks and the Three Bears* (see Galdone, 1972), and the *Little Red Hen*, (Galdone, 1973) are excellent for shared big-book experiences because they have tightly knit plot structures and predictable events which enable the children to remember the story and to join in on the predictable lines.
6. After the children are familiar with the story, begin to focus on certain words, letter/sound correspondences, comprehension skills, and print concepts within the text, as a basis for skill instruc-

tion (see also Bridge, 1986; McCracken & McCracken, 1986; Rhodes, 1981; Tompkins & Webeler, 1983).

## SELECTING AND USING
## MEANINGFUL, PREDICTABLE MATERIALS

### Meaningfulness

Beginning reading instruction should employ meaningful, functional texts (Goodman, 1976; Holdaway, 1986). This means that, in addition to the readiness materials, the preprimers, the primers, and first readers, teachers must expose the children to real texts that are representative of a variety of genres: storybooks, trade books, jokes, riddles, poetry, newspapers, comic strips, dictionaries, instructions, recipes, TV guides, catalogs, menus, letters, environmental print, and so forth.

Smith (1982) contends that, before they can learn to read, children must understand that print is meaningful. Unless children see teachers and parents using real texts to accomplish real purposes in their daily lives, it will be difficult for them to discover that print is meaningful and functional in their own lives. While children are in the early stages of reading acquisition, it will be necessary to read most of these real texts to them, but the modeling helps the child see that you can find out needed information by reading certain kinds of materials and that you can entertain yourself by using other types of materials. Because literacy is essentially a social skill, it will be learned best in social settings in which literacy occurs naturally and satisfies a social purpose. Holdaway (1986) says it well: "Reading and writing must deeply enhance the social well-being of potential learners if skill is to be hungrily sought" (p. 69).

### Predictable Materials

The first texts with which children are taught to read should be highly predictable; that is, they should contain an underlying structure which enables the reader to predict the next word, line, phrase, or episode. According to Rhodes (1979), the factors that influence the predictability of material for first graders are repetition of large chunks of language; repetition of episodes; and familiarity of story lines, story sequences, and concepts. Materials that contain these characteristics are called "patterned" or "structured language" materials.

There are many types of patterns that are based on the cultural, linguistic, and rhythmic structures with which students are already familiar when they arrive at school (Bridge, 1979). One of the simplest patterns involves the repetition of a certain phrase or sentence at various points throughout the selection, as in *Oh, A-Hunting We Will Go*. Cumulative-repetitive patterns also involve the repetition of a word, phrase, or sentence, but, in addition, a new word, phrase, or sentence is added to each succeeding episode, as in the old favorites, *The House That Jack Built* and *I Know an Old Lady* (Bonne, 1961). Patterns based on rhyme and rhythm are frequently used, and rhyme is sometimes combined with repetitive and cumulative-repetitive structures, as in *A Bug in a Jug*.

Other patterns are based on common cultural and linguistic sequences, such as the alphabet, the cardinal and ordinal numbers, the days of the week, the months of the year, the four seasons, and the basic colors. A final type of structure involves selections in which the events occur in such a way as to enable the reader to predict future events, as in the classic tales of *The Little Red Hen* and *The Three Billy Goats Gruff*, and the contemporary favorites, *Nobody Listens to Andrew* and *Who Took the Farmer's Hat?*. A list of these predictable books can be found at the end of this chapter. Other lists are available in Bridge (1986), Bridge, Winograd, and Haley (1983), Rhodes (1981), and Tompkins and Webeler (1983).

Predictable books can be used to accomplish many instructional purposes, such as building sight vocabulary and fluency; teaching rhyme and word families; teaching comprehension skills including prediction, cause-and-effect relationships, and sequence; and integrating reading and writing. But perhaps the most important value of using predictable materials in initial reading instruction is that they help beginning readers develop positive feelings about themselves as readers. Because of the repetition, children can "read" these predictable books with fluency, even before they can recognize all of the individual words (Leu, DeGroff, & Simons, 1986). They are able to read along with the predictable lines, thus role playing themselves as successful readers, even while becoming readers. Children experience a high rate of success when reading aloud from predictable materials, and high success rates have been shown to correlate positively with overall reading achievement (see Allington, 1977; Nichols, 1983; Johnston & Winograd, 1985).

When children do lots of impromptu choral reading of predictable texts, they are able to read fluently rather than in the halting manner characteristic of round-robin oral reading. As R. V. Allen (personal communication, 1976) insightfully points out, "There's nothing worse than a bunch of poor readers sitting in a circle hearing other poor readers read poorly." Children engaged in multiple choral rereadings of predictable texts do not experience the embarrassment and frustration of stumbling through a poor oral reading performance in front of a group. The poor readers are aided by the support of the more fluent readers in the group, as well as by the familiarity and predictability of the text.

The following steps can be followed in helping to improve oral reading fluency through the use of predictable texts:

1. *Teacher reading aloud.* The teacher reads the chosen book aloud, gathering the children closely around so they can see the illustrations and follow along as the teacher runs a hand along under the print. This is where the big books come in handy; they make it easier for all children to see the print.
2. *Reading together.* After the initial reading of the text, the teacher should read the book again to the children, inviting them to join in when they think they know what the print is going to say. After several of the children have begun to pick up on the pattern and read along, the teacher can ask how they figured out what would come next. For example, in *A Bug in a Jug,* the text is organized around five-line rhyming sequences such as the following:

    Page 1: This is a bug.
    Page 2: This is a jug.
    Page 3: This is a bug in a jug.
    Page 4: This is a rug.
    Page 5: This is a bug in a jug on a rug.

After reading pages 1 and 2, the teacher can turn to page 3 and ask the children to predict what this line would say. By using the repetitive line, the rhyme, and the illustration, the children can usually read the rest of the pages along with the teacher. Asking the children how they figured out what the print would say helps them bring to a conscious level their intuitive understanding of the way the author has organized the text. Ask,

What do you think this page will say?

How did you figure that out?

If children have trouble verbalizing how they figured out what the page would say, focus their thinking by asking,

Did the picture help you?

Did the rhyming words help you?

Did it help to have the same words repeated in each line?

3. *Children reading chorally and alone.* After reading the book to and with the children, the teacher should have the children read the text chorally and individually. Different lines can be assigned to small groups or to individuals. Multiple rereadings of the book provide lots of oral reading practice and build fluency and confidence in beginning readers.

After the children have become familiar with the predictable book through choral reading, then this can be used to develop sight vocabulary. For example, notice the words that were repeated over and over in *A Bug in a Jug*, namely *that, is, a, in,* and *on.* These are high-frequency words that all beginning readers must learn to recognize instantly, on sight. By rereading them over and over within the meaningful context of the predictable lines, children learn the words of the rhyme easily (Bridge & Burton, 1982; Bridge, Winograd, & Haley, 1983). To ensure that the sight vocabulary words are learned, teachers use the following steps, in addition to the three just presented:

1. After the children are able to read the book fluently, write the text of the book on a large chart, with space between the lines. Also write each line of the text on a separate sentence strip.
2. Have the children read the text from the chart, then match the sentence strips to the corresponding line on the chart.
3. When they are able to match the lines successfully, give them cards containing individual words from the text and have them match the card to the corresponding word on the chart.

Notice that the sequence of instruction in these lessons proceeds from whole-to-part. The teacher first reads the original book to the children, inviting them to join in as they gain familiarity with the text. Their first exposures to the text involve the total contextual support of the illustrations and the teacher's oral presentation of the whole text. Gradually the print is decontextualized by being written on the chart, without illustrations but with an intact text which the children can reread for contextual support. Finally, the teacher directs the children's attention to the individual words, while still giving them access to the total text on the chart. This gradual decontextualization always allows the children to refer to a meaningful piece of text.

## BUILDING MEANING VOCABULARY, WORD RECOGNITION, AND COMPREHENSION

### Meaning Vocabulary

Meaningful context is also important in teaching meaning vocabulary. Children need multiple exposures and rich semantic associations to learn the meanings of new words (McKeown, Beck, Omanson, & Perfetti, 1983; Stahl, 1983). Vocabulary words should be presented in many contexts, both oral and written, in order to increase the number of meaningful semantic associations the youngsters have with the words and to encourage their use of contextual clues. The children's attention should also be directed to the graphophonic and structural characteristics of the word, so that they will be developing multiple strategies for figuring out unfamiliar words.

The following approach can be used to preteach new words that are judged to be vital to the comprehension of a basal reader selection or content-area lesson:

1. Select the words that need to be pretaught. Not all new words do. You should introduce only those words that are vital to the comprehension of the selection and high-frequency words that the students will need to read other materials. If a word can be figured out from context, it does not require introduction. A limited number of new words should be introduced at one time.
2. Write the words on the board or on cards. One classroom set of word cards can be used for the entire class, if all children in the instructional group can see them; however, a set of word cards for each child is desirable so that every pupil can respond. This requires active involvement by every pupil.
3. Present oral definitions and oral cloze sentences in a fast-paced manner, and ask the students to point to the word that fits in the blank. This enables the children to develop rich and flexible associations. Some of the types of semantic associations that should be developed are classification and categorization, exemplars, synonyms, and antonyms.
4. Students should also generate sentences using the new words in context.
5. To help students focus on the phonic and structural characteristics of the words, ask them to point to and say the word that begins

with the same letters; has the same root word, prefix, or suffix; and so forth. Example statements are

Show me a word that begins like *black*.

Show me a word that has the same suffix as *aggravation*.

6. The students may also be asked to make predictions about the selection, based upon the vocabulary words that have been introduced (Wood & Robinson 1983). The predictions can focus upon the events in a story or upon aspects of story comprehension, such as setting, characterization, mood or feeling, and reality/fantasy. If the selection is factual, then the predictions could focus on structural elements such as cause and effect, comparison and contrast, sequence, and listing.

7. End the session with a quick review of the words, designed to develop fluent recognition. Go through the words in random order several times. You pronounce them; the children point to and say each word. Let a volunteer student pronounce each word while other students respond.

If every student is actively involved in multiple opportunities to read new vocabulary in meaningful contexts, then the children will be able to develop rich understanding and fluent recognition of these words.

### Word Recognition Skills

Knowing that children learn best when they can relate what they are learning to a meaningful context has led reading researchers and learning theorists to suggest that instruction in word recognition skills should proceed from whole-to-part (Botel & Seaver, 1984; Gibson & Levin, 1975; Holdaway, 1979; McCracken & McCracken, 1986). In a whole-to-part approach, children are first exposed to a whole text—the entire story, rhyme, finger play, language experience story, recipe, label, set of instructions, or other genuine text. Often the first exposure involves the teacher reading the selection aloud. As the children gain familiarity with the text, they begin to read along with the teacher and finally read the text without teacher support. Gradually, the teacher draws the children's attention to specific features of the text, depending on the purpose of instruction (e.g., initial consonants, short vowel sounds, or rhyme). As a result of moving from whole-to-part, children are able to relate skill instruction to a meaningful word, phrase, or text and they are better able to see a purpose for learning the skill.

*Initial Consonants.* Usually the first phonics instruction that children receive deals with initial consonant sounds, and appropriately so, since the initial sound and the context of the sentence are usually sufficient to enable a reader to figure out a word not recognized instantly at sight. For students who are just beginning to learn initial sounds, the following whole-to-part approach is suggested:

1. Select a rhyme that contains several words beginning with the target sound. For example, to teach the sound of *j*, choose a rhyme like "Jack and Jill." Write the rhyme on a large chart or on the chalkboard.
2. Read the rhyme aloud to children two or three times, while running your hand or a pointer along under the words.
3. Invite the children to join in and read along with you several times. It doesn't matter that they don't know all the words at this point. Use the pointer to keep their attention focused on the print you are currently reading.
4. Point to the *j* in the word *Jack,* and ask if the children know what that letter is. Write a capital *J* and a lower-case *j* on the board, and tell them what each is called. Have them listen to the sound of *j* in *Jack.* Do the same with the word *Jill.*
5. See if the children can think of other words that begin with *j*. List them on the board as they name them. Include the names of any children in the class that begin with *j*.
6. After the children have read *j* words in a meaningful context, they will be better prepared for the workbook pages designed to provide more practice on the *j* sound.

Other ways of reinforcing initial consonant sounds by having students use the sound in meaningful contexts include:

1. Have students bring in labels and logos with names or words that begin with the target sound. Glue them on a large poster so all children can read them.
2. Have students bring in empty cans, bottles, and boxes with labels on them, and use them to set up a grocery store. When working on a specific sound, have students "shop" for items beginning with the target sound.
3. Have students look for words in their basal reading selections and language-experience stories that begin with the target sound. List them on a chart.
4. Display a tongue twister containing words that begin with the

target sound. Read it to the students. Let them practice it for several days. Have a contest to see who can read it without getting confused.

5. Have the class compose alliterative lines using words beginning with the target sound, for example, "Jack and Jill like jelly beans and juice."

*Combination of Strategies: Context plus Phonics.*   Children need to develop multiple strategies for figuring out words they don't recognize instantly at sight. Usually by combining context clues with the initial sound, the child is able to figure out an unfamiliar word. Teachers can encourage this practice by responding to miscues and hesitations as follows:

1. When children pause before an unfamiliar word, tell them to read to the end of the sentence and think of a word that would make sense in the sentence.
2. Then have them look at the beginning sound of the unknown word and see if the word that they thought of begins the same way. If not, have them think of another word that begins with that letter and makes sense in the sentence.
3. Avoid telling children to "sound it out," as that causes them to focus only on letter/sound correspondences, rather than using context clues to help them figure out a word that makes sense.

When children fail to self-correct miscues that interfere with meaning, you need to help the children focus their attention on meaning by responding as follows:

1. Allow the child to complete the sentence or paragraph before stopping her or him or allowing other children to do so.
2. If the child fails to self-correct the miscue at that point, repeat the sentence with the miscue and ask, Did that make sense?
3. Have the child reread the sentence and self-correct the miscue.

Children soon get the message that reading should make sense and that, when it doesn't, they need to reread in order to self-correct.

## Comprehension

*Emphasis on Meaning.*   The most important contribution to comprehension instruction in early classrooms is an overall emphasis on meaning in reading. Even in their initial encounters with print, children must be helped to understand that it should make sense. In the previous sections of this chapter, we have laid the groundwork for comprehension instruction by keeping the focus on meaning in multiple ways: through the use of meaningful materials, such as predictable books and genuine texts, and through daily read-aloud sessions in which the children are involved in making predictions and in confirming and rejecting their predictions, in discussing and visualizing events and characters, and in relating story events to events in their own lives.

*Direct Instruction.* In addition to stressing an overall emphasis on meaning and relating skill instruction to meaningful texts, teachers of beginning reading can also build in more direct instruction in comprehension. In her study of comprehension instruction in elementary classrooms, Durkin (1978/1979) found that teachers spent very little time actually teaching children *how to* comprehend text, but that most of their time was spent asking children questions *after* they had read. It should be noted that, after the reading is completed, it is too late to influence comprehension. To be effective, most of the comprehension instruction must occur before and during reading and must be designed to transfer responsibility for comprehension from the teacher to the students. Recently researchers have attempted to develop ways of helping teachers do a better job of teaching students *how to* comprehend text and monitor their own comprehension (Paris, Cross, & Lipson, 1984; Paris, Lipson, & Wixson, 1983; Schmitt, 1987; Schmitt & Baumann, 1986a, 1986b).

Schmitt and Baumann (1986a) suggest the following modified guided reading procedure, which can be used during basal reader instruction to promote better comprehension and to develop students' comprehension monitoring skills.

BEFORE READING
1. *Activate background knowledge.* Tell children that they can use what they already know about the topic of the selection to help them understand the selection better. Help them learn to use the title and the pictures to think about what they already know. Have a brief discussion of their related prior knowledge. To help them learn to transfer the practice of arousing their own prior knowledge before starting to read, explain that thinking about what they already know before they read can help them better understand any material they read.

2. *Make predictions about selection content.* Have students use the prior knowledge aroused by the title and pictures to predict what might happen in the story or, if the selection is an informational article, what information might be presented. Write down their predictions on the chalkboard or on a large tablet so that they can refer back to them as they read. Ask students to justify their predictions by telling why they think an event will happen or a topic will be covered. If they have trouble making predictions using the title and pictures, model for them what you would predict and explain what clues in the title and pictures you used to make that prediction. When reading stories, have the students focus their predictions on basic story elements, such as settings, characters' problems and goals, and possible attempts and outcomes. Again, to facilitate transfer, remind them that predicting will help them comprehend anything they read.

3. *Set purposes for reading.* Explain to students that they should always have a purpose for reading, because it helps them become actively involved in reading and helps them focus on the information that relates to their purpose. After students have made predictions, their purpose becomes reading to see if the selection turned out as they thought it would.

4. *Generate prereading questions.* Tell students that before they begin to read they should ask themselves some questions that they want to answer as they read. This, too, helps them read more actively and recall more about what they read. Their questions should focus on basic story elements such as characters' goals and problems, how the characters attempt to solve their problems, and the final solution.

DURING READING

1. *Evaluate and revise predictions.* As students read, have them stop at logical breaking points, to see if the story events match their predictions. Ask them to cite evidence from the selection that supports or rejects their predictions. If the evidence calls for revision, the students should adjust their predictions in light of the accumulating information in the text. Encourage students to discuss their reasons for revising their predictions.

2. *Summarize at various points.* Help students learn to stop at various points and review the most important information up to that point in the text. Explain that this is a good way of seeing if they are comprehending what they have read. If they can't recall what they

have read, they need to reread the parts they can't remember or don't understand.

3. *Relate new information to prior knowledge.* Remind students that before they started reading they thought about what they already knew, to help them comprehend. Tell them that they should continue throughout the selection to compare what they are reading to what they already know.

4. *Answer prereading questions and generate new questions.* As new information is presented in the text, tell students they should find the answers to their prereading questions and that they should ask themselves new questions that arise as they read.

AFTER READING

1. *Evaluate predictions.* Have students discuss information from the selection which helped them confirm, reject, or revise their predictions. Have them tell when and why they made any revisions in their predictions.

2. *Answer purpose-setting questions.* Have students judge how well they achieved their prereading purpose and whether they were able to answer their prereading questions.

3. *Summarize the total selection.* Have students summarize the total selection, focusing on the structural elements of the story, such as the characters' problems and goals, attempts, and final solution. For informational articles, have them focus on the most important information by using elements of the text structure, such as cause and effect, comparison and contrast, sequence, and simple listing.

In summary, the most important thing to remember about comprehension instruction in any reading situation is to help students to set purposes before reading, to read actively to achieve these purposes, and to self-monitor and self-evaluate how well they have achieved their purposes during and after reading. At all times, teachers should be modeling these procedures for students and helping them to assume responsibility for their own comprehension and for their own comprehension monitoring.

## BUILDING FLUENCY THROUGH PRACTICE

We not only want children to comprehend effectively, we want them to be efficient as well, and efficiency requires fluent reading. If they are to become fluent readers, children must practice reading.

Smith (1982) contends that children learn to read by reading. This contention has been supported by findings from teacher effectiveness research. Children who do more reading achieve better on reading achievement tests than children who read for less time each day (Anderson, Evertson, & Brophy, 1979; Barr, 1973/1974; Leinhardt, Zigmund, & Cooley, 1981). Our goal as teachers, then, should be to increase the number of minutes our students spend reading each day, the number of words they read each day, and the number of books they read over the course of the year.

The problem for teachers of beginning readers is that there are few materials the children can read in the early stages, when they recognize so few words. How can we, as teachers of young children, provide opportunities for them to practice reading in the initial stages of instruction? There are several methods we can use, including multiple rereadings of predictable books, dictated language experience stories, choral reading, readers' theater, and Hoffman's (1987) "listen-first/read-later" approach. I have already discussed multiple rereadings of predictable books in the section on building sight vocabulary. When children join in and read with you on the predictable parts and when they read these parts chorally together, they are getting a great deal of practice reading fluently. Let us now see what these other methods have to offer.

## Language Experience Stories

Another way of giving children practice reading while their sight vocabularies are still limited is to take dictation of language experience stories. These stories may be authored by a group or an individual. Individually authored stories have the advantage of a better match between the child's own language and the printed story; however, they are time-consuming and the teacher may feel that a group-authored story makes better use of limited instructional time. Either type of story produces highly predictable texts that enable beginning readers to practice reading fluently, since both the content of the story and the language used to express it come out of the children's own experience and thus are familiar and predictable. Proceed as follows:

1. The first step is always to provide or help the children select an experience worthy of writing about. It may be a firsthand experience such as a field trip to a "petting zoo," an unexpected snow, a big rainstorm, a new brother or sister, or a classroom pet giving

birth. You may provide a stimulus such as an object, filmstrip, slide, picture, story, or newspaper article.

2. Talk about the experience with the children, to get them to generate ideas. Then help them to decide on a few of the most important ideas that they want you to write down. Keep the story short enough that the children can experience success in reading it back.

3. On a large sheet of chart paper, write down exactly what each child dictates. Wait until the child has expressed a complete thought, then instruct the children to watch as you write down the sentence, pronouncing each word as you write it.

4. As you are recording the children's story, you can slip in some instruction on print concepts. For example, point out to children that

> Print is written and read from left to right and from top to bottom.
>
> Space is left between words in a sentence.
>
> Sentences begin with capital letters and end with periods.
>
> People's names start with capital letters.
>
> What can be said can be written down and read back later.

Of course, you will not point out all of these things at once. Introducing one concept at a time is desirable, with occasional review of previously taught concepts.

5. Read the story back to the children, running your hand or a pointer under the print as you read at a normal rate. You will want to repeat the process of reading aloud to the children until they are able to read the story with you.

6. Have the children join in and read out loud with you, while you still direct the children's attention to the print with your hand or a pointer. Repeat until the children are able to read the story, as a group or individually, without your reading along.

7. Let individual volunteers read the story orally. If the children have difficulty with a word, supply it immediately. The goal is to allow the children to role play themselves as successful readers, even in the early stages of becoming readers. Through repeated readings of the words in the familiar context of the dictated language experience stories, children will add the words to their sight vocabularies and develop oral reading fluency and confidence in themselves as readers.

8. Display the language experience stories in the room so that the children can reread them whenever they wish. It is also a good idea to retype or photocopy all the dictated pieces and bind them

together in book form. This provides the children with a sense of satisfaction as they see the booklet grow and the number of stories they can read successfully increase. Putting a library card in the back so that the book can be checked out and taken home to be shared with parents enables the children to view themselves as authors as well as readers.

9. Reread the stories often, individually and chorally, to review and reinforce sight vocabulary and to build oral reading fluency.
10. The words in the stories can be used later for phonics lessons to teach various letter/sound correspondences.

## Choral Reading and Warm-ups

Choral reading is a natural and enjoyable way of providing more practice reading and increasing the number of words students read each day and the number of minutes they spend actually reading connected discourse. Having students chorally read and reread a poem or predictable book can easily triple or quadruple the number of words they read for the day. For example, if the children chorally read the nursery rhyme "Mary Had a Little Lamb" five times, they will be reading approximately 250 words in a five- to ten-minute period. Compare that to a typical preprimer or primer selection, which usually has fewer than fifty words. If the children read one selection per day, they would read only fifty words during the typical twenty- to thirty-minute reading period, or 100 words if they reread the story orally.

Furthermore, choral reading gets all students actively involved in reading in a relaxing, enjoyable, and noncompetitive way. The whole class can do choral reading together, so the teacher is able to work with all reading ability levels at the same time. Less able readers are helped by the multiple rereadings of a familiar selection and by reading along with more fluent readers. Soon even word-by-word readers are able to read the selection fluently.

The following steps can be used to conduct a choral reading lesson:

1. Write the selection on a large chart, on the chalkboard, or on a transparency. A chart is often preferable, since it can be displayed subsequently in the classroom.
2. Before displaying the written copy, read the whole poem aloud to the class, setting the mood and the basic rhythmic pattern. You may want to read it aloud more than once, to familiarize the

children further with the selection before you invite them to read along.

3. Discuss the selection *briefly* with the children, including its setting, mood, or poetic type, if you think that will help them to read it with more expression. Explain any difficult vocabulary or concepts, if necessary. Point out if the poet is one the children have read before or one they will be reading often.

4. Display the written copy of the poem and invite the children to join in and read aloud with you. Run your hand or a pointer under the words to help the children keep their place and stay together. Repeat as many times as you think appropriate.

5. If the selection lends itself to parts, solos, and choruses, assign them and reread. You may want to reassign roles and read it again, if the children's interest and enthusiasm remain high.

6. Keep a copy of the selection on display in the classroom, or have individual copies for the students. You'll be pleased to see how often the children will reread the poem on their own and take their copies home to read to their parents.

7. Think of ways of enriching and expanding the selection through drama, art, music, movement, pantomime, puppetry, finger plays, cooking, and writing takeoffs on the pattern or theme.

Many teachers are now using choral reading selections as "warm-ups" at the beginning of the reading instructional period. The children chorally reread a selection to which they have formerly been introduced. This gets them in the mood for reading and provides practice in reading connected discourse. This opportunity to reread a familiar selection fluently is especially helpful for beginning and poor readers, who rarely have the experience of reading something easily and fluently.

Be sure to use lots of humorous poems for choral reading. Poems by Jack Prelutsky, Shel Silverstein, William Cole, and Judith Viorst will make children laugh while helping them learn to read. The following are just a few of the good collections of poems to use for choral reading:

Cole, W. (1981). *Poem stew.* New York: J. B. Lippincott.
Prelutsky, J. (1983). *The Random House book of poetry for children.* New York: Random House.
Prelutsky, J. (1986). *Ride a purple pelican.* New York: Greenwillow Books.
Silverstein, S. (1974). *Where the sidewalk ends.* New York: Harper & Row.
Silverstein, S. (1981). *A light in the attic.* New York: Harper & Row.

Viorst, J. (1981). *If I were in charge of the world and other worries.* New York: Atheneum.

## Readers' Theater

Readers' theater is another enjoyable way of promoting reading practice through multiple rereadings of the same selection. It can be used for rereading the basal selections, or other simple stories can be adapted to it. Readers' theater is like presenting a play except that the players read their parts rather than memorize them and there are usually no costumes or props, thus preparation time is kept to a minimum. In readers' theater, the success of the presentation depends upon the presenter's ability to read expressively so that the audience can visualize what is going on; thus the focus is on reading well.

The following suggestions can help you use readers' theater effectively:

1. Select a story with several characters and dialogue. Eliminate all dialogue markers, such as "she said" or "he shouted."
2. Assign each character's part to one child and designate a narrator to read the passages containing no dialogue.
3. Rehearse the presentation by practicing rereading the parts until all players are reading with expression.
4. After two or three rehearsals, read the story to the rest of the class, another class in the school, or parents.

In readers' theater, children are highly motivated to perform before an audience, so their reading practice is purposeful and is aimed toward a meaningful interpretation of the story.

## Listen-First/Read-Later Approach

For beginning and poor readers, Hoffman (1987) has developed an alternative to the initial guided silent reading of the basal selection. Instead of having these students struggle through the initial reading of the text, he suggests the following series of steps:

1. Begin by reading the selection aloud to the children while they listen with books closed.
2. Together with the children, construct a story map of the selection, containing the characters; the setting; the initiating event, problem, goal of the main character; the attempts of the character to

achieve the goal or solve the problem; and the final resolution of the story. Write the map on the chalkboard as the students discuss the parts of the story.

3. Using the story map as a guide, have the children dictate a summary of the story; write this on the board or on a transparency. Then have the children reread the story summary.

4. Engage the students in guided silent reading and discussion of the story.

5. After reading silently, ask the students each to select a section of the story to practice rereading, in preparation for reading orally to the group.

6. Have the group read the story orally. While the individual who has practiced the section reads aloud, the rest of the group listens with books closed.

By first hearing the selection read aloud well by the teacher, the children are presented with a good reading model and are able to concentrate on the meaning of the selection from the beginning. After they fully comprehend the selection, they are able to focus on reading accuracy and fluency.

## SUMMARY

Beginning readers must see that reading is meaningful and functional in their lives. Because of certain limitations inherent in basal reading series and other limitations caused by their misuse, it is difficult for children to discover the meaningfulness and functionality of print if teachers rely solely on the basal materials and procedures. Therefore, teachers should view the basal only as a foundation for reading instruction and should extend basal instruction by creating a literate environment filled with meaningful, functional materials and providing many legitimate opportunities for the children to use them. Furthermore, teachers should read aloud daily to students, use predictable books and stories, and provide many opportunities for students to practice reading in context. Teachers should enrich vocabulary instruction by providing multiple exposures to the words in meaningful contexts and should relate skills instruction to meaningful texts. They should teach comprehension by promoting active involvement before, during, and after reading. Most important, teachers must always focus on meaning during reading instruction and help students experience the pleasures and purposes of print.

# REFERENCES

Allen, R. V. (1976). Personal communication.

Allington, R. L. (1977). If they don't read much how they ever gonna get good? *The Journal of Reading, 21,* 57–61.

Anderson, L., Evertson, C., & Brophy, J. (1979). An experimental study of effective teaching in first grade reading groups. *Elementary School Journal, 79,* 193–223.

Barr, R. C. (1973/1974). Instructional pace differences and their effect on reading acquisition. *Reading Research Quarterly, 9,* 526–554.

Botel, M., & Seaver, J. T. (1984). *Phonics revisited: Toward an integrated methodology.* Paper presented at the annual meeting of the Keystone State Reading Association, Hershey, PA. (ERIC Document Reproduction Service No. ED 252 819).

Brennan, A. D. H., Bridge, C. A., & Winograd, P. N. (1986). The effects of structural variation on children's recall of basal reader stories. *Reading Research Quarterly, 21,* 91–104.

Brewer, W. F., & Lichtenstein, E. H. (1980). Event schemas, story schemas, and story grammars (Tech. Rep. No. 197). Champaign, IL: University of Illinois, Center for the Study of Reading.

Bridge, C. (1979). Predictable materials for beginning readers. *Language Arts, 56,* 503–507.

Bridge, C. A. (1986). Predictable books for beginning readers and writers. In M. L. Sampson (Ed.), *The pursuit of literacy: Early reading and writing* (pp. 81–96). Dubuque, IA: Kendall/Hunt.

Bridge, C. A., & Burton, B. (1982). Teaching sight vocabulary through patterned language materials. In J. A. Niles & L. A. Harris (Eds.), *New inquiries in reading research and instruction: The thirty-first yearbook of the National Reading Conference* (pp. 119–123). Washington, DC: National Reading Conference.

Bridge, C. A., Winograd, P. N., & Haley, D. (1983). Using predictable materials to teach beginning reading. *The Reading Teacher, 36,* 884–891.

Bruce, B., & Rubin, A. (1981). Jobs you shouldn't count on readability formulas to do. In A. Davison, R. Lutz, & A. Roalef (Eds.), *Text readability: Proceedings of the March 1980 Conference* (Tech. Rep. No. 213) (pp. 45–73). Champaign, IL: University of Illinois, Center for the Study of Reading.

Clark, M. M. (1976). *Young fluent readers.* London: Heinemann Educational Books.

Cohen, D. (1968). The effect of literature on vocabulary and reading achievement. *Elementary English, 45,* 209–213, 217.

Durkin, D. (1966). *Children who read early.* New York: Teachers' College Press.

Durkin, D. (1978/1979). What classroom observations reveal about reading comprehension instruction. *Reading Research Quarterly, 14,* 481–533.

Gibson, E. J., & Levin, H. (1975). *The psychology of reading.* Cambridge, MA: MIT Press.

Goodman, K. S. (1976). *Reading: A conversation with Kenneth Goodman.* Glenview, IL: Scott, Foresman.

Hoffman, J. V. (1987). Rethinking the role of oral reading in basal instruction. *Elementary School Journal, 87,* 367–374.

Holdaway, D. (1979). *The foundations of literacy.* New York: Ashton Scholastic.

Holdaway, D. (1986). The structure of natural language as a basis for literacy instruction. In M. L. Sampson (Ed.), *The pursuit of literacy: Early reading and writing* (pp. 56–72). Dubuque, IA: Kendall/Hunt.

Johnston, P., & Winograd, P. (1985). Passive failure in reading. *Journal of Reading Behavior, 17,* 279–301.

Lamme, L. (1976). Reading aloud to young children. *Language Arts, 53,* 886–891.

Leinhardt, G., Zigmund, N., & Cooley, W. W. (1981). Reading instruction and its effects. *American Educational Research Journal, 18,* 343–361.

Leu, D. J., DeGroff, L. C., & Simons, H. D. (1986). Predictable texts and interactive-compensatory hypothesis: Evaluating individual differences in reading ability, context use, and comprehension. *Journal of Educational Psychology, 78,* 347–352.

McCormick, S. (1977). Should you read aloud to your children? *Language Arts, 54,* 139–143.

McCracken, R. A., & McCracken, M. J. (1986). *Stories, songs, and poetry to teach reading and writing.* Chicago, IL: American Library Association.

McKeown, M. G., Beck, I. L., Omanson, R. C., & Perfetti, C. A. (1983). The effects of long-term vocabulary instruction on reading comprehension: A replication. *Journal of Reading Behavior, 15,* 3–17.

Nichols, J. N. (1983). Using prediction to increase content area interest and understanding. *Journal of Reading, 27,* 225–228.

Paris, S. G., Lipson, M. Y., & Wixson, K. K. (1983). Becoming a strategic reader. *Contemporary Educational Psychology, 8,* 293–316.

Paris, S. G., Cross, D. R., & Lipson, M. Y. (1984). Informed strategies for learning: A program to improve children's reading awareness and comprehension. *Journal of Educational Psychology, 76,* 1239–1252.

Rhodes, L. K. (1979). Comprehension and predictability: An analysis of beginning reading materials. In J. C. Harste & R. F. Carey (Eds.), *New perspectives on comprehension* (pp. 100–131). Bloomington: Indiana University School of Education.

Rhodes, L. K. (1981). I can read! Predictable books as resources for reading and writing instruction. *The Reading Teacher,* 511–518.

Sampson, M. R., Briggs, L. D., & Sampson, M. B. (1986). Language, children, and text: Match or mismatch? In M. R. Sampson (Ed.), *The pursuit of literacy: Early reading and writing* (pp. 97–101). Dubuque, IA: Kendall/Hunt.

Schmitt, M. C. (1987, December). *The effects of an elaborated directed reading activity on the metacomprehension skills of third graders.* Paper presented at the annual meeting of the National Reading Conference, St. Petersburg, FL.

Schmitt, M. C., & Baumann, J. F. (1986a). How to incorporate comprehension monitoring strategies into basal reader instruction. *The Reading Teacher, 40,* 28–31.

Schmitt, M. C., & Baumann, J. F. (1986b, December). *Metacomprehension in basal reader instruction. Do teachers promote it?* Paper presented at the annual meeting of the National Reading Conference, Austin, TX.

Simons, H. D., & Ammon, P. R. (1987). *The language of beginning reading texts* (Final Report). Urbana, IL: National Council of Teachers of English Research Foundation.

Slaughter, J. P. (1983). Big books for little kids: Another fad or a new approach for teaching beginning reading? *The Reading Teacher, 36,* 758–763.

Smith, F. (1982). *Understanding Reading* (3rd ed.). New York: CBS College Publishing.

Stahl, S. (1983). Differential word knowledge and reading comprehension. *Journal of Reading Behavior, 15,* 33–50.

Tompkins, G. E., & Webeler, M. (1983). What will happen next? Using predictable books with young children. *The Reading Teacher, 36,* 498–502.

Wood, K. D., & Robinson, N. (1983). Vocabulary, language, and prediction: A prereading strategy. *The Reading Teacher, 36,* 392–395.

## PREDICTABLE BOOKS

*Books with a repetitive pattern in which a certain phrase or sentence is repeated throughout the story*

Ahlberg, Janet & Allan. *Peek-a-boo*. Viking Press, 1981.
Allen, Roach Van. *I Love Ladybugs*. DLM Teaching Resources, 1985.
Balina, Lorna. *Mother's Mother's Day*. Abingdon Press, 1982.
Barrett, Judi. *Animals Should Definitely Not Act Like People*. Atheneum, 1980.
Barrett, Judi. *Animals Should Definitely Not Wear Clothes*. Atheneum, 1981.
Barrett, Judi. *A Snake Is Totally Tail*. Atheneum, 1983.
Barton, Byron. *Harry Is a Scaredy-Cat*. Macmillan, 1974.
Berenstain, Stan & Jan. *Old Hat New Hat*. Random House, 1970.
Brooke, Leslie. *Johnny Crow's Garden*. F. Warne & Co., 1941.
Brooke, Leslie. *Johnny Crow's New Garden*. F. Warne & Co., 1938.
Brown, Margaret Wise. *The Friendly Book*. Western Publishing, 1954.
Brown, Margaret Wise. *Goodnight Moon*. Harper & Row, 1947.
Brown, Margaret Wise. *The Important Book*. Harper & Row, 1949.
Brown, Margaret Wise. *Where Have You Been?* Hastings House, 1952.
Brown, Ruth. *A Dark Dark Tale*. Dial Press, 1981.
Caldwell, Mary. *Henry's Busy Day*. Viking Press, 1984.
Carle, Eric. *The Grouchy Ladybug*. Thomas Y. Crowell Co., 1977.
Crews, Donald. *Light*. Greenwillow Books, 1981.
Degen, Bruce. *Jamberry*. Harper & Row, 1983.
Domanska, Janina. *If All the Seas Were One Sea*. Macmillan, 1971.
Eastman, P. D. *Go, Dog, Go!* Random House, 1961.
Galdone, Paul. *The Teeny-Tiny Woman*. Clarion Books, 1984.
Ginsburg, Mirra. *The Chick and the Duckling*. Macmillan, 1972.
Hamsa, Bobbie. *Dirty Larry*. Children's Press, 1983.
Harper, Anita. *How We Work*. Harper & Row, 1977.
Harper, Anita & Roche, Christine. *How We Live*. Harper & Row, 1977.
Hutchins, Pat. *Goodnight Owl*. Macmillan, 1972.
Isadora, Rachel. *I See*. Greenwillow Books, 1985.
Kraus, Robert. *I'm a Monkey*. Windmill Books, 1975.
Krauss, Ruth. *I Write It*. Harper & Row, 1970.
Krauss, Ruth. *A Hole Is to Dig*. Harper & Row, 1952.
Krauss, Ruth. *The Happy Day*. Harper & Row, 1949.
Langstaff, John M. *Oh, A-Hunting We Will Go*. Atheneum , 1977.
Malloy, Judy. *Bad Thad*. E. P. Dutton, 1980.
Martin, Bill. *King of the Mountain*. Holt, Rinehart & Winston, 1970.
Martin, Bill. *Brown Bear, Brown Bear*. Holt, Rinehart & Winston, 1970.
Martin, Bill. *Up and Down the Escalator*. Holt, Rinehart & Winston, 1970.
Martin, Bill. *Silly Goose and the Holidays*. Holt, Rinehart & Winston, 1970.
Martin, Bill. *The Haunted House*. Holt, Rinehart & Winston, 1970.
Mosel, Arlene. *Tikki Tikki Tembo*. Holt, Rinehart & Winston, 1968.

Muntean, Michaela. *I Like School.* Golden Press, 1980.
Paterson, Diane. *If I Were a Toad.* Dial Press, 1977.
Peek, Merle. *Mary Wore Her Red Dress.* Clarion Books, 1985.
Preston, Edna Mitchell. *Where Did My Mother Go?* Four Winds Press, 1978.
Regniers, Beatrice Schenk. *Going for a Walk.* Harper & Row, 1961.
Quackenbush, Robert. *Skip to My Lou.* J. B. Lippincott, 1975.
Rockwell, Anne. *Thump Thump Thump!* E. P. Dutton, 1981.
Scheer, Julian. *Rain Makes Applesauce.* Holiday House, 1964.
Seuss, Dr. *The Foot Book.* Random House, 1968.
Shaw, Charles G. *It Looked Like Spilt Milk.* Harper & Row, 1947.
Simon, Norma. *I Know What I Like.* Whitman, 1971.
Titherington, Jeanne. *Big World, Small World.* Greenwillow Books, 1985.
Udry, Janice May. *A Tree Is Nice.* Harper & Row, 1956.
Watanabe, Shigeo. *I Can Ride It!* Philomel Books, 1981.
Watanabe, Shigeo. *Where's My Daddy?* Philomel Books, 1979.
Williams, Barbara. *Never Hit a Porcupine.* E. P. Dutton & Co., 1977.


*Books with predictable plots in which the events occur in such a way as to enable the reader to predict future events.*

ALIKI. *At Mary Bloom's.* Greenwillow Books, 1976.
Allard, Harry. *I Will Not Go to Market Today.* Dial Press, 1979.
Aylesworth, Jim. *Hush Up!* Holt, Rinehart & Winston, 1980.
Balian, Lorna. *Where in the World is Henry?* Abingdon, 1972.
Barton, Byron. *Buzz, Buzz, Buzz.* Puffin Books, 1979.
Brown, Margaret Wise. *The Runaway Bunny.* Harper & Row, 1972.
Burningham, John. *Mr. Gumpy's Outing.* Scholastic, 1974.
Charlip, Remy. *Fortunately.* Four Winds Press, 1964.
Emberley, Ed. *Klippity Klop.* Little, Brown and Co., 1974.
Fregosi, Claudia. *Are There Spooks in the Dark?* Four Winds Press, 1977.
Galdone, Paul. *The Three Bears.* Scholastic, 1972.
Galdone, Paul. *The Three Billy Goats Gruff.* Scholastic, 1963.
Galdone, Paul. *The Three Little Pigs.* Seabury Press, 1970.
Ginsburg, Mirra. *Where Does the Sun Go at Night?* Greenwillow Books, 1981.
Joslin, Sesyle. *What Do You Do, Dear?* Young Scott Books, 1961.
Klein, Leonore. *Brave Daniel.* Scholastic, 1958.
Lobel, Arnold. *A Treeful of Pigs.* Greenwillow Books, 1979.
Mayer, Mercer. *Just for You.* Golden Press, 1975.
Nodset, Joan. *Who Took the Farmer's Hat?* Scholastic, 1963.
Silverstein, Shel. *Who Wants a Cheap Rhinoceros?* Macmillan, 1983.
Stevenson, James. *Could Be Worse!* Greenwillow Books, 1977.
Tobias, Tobi. *A Day Off.* G. P. Putnam's Sons, 1973.
Zolotow, Charlotte. *Do You Know What I'll Do?* Harper & Row, 1958.

*Books with a repetitive-cumulative pattern in which a word, phrase, or sentence is repeated in each succeeding episode and with each episode adding a new word, phrase, or sentence to the sequence.*

Aardema, Verna. *Bringing the Rain to Kapita Plain.* Dial Press, 1981.
Aardema, Verna. *Why Mosquitos Buzz in People's Ears.* Scholastic, 1975.
Berenstain, Stan & Jan. *The B Book.* Random House, 1971.
Berenstain, Stan & Jan. *C is for Clown.* Random House, 1972.
Berenstain, Stan & Jan. *Inside Outside Upside Down.* Random House, 1968.
Bonne, Rose. *I Know an Old Lady.* Scholastic, 1961.
Brenner, Barbara. *The Snow Parade.* Crown Publishers, 1984.
Dodd, Lynley. *Hairy Maclary from Donaldson's Dairy.* Gareth Stevens, Inc., 1983.
Emberley, Barbara. *Drummer Hoff.* Prentice-Hall, Inc., 1967.
Ets, Marie Hall. *Elephant in a Well.* Viking, 1972.
Galdone, Paul. *Chicken Little.* Seabury Press, 1968.
Galdone, Paul. *The Greedy Old Fat Man.* Clarion Books, 1983.
Galdone, Paul. *The Old Woman and Her Pig.* McGraw-Hill, 1960.
Granowsky, Alvin. *Pat's Date and Plate.* D. C. Heath & Co., 1975.
Guilfoile, Elizabeth. *Nobody Listens to Andrew.* Scholastic, 1957.
Hogrogian, Nonny. *One Fine Day.* Collier Books, 1971.
Hoguet, Susan R. *I Unpacked My Grandmother's Trunk.* E. P. Dutton, 1983.
Kalan, Robert. *Jump, Frog, Jump.* Greenwillow Books, 1981.
Kent, Jack. *The Fat Cat.* Scholastic, 1971.
Kent, Jack. *Jack Kent's Twelve Days of Christmas.* Scholastic, 1973.
Lobel, Arnold. *The Rose in my Garden.* Greenwillow Books, 1984.
Parnall, Peter. *The Mountain.* Doubleday, 1971.
Patrick, Gloria. *A Bug in a Jug and Other Funny Rhymes.* Scholastic, 1970.
Peppe, Rodney. *The House that Jack Built.* Delacorte Press, 1970.
Quackenbush, Robert. *No Mouse for Me.* Franklin Watts Publishers, 1981.
Sadler, Marilyn. *It's Not Easy Being a Bunny.* Random House, 1983.
Seuss, Dr. *Green Eggs and Ham.* Random House, 1960.
Shoemaker, Kathryn. *Children, Go Where I Send Thee.* Winston Press, 1980.
Silverstein, Shel. *A Giraffe and a Half.* Harper & Row, 1964.
Tolstoy, Alexi. *The Great Big Enormous Turnip.* Franklin Watts, 1968.
Wood, Audrey. *The Napping House.* Harcourt Brace Jovanovich, 1984.

*Books with a repetitive refrain in which a certain phrase or sentence is repeated at various points in the story.*

Aardema, Verna. *The Vinganese and the Tree Toad.* Frederick Warne & Co., 1983.
Aardema, Verna. *Who's in Rabbit's House?* Dial Press, 1969.

Bang, Betsy. *The Old Woman and the Rice Thief.* Greenwillow Books, 1978.

Brown, Margaret Wise. *Wait Till the Moon Is Full.* Harper & Row, 1948.

Brown, Margaret Wise. *Home for a Bunny.* Golden Press, 1980.

daPaola, Tomie. *Marianna May and Nursey.* Holiday House, 1983.

Gag, Wanda. *Millions of Cats.* Coward, McCann & Geoghegan, 1977.

Littledale, Freya. *The Magic Fish.* Scholastic, 1967.

Shannon, George. *The Piney Woods Peddler.* Greenwillow Books, 1981.

*Books with patterns based on familiar cultural sequences (cardinal and ordinal numbers, alphabet, months of the year, days of the week, seasons and colors).*

## Numbers:

Anno, Mitsumasa. *Anno's Counting Book.* Thomas Y. Crowell Co., 1975.

Anno, Masaichiro & Mitsumasa. *Anno's Mysterious Multiplying Jar.* Philomel Books, 1983.

Bang, Molly. *Ten, Nine, Eight.* Greenwillow Books, 1983.

Berenstain, Stan & Jan. *Bears on Wheels.* Random House, 1969.

Bruna, Dick. *I Can Count.* Methuen Children's Books, 1968.

Carle, Eric. *1, 2, 3 to the Zoo.* Philomel Books, 1968.

Cleveland, David. *The April Rabbits.* Coward, McCann & Geoghegan.

Duvoisin, Roger. *Two Lonely Ducks.* Alfred A. Knopf, 1955.

Emberley, Barbara. *One Wide River to Cross.* Scholastic, 1966.

Feelings, Muriel. *Moja Means One: Swahili Counting Book.* Dial Press, 1971.

Ginsburg, Mirra. *Kitten from One to Ten.* Crown Publishers, Inc., 1980.

Hoberman, Mary Ann. *The Looking Book.* Alfred A. Knopf, 1973.

Hopkins, Lee Bennett. *Small Circus.* Macmillan, 1975.

Hughes, Shirley. *When We Went to the Park.* Lothrop, Lee & Shepard Books, 1985.

Hutchins, Pat. *1 Hunter.* Greenwillow Books, 1982.

Keats, Ezra Jack. *Over in the Meadow.* Scholastic, 1971.

Kredenser, Gail & Mack, Stanley. *1 One Dancing Drum.* S. G. Phillips, 1971.

LeSieg, Theo. *I Can Write!* Random House, 1971.

Lewin, Betsy. *Cat Count.* Dodd, Mead & Co., 1981.

Martin, Bill. *Ten Little Squirrels.* Holt, Rinehart & Winston, 1970.

McLeod, Emilie Warren. *One Snail and Me.* Little, Brown & Co., 1961.

Nedobeck, Don. *Nedobeck's Numbers Book.* Ideals Publishing Co., 1981.

Peek, Merle. *Roll Over! A Counting Song.* Clarion Books, 1981.

Scarry, Richard. *Best Counting Book Ever.* Random House, 1975.

Schertle, Alice. *Goodnight, Hattie, My Dearie, My Dove.* Lothrop, Lee & Shepard Books, 1985.

Smollin, Michael J. *I Can Count to 100 . . . Can You?* Random House, 1979.

## Alphabet:

Anno, Mitsumasa. *Anno's Alphabet.* Thomas Y. Crowell Co., 1974.

Arnosky, Jim. *Mouse Writing.* Harcourt Brace Jovanovich, 1983.

Attwell, Lucie. *Lucie Attwell's ABC 123 Pop-up Book.* Deans International Publishers, 1984.

Balian, Lorna. *Humbug Potion an A B Cipher.*

Baskin, Leonard. *Hosie's Alphabet.* Viking Press, 1972.

Bridwell, Norman. *Clifford's ABC.* Scholastic, 1983.

Brown, Marcia. *All Butterflies—an ABC.* Charles Scribner's Sons, 1974.

Carle, Eric. *All About Arthur (An Absolutely Absurd Ape).* Franklin Watt.

Duke, Kate. *The Guinea Pig ABC.* E. P. Dutton, 1983.

Duvoisin, Roger. *A for the Ark.* Lothrop, Lee & Shepard Co., 1952.

Eastman, P. D. *The Alphabet Book.* Random House, 1974.

Eichenberg, Fritz. *Ape in a Cape—An Alphabet of Odd Animals.* Harcourt Brace & World, 1952.

Elting, Mary & Folsom, Michael. *Q is for Duck.* Clarion Books, 1980.

Emberley, Ed. *Ed Emberley's ABC.* Little, Brown & Co., 1978.

Gretz, Susanna. *Teddy Bears ABC.* Follett, 1977.

Hoban, Tana. *A.B. See!* Greenwillow Books, 1982.

Isadora, Rachel. *City Seen from A to Z.* Greenwillow Books, 1983.

Kitchen, Bert. *Animal Alphabet.* Dial Books.

Miller, Elizabeth & Cohen, Jane. *Cat and Dog and the ABC's.* Watts Publishing Co., 1981.

Munari, Bruno. *Bruno Munari's ABC.* Collins/World Publishing Company, Inc., 1960.

Ruben, Patricia. *Apples to Zippers.* Doubleday, 1976.

Schmiderer, Dorothy. *The Alphabeast Book.* Holt, Rinehart & Winston, 1971.

Sendak, Maurice. *Alligators All Around.* Harper & Row, 1962.

Seuss, Dr. *ABC.* Random House, 1963.

Stevenson, James. *Grandpa's Great City Tour.* Greenwillow Books, 1983.

Tallon, Robert. *Rotten Kidphabets.* Holt, Rinehart & Winston, 1975.

Warren, Cathy. *Victoria's ABC Adventure.* Lothrop, Lee & Shepard, 1984.

Wildsmith, Brian. *Brian Wildsmith's ABC.* Franklin Watts, 1962.

Yolen, Jane. *All in the Woodland Early.* Collins, 1979.

## Colors:

Miller, J. P. & Howard, Katherine. *Do You Know Colors?* Random House, 1978.

O'Neill, Mary. *Hailstones and Halibut Bones.* Doubleday & Co., 1961.
Rossetti, Christina G. *What Is Pink?* Macmillan, 1971.

**Days:**

Carle, Eric. *The Very Hungry Caterpillar.* Philomel Books, 1983.
Clifton, Lucille. *Some of the Days of Everett Anderson.* Holt, Rinehart &
     Winston, 1970.
Domanska, Janina. *Busy Monday Morning.* Greenwillow Books, 1985.
Elliott, Alan C. *On Sunday the Wind Came.* William Morrow & Co., 1980.
Hooper, Meredith. *Seven Eggs.* Harper & Row, 1985.
Quackenbush, Robert. *Too Many Lollipops.* Scholastic, 1975.
Sharmat, Mitchell. *The Seven Sloppy Days of Phineas Pig.* Harcourt Brace
     Jovanovich, 1983.
Yollen, Jane. *No Bath Tonight.* Thomas Y. Crowell, 1978.

**Months and Seasons:**

Clifton, Lucille. *Everett Anderson's Year.* Holt, Rinehart & Winston, 1974.
Lionni, Leo. *Mouse Days.* Pantheon Books, 1981.
Sendak, Maurice. *Chicken Soup with Rice.* Scholastic, 1962.
Wolff, Ashley. *A Year of Birds.* Dodd, Mead & Co., 1984.
Zolotow, Charlotte. *Summer Is . . .* Abelard-Schuman, 1967.

*Books with rhyming patterns, many of which have rhyme combined
with repetition and cumulative-repetition.*

ALIKI. *Hush Little Baby.* Prentice-Hall.
Battaglia, Aurelius. *Old Mother Hubbard.* Golden Press, 1972.
Cameron, Polly. *"I Can't" Said the Ant.* Scholastic, 1961.
Cole, William. *The Square Bear and Other Riddle Rhymers.*
Cranstoun, Margaret. *1, 2, Buckle My Shoe.* Holt, Rinehart & Winston, 1967.
Einsel, Walter. *Did You Ever See?* Scholastic, 1962.
Hawkins, Colin & Jacqui. *Pat the Cat.* G. P. Putnam's Sons, 1983.
Kessler, Leonard. *Hey Diddle Diddle.* Garrard Publishing, 1980.
Krauss, Ruth. *Bears.* Harper & Row, 1948.
Petersham, Maud & Miska. *The Rooster Crows: A Book of American Rhymes
     and Jingles.* Macmillan, 1971.
Schermer, Judith. *Mouse in a House.* Houghton Mifflin, 1979.
Sendak, Maurice. *Pierre.* Harper & Row, 1962.
Seuss, Dr. *I Can Read with My Eyes Shut!* Random House, 1978.
Seuss, Dr. *The Cat in the Hat.* Random House, 1957.
Spier, Peter. *London Bridge Is Falling Down.* Doubleday & Co., 1967.

Stadler, John. *Cat at Bat.* E. P. Dutton, 1979.
Withers, Carl. *Favorite Rhymes from A Rocket in My Pocket.* Scholastic, 1967.
Zolotow, Charlotte. *Some Things Go Together.* Thomas Y. Crowell, 1969.
Zuromskis, Diane. *The Farmer in the Dell.* Little, Brown & Co., 1978.

*Books with a wordplay pattern in which pictures illustrate characteristics of words.*

Gwynne, Fred. *The King Who Rained.* Windmill Books, 1970.
Hanson, Joan. *Antonyms.* Lerner Publishing Co., 1972.
Hanson, Joan. *Homographic Homophones.* Lerner Publishing Co., 1973.

Chapter 7

# *Creating a Bridge to Children's Literature*

LESLEY MANDEL MORROW

In the classroom pressure of schedules and testing, it is sometimes easy to lose sight of the fact that the main goal of reading instruction is to enable and encourage students to *read*, not just to learn *how* to read. This chapter identifies the roles literature plays in helping students not only to develop and practice reading skills but to become individuals who *choose* to read. It explains why those roles are important and how they can be integrated into classroom reading instruction. It describes, among other components and procedures, how the classroom teacher can design and manage a library corner; teacher-directed activities that extend, elaborate, or supplement basal reading instruction; and practices that have been proven to increase students' skills and willingness as readers. Such techniques as reading stories aloud, retelling, and roleplaying not only are compatible with basal reading programs but also work as learning devices, because they involve children and adults together in the activity and enjoyment of reading.

## BACKGROUND

Literature opens worlds of imagination and information, and it makes reading a pleasurable experience. It also enables youngsters to practice and develop fundamental reading skills. It has long been known that youngsters who are exposed early in their lives to literature and activities related to literature develop more sophisticated language structures, including vocabulary and syntax, than youngsters who are not exposed to literature. They accumulate background knowledge not only about the content at hand but also about how language works and how written language differs from spoken. They demonstrate increased interest in learning to read, and develop a better sense of story structure (see Bower, 1976; Chomsky, 1972; Cohen, 1968; Durkin, 1966).

Youngsters who choose to read are successful readers. Studies of children identified as voluntary readers in elementary and middle grades found them achieving high reading scores on standardized tests (Greaney, 1980; Whitehead, Capey, & Maddren, 1975). I found that kindergartners who demonstrated voluntary interest in books not only scored significantly higher on standardized reading readiness tests than children with low interest in literature, but were also rated higher by teachers on work habits, general school performance, and social and emotional development (Morrow, 1983).

More recent data suggest a strong relationship between the amount of silent reading a student does, both in and out of school, and that student's reading achievement. The average number of minutes per day spent reading books has been found to relate positively to readers' comprehension, vocabulary development, and gains in reading achievement. Significant gains in comprehension and vocabulary were also made by children participating in a program that utilized free reading of literature, when they were compared with a control group that did not participate (Anderson, Wilson, & Fielding, 1985).

Unfortunately, substantial numbers of children choose not to read for either pleasure or information. Of the fifth-grade students he surveyed, Greaney (1980) found that 22 percent chose not to read at all; those who did read spent only 5 percent of their free time doing so. A Gallup survey reported by Spiegel (1981) indicated that 80 percent of the books read in the United States were read by only 10 percent of the population. Half the adults sampled claimed never to have read a book from cover to cover. The Book Industry Study Group (1984) reported that the number of Americans under twenty-one who could be identified as readers had dropped 12 percent in the interim since a similar 1976 study.

It is equally unfortunate that, in spite of data that support the value of literature and encourage opportunities for independent reading, teachers tend not to utilize classroom strategies appropriate to that data. They tend neither to assign literature-related experience a high priority in their classrooms nor to see it as an integral component of instructional programs (Morrow, 1982, 1983, 1986). Use of literature and systematic development of voluntary reading remain quite limited in early childhood and elementary classrooms.

One explanation often cited for this unfortunate situation is that teachers rely almost exclusively on basal reading programs as instructional materials because they and their students are often evaluated on the array of psychological and linguistic skills and subskills represented in many of those materials and the teacher's guides that accompany them. Classroom library corners are either poorly designed or nonexistent. Time is seldom allotted for youngsters to read on their own. Little use is made of storytelling, role-playing stories, or anecdotal records of books read independently by children. Rather than encouraging youngsters' immersion into the reading experience, "learning to read" is seen almost exclusively as teacher-dominated direct instruction of skills on which students will be drilled and tested. The experience and enjoyment of literature-related activities are more often than not considered supplementary or fringe benefits, rather than central to the development of lifelong voluntary reading. Ironically, schools spend a great deal of time teaching literacy skills, then leave little room for children to practice those skills.

Some popular basal series do include the suggestion, often in teacher's manuals, that lessons from the basal be integrated with literature, writing, attitude development, and creativity (Morrow, 1987a). Some recommend that independent reading be incorporated into a program as a means of developing and reinforcing comprehension and meaning. Others point out that reading skills need to be enriched, reinforced, and applied in activities in language, literature, and creativity. Certain selections in the basals themselves represent high-quality fiction and nonfiction, including poetry.

Few goals are so prevalent, traditional, and basic in American schools as teaching people to read, and none is more important. It is remarkable that so little programmatic attention is paid, especially in the early years of schooling, to developing youngsters who will choose, on their own, to read widely and often. A recent report by Daniel J. Boorstin (1984) during his tenure as Librarian of Congress suggests that aliteracy choosing not to read—rivals illiteracy as a threat to our democratic tradition, a tradition, he points out, that has been built on books and reading.

There is an obvious need to help teachers build instructional bridges between basal reading programs and the classroom exploration of literature.

## RATIONALE

Basal readers have played a major role in reading instruction in American classrooms for at least 125 years (Farr & Roser, 1979). Yarington (1978) reported about ten years ago that basal readers were the main source of reading instruction in at least 95 percent of our elementary schools. In spite of the negative criticism they often receive, basals dominate reading instruction and probably will continue to do so. One reason for their widespread use is that they provide teachers with complete packages of materials and directions for instruction. Newer editions have also attempted to meet criticism by reflecting social change, current research, and newer theoretical frameworks for instruction (Farr & Roser, 1979).

While basals play a dominant role in reading instruction, overreliance on the extensive guidelines for their use sometimes inhibits both the techniques and scope of a teacher's instruction. Furthermore, basal materials are not normally associated in a student's mind with reading as pleasure. Those few literary examples incorporated in certain basal lessons cannot begin to represent the variety, depth, and fullness available in literature as a whole. In an analysis of 2,733 selections from six different sets of current basal readers, I found that only five of fourteen potential literary activities were ever recommended, and those five appeared only infrequently, in the supplementary sections of teacher's manuals where they will probably go unread and thus untried (Morrow, 1987a). Because they have so many other goals to accomplish, basals are at best a jumping-off point for literary exploration. Of equal importance to the use of basals in reading instruction is a strong planned program of literature and related activities.

Much has been written in favor of using literature in the classroom. Bloom (1964) wrote that a child's lifetime reading habits develop early; that is, by sixth grade one has already become the kind of reader one is going to become. Arbuthnot and Sutherland, 1977; Cullinan, 1977; Huck, 1976; Smith and Parker, 1977; and Stewig and Sebesta, 1978 all have stressed the importance of programs planned to give youngsters pleasurable experiences with literature. They and others recommend that teachers read to children daily and lead discussions of stories they read. Children should be encouraged to read and tell stories to each other, either in small groups or to the whole class. Books should be easily accessible to children, borrowed for home use, shared frequently, and integrated with content-area teaching. Where such programs and practices are lacking, children are not being offered complete instruction in learning to read (Hall, 1971; Lamme, 1976; Morrow, 1982; Spiegel, 1981).

Because they accumulate information, develop positive attitudes toward reading, and associate reading with pleasure, youngsters to whom stories have been frequently read are more interested in learning to read, begin to read earlier, and learn to read with greater ease than youngsters who have not had such experiences (Clark, 1984; Durkin, 1966; Hiebert, 1981; Shickendanz, 1978; Teale, 1984). Mason (1983) found that being read to contributes to a child's metacognition in three areas of early reading that she feels are most important, namely, the function, form, and conventions of print. Reading aloud to children helps them learn how to approach reading tasks and interact with teachers.

Active participation in literary experiences through role playing, retelling, or reconstruction of stories with pictures aids a child's comprehension, integration of information, and sense of story structure (Brown, 1975; Morrow, 1985; Pellegrini & Galda, 1982). The interaction among questions, comments, and responses in reading aloud between parent and child or teacher and child helps establish purpose, encourage interpretation, add to background experience, and reconstruct the meaning behind words (Altwerger, Diehl-Faxon, & Dockstader-Anderson, 1985). Literary activities have been found to help children develop oral language as well as comprehension and a sense of story structure (Blank & Sheldon, 1971; Morrow, 1985). In addition to building skills, active involvement in literature creates voluntary readers (Morrow & Weinstein, 1982, 1986).

There are theoretical frameworks for bridging literature and basal readers. The basic rationale behind much basal instruction is that literacy builds from competencies in certain cognitive operations with letters, words, sentences, and texts—competencies that can subsequently be applied in a variety of situations. By contrast, Teale (1982) argues for "natural literacy development," that is, learning to read without formal instruction. He writes,

> The typical literacy curriculum with its progression from part to whole and its hierarchy of skills does not reflect the way children learn to read. A critical mistake here is that the motives, goals, and conditions have been abstracted away from the activity in the belief that this enables the students to "get down to" working on the essential processes of reading and writing. But these features are critical aspects of the reading and writing themselves. By organizing instruction which omits them, the teacher ignores how literacy is

practiced (and therefore learned) and thereby creates a situation in which the teaching is an inappropriate model for the learning. [p. 567]

In Teale's view, literacy results from children's involvement in reading activities that are mediated by "literate others." It is the interaction accompanying these activities that makes them so significant to the child's development. Not only do interactive literacy events teach children the societal functions and conventions of literature, they also link reading and writing with enjoyment and satisfaction and thus increase children's desire to engage in literacy activities.

Teale's (1982) theory of literacy development is consistent with Holdaway's (1979). According to Holdaway,

> The way in which supportive adults are induced by affection and common sense to intervene in the development of their children proves upon close examination to embody the most sound principles of teaching. Rather than provide verbal instructions about how a skill should be carried out, the parent sets up an emulative model of the skill in operation and induces activity in the child which approximates toward the use of the skills. The first attempts of the child are to do something that is like the skill he wishes to emulate. This activity is then "shaped" or refined by immediate rewards. . . . From this point of view, so-called "natural" learning is in fact supported by higher quality teaching intervention than is normally the case in the school setting. [p. 22]

Holdaway (1979) contends that this form of "developmental teaching" is appropriate for school-based literacy instruction. He proposes less teaching and more learning, learning that is self-regulated rather than adult regulated. In such a setting, the teacher provides an environment rich with materials and activities from which children are invited to select, and a social context where children are actively involved with other children, with the teacher, and with materials. The environment he recommends is emulative rather than instructional, providing lively examples of reading skills in action and use. Teachers present themselves as models involved in literary activities. They also serve as sources of support and positive reinforcement for appropriate behavior patterns in the child.

The literature program described in the following section is a bridge from basal reading instruction, which incorporates Holdaway's (1979) and Teale's (1982) notions of a developmental approach to literacy. Through regularly scheduled literary activities and ready access to attractive and comfortable classroom library corners stocked with books and materials that inspire interest and active participation, children in the program will associate instruction with pleasure and develop an appreciation for books. Given time to use the library corner and participate in recreational reading activities in a social setting, children will reinforce reading skills through enjoyable, self-selected practice. They will become children who not only are capable of reading but choose to read voluntarily.

## COMPONENTS OF A LITERATURE PROGRAM

Given the value of literature, both as an instructional medium and a motivational tool, the remedy for its current lack of use in early classroom reading instruction is to develop and use appropriate instructional activities, adjust or reallocate resources, redirect preparation of teachers, and foster attitudes of mutual support among all concerned—especially teachers, administrators, and parents (Morrow, 1986). In doing so, it is important to keep in mind four basic principles evident from research on children's choosing to read and the use of literature in early childhood and elementary classrooms. Those principles include (1) providing for easy access to a wide variety of attractive choices in literature, (2) providing for interaction between children and adults during experiences with literature, (3) encouraging active involvement of individual youngsters in those activities, and (4) cultivating the responsiveness of a child that typically results from practices implied in the first three principles.

In order to provide a program of reading instruction with a strong literature component, teachers using basal reading programs can motivate and integrate the use of children's literature in the classroom in several ways. First, they can follow suggestions already made or implied in basal readers and in at least some of the teacher's manuals that accompany them. Second, they can encourage recreational reading of children's literature as seatwork during the basal reading period. Finally, they can capitalize on selections of children's literature found in the basals themselves by acquiring and making available to children additional books by the same authors, on the same topics, or in the same styles or genres.

The cornerstones of a program for building a strong complementary program in literature to extend the basal's scope and reinforce its basic purpose of enabling youngsters to read are classroom library corners; literature-related, teacher-directed activities; and recreational reading.

## Classroom Library Corners

Immediate access to books increases the amount of independent reading by children, both at home and at school. It is clear that children in classrooms that include library corners and children from homes where books are available in many different rooms in the house read more than children who do not experience such environments (Beckman, 1972; Bissett, 1969; Morrow, 1983; Morrow & Weinstein, 1986; Powell, 1966). Stauffer (1970) suggests that classroom libraries become the focal area in a classroom because they represent a principal source of knowledge. Beckman (1972) concurred, pointing out that, although it is very important to maintain a central library in a school, classroom mini-libraries are essential for providing immediate access to materials. Such recommendations were foreshadowed by Bissett (1969), who determined that children in classrooms that contained literature collections read 50 percent more books than those in classrooms without such resources.

Classroom access alone is not enough, however. The way the library corner is set up must be considered carefully. Through empirical study, I have identified positive relationships between the frequency of literature use and certain physical design characteristics of library corners (Morrow, 1982). An excellent design is shown in Figure 7.1. The following lists describe the attributes and resources of a good classroom library corner, many of which can be seen in the figure.

*Physical Characteristics.* It is of great importance that a library corner

- Be visually and physically accessible
- Be able to hold at least six children
- Provide comfortable seating, such as a rocking chair, pillows, and a throw rug
- Be partitioned off on two or three sides for privacy
- Include an open-faced bookshelf to feature new or special books

**Figure 7.1** Design for a Library Corner

*Source* Morrow, L. M. (1988). *Literacy development in the early years: Helping young children read and write.* Englewood Cliffs, NJ: Prentice-Hall. Il ustrator, Pamela Cromey. Used with permission.

*Contents.* A library corner should

• Hold varied types and levels of children's literature, including picture books, picture story books, fiction, nonfiction, biography, poetry, number books, fairy tales, nursery rhymes, folktales, riddle books, series books, craft books, books related to television programs, magazines, newspapers, and student-generated materials
   • Include literature-related bulletin boards and posters
   • Include story props such as a felt board, roll movies, and taped stories on cassettes, with tape players and headsets for listening

*Organization and Circulation.*

• A library corner should contain categorized books for easy selection by author, type, topic, and so forth. This can be accomplished by coding categorized books with different colored stickers.
   • Teachers should provide clear, simple procedures for checking books in and out of the library corner. For example, one might label two file boxes, one with the title "Out" and one titled "In." When children elect to take a book home, they fill out an index card with the title of the book, the date, and their name. The card is placed in the "Out" box. When the book is returned, the child indicates the date of return on the index card and moves it to the "In" box. A clipboard with a sign-out sheet is another easily used system.
   • When materials have been in circulation for some time, they should be changed, so as to introduce new or different books regularly (Morrow & Weinstein, 1982, 1986).

Letting children help plan, design, and manage the corner ensures its appreciation and use. Instead of putting the corner into place prior to the beginning of school, discuss its creation with the children soon after the school year begins. Let them make the decision as to its placement in the room, allow them to organize materials on shelves, give them the responsibility for keeping it neat, and allow them to choose a name for the area. Hooks and index cards, one set for each student, allow youngsters to keep visible track, through their recording of dates and titles, of books they have read.

The classroom library corner becomes both the repository and source of materials and a center of student activity. With its collection of print literature as well as its stock of felt-board materials, roll movies, and other physical or audiovisual devices, children can be encouraged to share stories within its borders, to write their own stories, bind their own books, and make their own felt-board stories. Books from home can be displayed there, as well as books featured in teacher-directed activities.

Lists of books recommended for children and appropriate for classroom library inventories are available from associations listed under "Teacher Resources" at the end of the chapter.

### Teacher-Directed Activities

A study of the summer recreational reading program in urban day-care centers (Morrow, 1987b) indicates that no other factor is more influential in helping students choose a book from among other books than a teacher's reading books to the children. The critical role that teachers play in shaping children's attitudes toward reading is inestimable. If, through a teacher's presentations, children learn to associate reading only with repetitive skill drills and testing, they will probably not be encouraged to reach for books on their own. On the other hand, if the teacher becomes a role model who obviously enjoys reading and sharing books, children are likely to emulate that adult behavior. My research (Morrow, 1982; Morrow & Weinstein, 1982, 1986) indicates that, of various specific teacher activities during recreational reading periods in nursery through third grade, reading to children daily was of utmost importance.

When reading aloud, provide varied formats, styles, and techniques. The following are some good examples:

1. Tell stories either by themselves or with such props as roll movies, felt boards, puppets, filmstrips, and tapes. Reading stories from the text is, of course, of equal value. The physical presence of a book during its telling and its announced availability to students through the classroom library encourage students to pick it up on their own.

2. To heighten interest, have discussions that focus on interpretive and critical issues within stories.

3. Have discussion about authors and illustrators, comparing their techniques, styles, and purposes.

There are additional activities that promote interest in books. For example, literature may be used in content areas and activities. When studying the life cycle of a caterpillar, some teachers find Eric Carle's *The Very Hungry Caterpillar* (1970) not only useful but entertaining and illustrative to students. *Blueberries for Sal*, by Robert McClosky (1948) lends itself well to the topic of food preparation, which involves the use of math and science concepts. You can follow the reading of this story by baking and eating blueberry muffins in class.

Another idea is to encourage children to read, during instructional time, stories they have written themselves or brought from home.

The same sorts of outlines that are used for asking comprehension questions and leading discussions of basal selections can be used for other literature. The traditional format may be used, but also be sure to include those emphasizing story structure as well. Here is an example of a traditional outline:

- Literal level
     - Facts and detail
     - Cause-and-effect relationships
     - Classification
- Inferential comprehension
     - Interpreting characters' feelings
     - Relating to children's experiences
- Critical level—problem solving

An outline emphasizing story structure might look like this:

- Setting
     - Time and place
     - Characters in the story
- Theme—goal or problem facing main character
- Plot episodes—sequence of events that leads the main character to solving a problem or reaching a goal
- Resolution—how main character reaches goal or solution; story ending

The questions posed will depend on the area selected. An "inferential" question, for example, dealing with the interpretation of characters' feelings, would be, How would you have felt if you were Cinderella, when the clock was striking twelve, the night of the ball? Explain your answer. A structural question dealing with "theme" and concerning the story *The Little Red Hen* might be, What did the little red hen want to do at the beginning of the story; what was her goal? Note that not all types of questions should be asked about a story after just one reading. Over the course of several readings of many stories, try to include as many types of questions as possible, to help children develop competence with different ways of eliciting meaning from narratives.

Read literature selections from the basal aloud to children occasionally, during reading group instruction. Reading to small groups of children encourages responses that reflect literal, interpretive, and critical comprehension skills.

Have additional books by a popular author available for children when one of her or his stories is featured in a basal selection. If a basal lesson features selections by more than one author, students can be led to compare the selections for writing style, illustrations, and plots.

When a basal selection features a biography, suggest that students read other biographies found in the library corner. Nonfiction selections that deal with real-life issues can lead to further exploration of literature dealing with realistic topics such as divorce, death, loneliness, aging, and fear. Poetry, often neglected, appears occasionally in many basals, offering the teacher an opportunity to guide children to volumes of poetry, or to make classroom or individual collections of poetry, some of it original. Similar techniques and ideas hold for all other types of basal selection—myths, dialogues or plays, folktales, and fables. The teacher must, however, collect the type of featured literature for the classroom library, so the material is readily accessible for the children.

Provide for adult/child interactions during story reading by reading to small groups of children. This format provides for personal interaction and has been found to promote responses to literature that are vitally important to literacy development. Whenever aides are available, and when individual students can read to each other, these strategies should be put to use. Use some of the time during reading groups for this type of story reading. The interactive process of one-to-one readings gains in effectiveness through questions posed by either adult or child, through scaffolding (demonstrating the kind of responses expected of the child), and praise. Offering information, directing discussion, sharing personal reactions, and relating concepts in a story to personal experiences have all been shown to be beneficial to a child's becoming a better, more habitual reader (Cochran-Smith, 1984; Flood, 1977; Morrow, 1988; Ninio, 1980; Teale, 1981). Children's questions and comments during a story-reading activity are critical aspects of the interactive process. They reflect what Torrey (1969) suggests: that literacy must be learned, not just taught. Children's questions provide them with a direct channel for obtaining information (Yaden, 1985).

Utilize literature for skill development. A basal lesson in a specific skill such as initial consonants, digraphs, vowels, or a specific level of comprehension lends itself to development of that skill within an example taken from literature outside the basal. If rhyming or word families are the topic of a basal lesson, verse abounds in children's literature. Stories in verse, such as *Madeline* (Bemelmans, 1978), can be used for reinforcement as well as enjoyment. Lessons aimed at developing critical levels of comprehension can lead to the introduction of literature that deals with critical issues and stimulates critical thought, such as *William's Doll* (Zolotow, 1972). Lessons in story structure can be complemented with well-plotted stories from the classroom library corner (Morrow, in press).

All these techniques depend upon you as the teacher to put them to use and make them work to the benefit of your students.

### Recreational Reading

A total literature program requires time for recreational reading. Even though an effective recreational reading program denotes a degree of independent choice and activity by youngsters, establishing and maintaining the program depends on the leadership of the classroom teacher. I suggest the following nine procedures for teachers (Morrow, 1985; used with permission):

1.   Introduce the recreational reading period by explaining the use of a small number of activities available to the children in the library corner. Gradually add items to the corner as children become used to working independently. The first day that the children use the library corner, introduce them to the book check-out system, the method for recording books read, the open-faced bookshelves, the color-coding system for book selection, and the feltboard stories. On another day introduce a roll movie, taped stories with tape players and headsets, and materials for making their own books. The introduction of a few materials at a time on subsequent days will avoid confusion.

2.   Stress with students that during recreational reading the classroom should be relatively quiet, with minimal movement.

3.   Orally introduce new books and other materials as they are added to the classroom library corner.

4.   Explain how to care for books and other materials, and show where they are located in the classroom library corner so that everyone knows where to find them and where to return them.

5.   Provide a checklist of library corner activities so children can indicate their choices of things to do for a given recreational reading

period. When children have selected their activities in advance they know where to go and what to do.

6.   Encourage children to stay with their choices for each entire recreational reading session.

7.   Allow children to work alone or with other children, and either in the library corner, at their own desks, or at other locations in the classroom.

8.   Because the library corner will not accommodate all the children at a time, post a schedule naming the youngsters allowed to work in the library corner on each given day.

9.   Restate often the objectives of the recreational reading period: to read, to enjoy reading, and to practice skills learned in reading groups.

There are a number of ways to tie a recreational reading period to traditional basal instruction. A teacher should often substitute such a period for the seatwork typical in the basal program, or use one of the suggestions from the basal manual itself for extension of a basal lesson into activities involving literature. While such suggestions are typically found in supplementary sections of the teacher's manual rather than main texts, they are there to be applied. Basals often suggest books for further reading. Recreational reading periods offer excellent opportunities for making those books available to youngsters and calling their attention to them.

The importance of social interaction and active, personal involvement during experiences with literature indicates the value of letting children work in pairs, threes, or fours, if they choose, during recreational reading periods. Materials for writing, binding, and illustrating books can be put to use. Other possibilities include the writing of student diaries and logs, keeping individual records, and checking books in or out. Children can lead discussions of books with other children, or simply share comments on books, authors, or illustrators they have liked. They can engage in storytelling or help each other with basal selections or exercises.

A less common but very rewarding activity can be the creation and maintenance of a classroom bookstore—staffed by a teacher, adult volunteer, administrator, or mature students—in which books can be bought, sold, or traded.

It is often the experience of teachers who develop and regularly schedule recreational reading periods that, once children are accustomed to their rules, responsibilities, and opportunities, they become self-managed and self-perpetuating so that teachers themselves can find time for quiet personal reading during the time allotted. This is recommended, as by so doing the teacher provides a model for children to emulate.

## GENERAL SUGGESTIONS AND SUMMARY OF ACTIVITIES

The following list reviews and provides additional general and specific suggestions for creating a bridge from basal reading instruction to literature.

- Encourage adoption of basal series that include strong and frequent literary selections and suggested activities.
- Be aware of and use literary activities, sources, and selections already suggested in the basal materials, especially in supplements to the teacher's manual.
- Gather materials representative of literary selections within the basal, such as stories by the same authors or illustrators, on the same topics, or of the same types. Promote those materials and make them available to students.
- Inform parents about how literature is being used in reading instruction, to heighten their interest and appreciation.
- Organize and promote such schoolwide or full-day activities as book fairs, author or illustrator visits, and book days when youngsters dress up as book characters and spend the day reading, telling, or role playing stories.
- Read literature selections from basals and other books to children regularly, and lead discussions about stories both before and after you read them.
- Plan, establish, and maintain a classroom library corner.
- Provide recreational reading periods as regular components of the instructional program in reading. Schedule them at the time when children usually do seatwork during reading groups.
- Encourage children to borrow books from the classroom library corner and to keep records of the books they read.
- Plan learning activities that make use of art, music, and content topics in relation to various pieces of relevant literature. Whenever the basal has a selection that lends itself to this, take advantage of the situation.

• Encourage children to read books and basal selections to each other, write books for the classroom library corner, tell stories, visit school and public libraries often, and discuss authors and illustrators.

• Ask the school principal, custodian, nurse, secretary, or a parent to serve as a visiting storyteller or reader for your class.

• Encourage children to write to their favorite authors or illustrators of basals and other literature selections.

• Organize and direct a book fair, book swap shop, author's or illustrator's visit, or book celebration day.

• Take class field trips to community libraries, binderies, publishing houses, or print shops.

• Establish cooperative efforts between home and school that will lead to a systematic, integrated program for developing recreational readers. Ideas include (1) distributing a newsletter to parents and other members of the community about literature-related activities in the school; (2) involving parents in classroom activities and money-raising drives for purchase of books for the library corner; (3) holding a workshop for parents in which you explain the roles of literature in life and in learning to read, and describe an ideal home recreational reading program.

## SUMMARY

The use of literature is crucial to reading instruction, both for its motivational and pedagogical values and uses, and because it represents the purposes for learning to read in the first place. Students must not only learn how to read but choose to read. Basals can serve as a catalyst for classroom use of literature. Creating a bridge from basal readers to literature in a program of reading instruction helps meet that dual purpose. It involves the establishment, management, and regularly scheduled use of classroom library corners, teacher-directed activities, and recreational reading periods.

## REFERENCES

Altwerger, A., Diehl-Faxon, J., & Dockstader-Anderson, K. (1985). Read-aloud events as meaning construction. *Language Arts, 62*, 476–484.

Anderson, R. C., Wilson, P. T., & Fielding, L. G. (1985, December). *A new focus on free reading.* Paper presented at the annual meeting of the National Reading Conference, San Diego, CA.

Arbuthnot, M. H., & Sutherland, Z. (1977). *Children and books* (5th ed.). Glenview, IL: Scott, Foresman.

Beckman, D. (1972). Interior space: The things of education. *National Elementary Principal, 52,* 45–49.

Bemelmans, L. (1978). *Madeline.* New York: Penguin Books.

Bissett, D. (1969). *The amount and effect of recreational reading in selected fifth grade classes.* Unpublished doctoral dissertation, Syracuse University, Syracuse NY.

Blank, M., & Sheldon, F. (1971). Story recall in kindergarten children: Effect of method of presentation on psycholinguistic performance. *Childhood Development, 42,* 299–312.

Bloom, L. (1964). *Stability and change in human characteristics.* New York: John Wiley.

Book Industry Study Group. (1984). *The 1983 consumer research study on reading and book purchasing.* New York: Author.

Boorstin, D. (1984). Letter of transmittal. In *Books in our future: A report from the Librarian of Congress to the Congress* (p. iv). Washington, DC: U.S. Congress, Joint Committee on the Library.

Bower, G. (1976). Experiments on story understanding and recall. *Quarterly Journal of Experimental Psychology, 28,* 511–534.

Brown, A. (1975). Recognition, reconstruction, and recall of narrative sequences of pre-operational children. *Child Development, 46,* 155–156.

Carle, E. (1970). *The very hungry caterpillar.* New York: Putnam.

Chomsky, C. (1972). Stages in language development and reading. *Harvard Educational Review, 42,* 1–33.

Clark, M. M. (1984). *Young fluent readers.* London: Heinemann Educational Books.

Cochran-Smith, M. (1984). *The making of a reader.* Norwood, NJ: Ablex.

Cohen, D. (1968). The effect of literature on vocabulary and reading achievement. *Elementary English, 45,* 209–213, 217.

Cullinan, E. (1977). Books in the life of the young child. In B. Cullinan & C. Carmichael (Eds.), *Literature and young children* (pp. 1–17). Urbana, IL: National Council of Teachers of English.

Durkin, D. (1966). *Children who read early: Two longitudinal studies.* New York: Teachers College Press.

Farr, R., & Roser, N. (1979). *Teaching a child to read.* New York: Harcourt Brace Jovanovich.

Flood, J. (1977). Parental styles in reading episodes with young children. *The Reading Teacher, 30,* 864–867.

Greaney, V. (1980). Factors related to amount and type of leisure reading. *Reading Research Quarterly, 15,* 337–357.

Hall, M. (1971). Literature experiences provided by cooperating teachers. *The Reading Teacher, 24,* 425–431.

Hiebert, E. H. (1981). Developmental patterns and interrelationships of preschool children's print awareness. *Reading Research Quarterly, 16,* 236–260.

Holdaway, D. (1979). *The foundations of literacy.* New York: Ashton Scholastic.

Huck, S. (1976). *Children's literature in the elementary school* (3rd ed.). New York: Holt, Rinehart & Winston.

Lamme, L. (1976). Are reading habits and abilities related? *The Reading Teacher, 30,* 21–27.

Mason, J. M. (1983, March). *Acquisition of knowledge about reading in the preschool period: An update and extension.* Paper presented at the annual convention of the Society for Research in Child Development, Detroit, MI.

McCloskey, R. (1948). *Blueberries for Sal.* New York: Viking Press.

Morrow, L. M. (1982). Relationships between literature programs, library corner designs, and children's use of literature. *Journal of Educational Research, 76,* 221–230.

Morrow, L. M. (1983). Home and school correlates of early interest in literature. *Journal of Educational Research, 76,* 221–230.

Morrow, L. M. (1985). Retelling stories: A strategy for improving children's comprehension, concept of story structure, and oral language complexity. *Elementary School Journal, 85,* 647–661.

Morrow, L. M. (1986). Relationships between principals', teachers', and parents' attitudes towards the development of voluntary reading. *Reading Research and Instruction, 25,* 116–130.

Morrow, L. M. (1987a). Promoting voluntary reading: Activities represented in basal reader manuals. *Reading Research and Instruction, 26,* 189–202.

Morrow, L. M. (1987b). Promoting inner city children's voluntary reading. *Reading Teacher, 41,* 266–274.

Morrow, L. M. (1988). Young children's responses to one-to-one story readings in school settings. *Reading Research Quarterly, 23,* 89–107.

Morrow, L. M. (in press). *Developing literacy in the early years: Helping children read and write.* Englewood Cliffs, NJ: Prentice-Hall.

Morrow, L. M., & Weinstein, C. S. (1982). Increasing children's use of literature through program and physical design changes. *Elementary School Journal, 83,* 131–137.

Morrow, L. M., & Weinstein, C. S. (1986). Encouraging voluntary reading: The impact of a literature program on children's use of library centers. *Reading Research Quarterly, 21,* 330–346.

Ninio, A. (1980). Picture-book reading in mother-infant dyads belonging to two subgroups in Israel. *Child Development, 51,* 587–590.

Pellegrini, A. D., & Galda, L. (1982). The effects of thematic-fantasy play training on the development of children's story comprehension. *American Educational Research Journal, 19,* 443–452.

Powell, W. R. (1966). Classroom libraries: Their frequency of use. *Elementary English, 43,* 395–397.

Schickedanz, J. (1978). Please read that story again: Exploring relationship between story reading and learning to read. *Young Children, 33,* 48–55.

Smith, J. A., & Parker, M. (1977). *Word music and word magic: Children's literature methods.* Newton, MA: Allyn & Bacon.

Spiegel, D. L. (1981). Reading for pleasure: Guidelines. Newark, DE: International Reading Association.

Stauffer, R. G. (1970). A reading teacher's dream come true. *Wilson Library Bulletin, 45,* 285–292.

Stewig, J. W., & Sebesta, S. (Eds.). (1978). *Using literature in the elementary classroom.* Urbana, IL: National Council of Teachers of English.

Teale, W. H. (1981). Parents reading to their children: What we know and need to know. *Language Arts, 58,* 902–911.

Teale, W. H. (1982). Toward a theory of how children learn to read and write naturally. *Language Arts, 59,* 555–570.

Teale, W. (1984). Reading to young children: Its significance for literacy development. In H. Goelman, A. Oberg, & F. Smith (Eds.), *Awakening to Literacy* (pp. 110–121). London: Heinemann Educational Books.

Torrey, J. (1969). Learning to read without a teacher. *Elementary English, 46,* 550–556, 658.

Whitehead, F., Capey, A. C., & Maddren, W. (1975). *Children's reading interests.* London: Evans and Methuen.

Yaden, D. (1985, December). *Preschoolers' spontaneous inquiries about print and books.* Paper presented at the annual meeting of the National Reading Conference, San Diego, CA.

Yarington, D. (1978). *The great American reading machine.* Rochelle Park, NJ: Hayden Books.

Zolotow, C. (1972). *William's doll.* New York: Harper & Row.

## RECOMMENDED READINGS

Anderson, W., Croff, P., & Robinson, R. (1972). *A new look at children's literature.* Belmont, CA: Wadsworth.

Applebee, A. N. (1978). *The child's concept of story: Ages two to seventeen.* Chicago, IL: University of Chicago.

Bettleheim, B. (1976). *The uses of enchantment.* New York: Knopf.

Chatterson, J. (1977). *Children and literature.* Newark, DE: International Reading Association.

Coody, B. (1983). *Using literature with young children.* Dubuque, IA: William Brown.

Cullinan, B. E. (1981). *Literature and the child.* New York: Harcourt Brace Jovanovich.

Hickman, J. (1984). Research currents: Researching children's response to literature. *Language Arts, 61*(3), 278–284.

Irving, A. (1980). *Promoting voluntary reading for children and young people.* Paris: UNESCO.

Lamme, L. L. (1981). *Learning to love literature.* Urbana, IL: National Council of Teachers of English.

Larrick, N. (1975). *A parent's guide to children's reading.* New York: Bantam Books.

Lukens, R. J. (1982). *A critical handbook of children's literature* (2nd ed.). Glenview, IL: Scott, Foresman.

Morrow, L. M. (1981). *Super tips for storytelling.* Duluth, MN: Instructor Books.

Morrow, L. M. (1985). *Promoting voluntary reading in school and home.* Bloomington, IN: Phi Delta Kappa Educational Foundation.

Morrow, L. M. (1986). Voluntary reading: Forgotten goal. *Educational Forum, 50,* 159–168.

Purves, A., & Beach, R. (1972). *Literature and the reader: Research in responses to literature, reading interests, and the teaching of literature.* Urbana, IL: University of Illinois.

Strickland, D. (1981). *The role of literature in reading instruction: Crosscultural views.* Newark, DE: International Reading Association.

Taylor, D., & Strickland, D. (1976). *Family storybook reading.* Portsmouth, NH: Heinemann Educational Books.

Trelease, J. (1985). *The read-aloud handbook.* New York: Penguin Books.

Williamson, P. M. (1981). Literature goals and activities for young children. *Young Children, 36*(4), 24–30.

## TEACHER RESOURCES

American Library Association, 50 East Huron Street, Chicago, IL 60611

Children's Book Council, 67 Irving Place, New York, NY 10003

International Reading Association, P.O. Box 8139, 800 Barksdale Road, Newark, DE 19814

National Council of Teachers of English, 1111 Kenyon Road, Urbana, IL 61801

Chapter 8

# Integrating Writing
# and Reading Instruction

TAFFY E. RAPHAEL
CAROL SUE ENGLERT

Why use writing to teach reading? What kinds of writing instruction and activities can help to improve reading? How can writing be used to help comprehension of both stories and informational articles? Questions such as these occur with increased frequency as teachers and other school staff become more sophisticated in their knowledge of the reading process and the relationship of reading to the other language processes. The purpose of this chapter is to discuss how writing can be made a prominent and integral part of the basal reading program. We first describe current practice in reading and writing instruction. Next we provide a three-phase structure for integrating reading and writing instruction, focusing on strategies and skills common to both. Third, we recommend procedures for linking reading and writing instruction, drawing from instructional research on strategies for developing classroom writing instruction, which we then relate to the processes emphasized during effective reading instruction. We include sample activities that teachers may incorporate into current basal reading programs, as well as a list of recommended readings for those who wish to pursue further the topic of integration of writing and reading instruction.

## BACKGROUND

In most elementary classrooms in the United States, reading instruction and writing instruction are compartmentalized into two separate programs. Generally, the formal reading program uses one of many basal reading series or trade book collections. The separate writing program, by contrast, involves either skill instruction within a published language arts series or, less frequently, writing-as-process instruction independent of the reading program. Criticism of formal developmental reading programs has stemmed from the amount, or lack, of actual comprehension instruction that occurs (Durkin, 1978/1979), as well as an analysis of the types of activities encouraged in the teacher's manuals accompanying basal reading programs (Beck, McKeown, McCaslin, & Burkes, 1979; Durkin, 1981) and in related workbook and skill sheets (Osborn, 1985). Textbook-driven writing instruction has received similar criticism, resulting in a shift from a focus on written products to a focus on writing processes. Within this shift, writing instruction has moved from a product orientation, stressing the response to writing that focuses on conventions such as spelling and grammar, to a process orientation that stresses the response during writers' planning, drafting, and revising and focuses on communicating writers' ideas (Hairston, 1982; Laine & Schultz, 1985). However, even the way process-writing instruction is often conceptualized has received criticism (e.g., Applebee, 1986; Hillocks, 1986).

In contrast to compartmentalized reading/language arts programs, classrooms in which reading and writing are integrated have often been described as using "whole-language" (Newman, 1985) or "literature-based" (DeFord, 1986) approaches. In general, such approaches stress immersion of students in a language-based program that deemphasizes skill instruction and stresses a supportive environment in which students are encouraged through different opportunities to develop personally relevant reasons for selecting books or topics about which to write. Activities in such classrooms include reading aloud to students, using language experience programs in which students dictate stories based on their own experiences, having students learn vocabulary through a collection of words (e.g., "word banks") taken from their dictated stories, and fostering sustained silent reading from student-selected trade books. The teacher's responsibility is not to "impart wisdom from his or her *fount of knowledge* but to arrange conditions to help learning to occur, to provide information when asked to do so by a student . . . and to help children realize the range of goals and functions that reading can serve" (Pearson & Leys, 1985, p. 4).

Historically, the compartmentalized and literature-based approaches have represented the existing alternatives to literacy instruction, with much debate as to which method was "the right one." The former was seen as primarily focused on the teaching of isolated reading skills (e.g., phonics, main ideas) and writing skills (e.g., punctuation, grammar), while the latter was seen as being more "child-centered" and "natural." Recently, researchers have begun to examine relationships across the two approaches, demonstrating links between the basic processes of reading and writing that go beyond such superficial relationships as teaching phonics for both reading and spelling (Pearson & Leys, 1985). Arguments have been made that reading is a composing process (Tierney & Pearson, 1983) and that composing and comprehending are possibly "two sides of the same basic process" (Squire, 1984), though not mirror images of one another. Currently, there is general agreement that reading and writing are both fundamental cognitive processes, depending upon cognitive activities such as selecting important information, organizing and retrieving it, summarizing or consolidating it, and so forth (de Beaugrande, 1982; Spiro, 1980). Thus, instruction in reading and writing becomes an important aspect of enhancing students' thinking skills.

## SIMILARITIES IN THE READING AND WRITING PROCESSES

A number of skills and strategies are involved in the complex cognitive processes of reading and writing. We find it useful to consider these skills and strategies in terms of three phases of a reading or a writing activity: The planning (prewriting or prereading), drafting (writing or guided reading), and revising (modifying and extending, or post-reading) phases.

### Planning

When writers or readers plan, they generate ideas. In writing, planning involves making decisions about ideas generated related to the topic selected, the audience, the purpose, and how the ideas might be organized (Scardamelia & Bereiter, 1986). In reading, planning involves similar decision making about the ideas readers have generated. For example, readers consider the topic of the selection to be read, predict what may be included in the text and how the information may be organized, and select information from their own background knowledge that can help them make sense of and remember what they read. These decisions are guided by the readers' purposes for reading the selection and the information they have about the author of the text.

## Drafting

During drafting, readers and writers "construct the meaning" of the text, whether the text is self- or other-generated, relying on their awareness of author/reader relationships, their knowledge of text structure or organization, their understanding of the types of questions a particular text should be able to answer, and the signal words that indicate where particular types of information can be found. (For example, *in contrast to* signals information that is in opposition to already presented material.) Tierney and LaZansky (1980) discuss the author/reader "contract" that exists between the author and his or her audience. Both authors and readers know and agree that not everything can or should be explicitly stated in the text. What is or is not included is a function of the author's sensitivity to the audience's needs. As authors create their drafts, they consider such audience needs as background knowledge, vocabulary knowledge, and experience with story or expository text features. They are expected to provide whatever information they believe their audience needs to comprehend what is written. Similarly, readers also understand the "contract," both as they read information on the page and read between the lines to infer whatever other information is needed to make sense of the text.

Drafting also requires that both writers and readers use their knowledge of how texts are structured, as well as the types of questions each type of text structure is designed to answer (Armbruster & Anderson, 1982; Raphael, Englert, & Kirschner, 1986). For example, authors of stories follow a structure that allows readers to predict and identify information about setting and characters, as well as characters' motives and plans, initiating events (i.e., problem), related actions, and resolutions. That is to say, authors create a mental "story map," as described by Beck and McKeown (1981) and Pearson (1981).

Similarly, when authors write an explanation, they follow a structure that allows readers to predict both the categories of information that will be discussed as well as the order in which ideas will be presented logically. Thus, writers are likely to state first *what* is being explained and then discuss what "supplies" or other materials will be needed, ending with a presentation of the steps one would follow. Readers who read the text use similar knowledge to recognize that the text is, in fact, an explanation. Once the type of text has been recognized, readers then expect to find information related to an explanation, including materials and steps. Writers use key words and phrases to signal their readers as to the location of specific information, making for "considerate" text (see Armbruster, 1984). Readers use these same key words and phrases to identify quickly where particular information can be found.

Such knowledge is fundamental to students' ability to monitor and evaluate the comprehensibility of text and to identify sources of problems in their writing and their reading.

### Revising

During revision, writers and readers focus on monitoring and evaluating how successfully they have constructed meaning with or from text. Revision processes occur during planning or predicting, such as when a writer determines that more categories of information are needed, or a reader decides a prediction should be revised based on initial reading of content. Revision also occurs as writers draft text. They reread it to consider whether or not their text answers the questions it has been designed to answer, achieves their general goals or purposes (e.g., to make the reader laugh, to provide information to a naive audience, to convince the reader to take a particular point of view), and presents their ideas in a logical sequence. In addition, other decisions are made, such as the selection of a particular word or phrase, the replacement of one word with another, or corrections in spelling and grammar. Readers similarly monitor and evaluate their understanding of text and reread portions when they discover discrepancies between the questions the text was designed to answer and their own text interpretation. Revisions also occur when readers discover a mismatch between the content in the text and the readers' own background knowledge.

### RATIONALE

Given the similarity in cognitive activities across the reading and writing processes, it is reasonable to expect that instruction and application of strategies learned in writing might help readers as they develop the reading strategies of planning, constructing meaning, and monitoring their comprehension of stories and informational text. Thus, it makes sense for us to consider what we have learned from instructional research that can inform our teaching and the integration of reading and writing instruction.

The volume of instructional research in writing has rapidly grown in the past decade, spurred by such large-scale projects as the National Writing Project (Camp, 1982) and the Writers Workshop (Graves,

1983). This literature is an important source of ideas for implementing an integrated reading and writing program. These large-scale programs have emphasized the importance of creating a general environment in which young writers can learn to take control of the subprocesses involved in planning, drafting, and "going public" with their written work. Fundamental to these programs are writing for real purposes and audiences, students' sharing of ideas and written work, students' ownership of their topics, frequent writing opportunities, and opportunities for extended writing. Consistent with this research are studies and papers that emphasize the integration of reading and writing instruction (e.g., Graves & Hansen, 1983; Rubin & Hansen, 1986).

From this relatively new but extensive body of research, several instructional ideas and recommendations can be drawn. We will discuss these in terms of *general* suggestions for creating a literate environment, *specific* suggestions for developing strategies related to planning, drafting, and revising; and *selected activities* with which to apply these general and specific suggestions within a basal reading program. Throughout this discussion, we note how these ideas and recommendations are linked to the development of the concepts of planning, drafting, and revising during writing and reading.

## CREATING A LITERATE ENVIRONMENT: GENERAL SUGGESTIONS

In order truly to link reading and writing instruction in classrooms, it is important first to establish an environment that emphasizes the importance of literacy, including the reading of a variety of materials, sharing thoughts and feelings about selections read, writing about issues of importance, and sharing writing with others. In other words, it is important for students to view their own and others' writing as part of a larger body of literary and informational written work, both professionally and informally published, that is legitimate reading material for their classrooms. This provides students with a purpose for planning their papers, namely that, since a real audience will read their work it is important to present information in an organized and interesting manner. It also gives purposes for drafting and revising, for, since their work will be "public," they experience the need to shape the work to represent best their own goals for their papers.

There are numerous ways of creating such an environment, from using traditional and easily accessible materials such as paper and pencils and bulletin boards, to using more sophisticated modern technology such as microcomputers. One example of a literate environment that was created using a microcomputer, but that is easily adapted to more routine classroom materials, is called QUILL (Rubin & Bruce, 1986). QUILL focuses on planning, text production, and "going public" with one's writing. For example, to address students' needs during planning, a series of prompts are used to engage students in thinking about their characters, the major events in their stories, the important information they should include in a report, and so forth. To emphasize the concept of audience, QUILL provides an electronic mail system through which students send messages to other individual students, to large groups, or to a general "bulletin board"; as well as a "library" program that encourages students to write informational pieces for a permanent collection. Whereas QUILL was designed for use with a personal computer, the ideas obviously can be implemented in any classroom. For example, a classroom bulletin board designated as a place where students can post messages, respond to each others' notes, write graffiti to invite response on specific topics, and so forth, establishes a sense of audience within the classroom. A permanent collection of informational texts written by students may be created at writing centers in which students add reports to notebooks that are arranged like a set of encyclopedias, including several volumes and an index. Students can add their selection to the appropriate volume, adding a reference in the index designed to attract other readers' attention. Such a setting stresses the purposeful nature of writing, both for communicating and for sharing information.

Another means for creating a literate environment, the "author's chair," was developed as part of the Writers Workshop (Graves & Hansen, 1983). The author's chair is a special chair in the classroom in which authors sit. From this chair, students present, discuss, and answer questions concerning written pieces that they themselves have authored or that represent favorite works by published authors. Such an activity is particularly helpful for developing the students' concept of drafting and revision, as it provides students with an opportunity to share their own writings, to receive comments about work in progress and ideas for future writing, and to discuss ideas present in writing. Thus, students see that writing occurs because an author has a purpose and an audience with whom she or he wishes to communicate. They learn through such discussion that writing is a decision-making process and that writers consider the needs and expectations of their audience when creating their stories and articles and that they monitor how well their ideas are communicated, revising when needed. Through writing and talking about writing, they learn to view published written materials through the eyes of the author as well as from the perspective of the reader.

A third means for creating a literate environment has been discussed recently in articles by such teachers and researchers as Atwell (1984), Fulwiler (1982), and Gambrell (1985). They describe the importance of and means for using "dialogue journals." These are used to encourage written conversations between teachers and students, or among students themselves. The journals can be used to encourage discussion of specific topics (e.g., an assigned selection the students have just read) or general comments (e.g., topics selected by the students, questions they wish to raise, and so forth). The journals themselves can be as simple as spiral notebooks, composition books, or sheets of notebook paper stapled together to form a notebook. They provide an important opportunity for students both to express their own ideas and to respond in writing to the ideas of others.

Gambrell (1985) suggests introducing students to dialogue journals by suggesting a format similar to letter writing and then encouraging them to use it to ask the teacher questions or write about something they wish to share with the teacher. Fulwiler (1982), in describing how dialogue journals can be used in subject-matter areas, suggests having students respond to a specific problem or question, such as, How would you explain prime numbers to a second grader? or, How are the problems of farmers today similar to the problems faced by farmers 100 years ago? How are they different? Atwell (1984) describes how dialogue journals can be used to explore students' reactions to stories they are reading, as well as to challenge students to consider alternate reactions and read related selections. In short, dialogue journals provide a "window" into the students' cognitive activities during writing and reading, giving them opportunities both to write and to write about reading, and giving teachers opportunities to highlight students' idea generation, planning, predicting, and monitoring of their own writing and reading.

In summary, there are a variety of means for developing a literate environment within which reading and writing instruction can be integrated. Fundamental to such an environment should be (1) writing for real purposes and audiences, (2) frequent opportunities to write and share one's writing, and (3) opportunities for extended writing. These goals can be accomplished through children's sharing of their work orally (e.g., author's chair) and in writing (e.g., dialogue journals, bulletin boards, classroom encyclopedias); and through their sharing with a range of audiences, from peers and teachers to family members and wider audiences in their school. The importance of these opportunities for sharing will become even more apparent during our discussion, in the final section of this chapter, of selected activities that can be incorporated into basal reading lessons. First, we will look at some more specific ideas for reading and writing strategies.

## DEVELOPING STRATEGIES FOR WRITING AND READING: SPECIFIC SUGGESTIONS

Within the general literate environment just described, skills related to planning, drafting, and monitoring or revising during reading and writing must be taught. For example, students need to develop skills for planning extended texts that extend beyond the simple answering of questions, or beyond a few lines in length. They need to learn strategies for revising a paper to fit the needs of their audiences; they need to understand the range of possibilities for both audience and purpose; they need to learn a variety of ways of expressing and responding to the potential ideas represented by this range in audience and purpose; and they need to learn the different ways in which information can be structured. In fact, Applebee (1986) suggests that "writing processes must be reconstrued as strategies that writers employ for particular purposes" (p. 106).

A number of specific instructional approaches provide insight into ways of instructing our students in the skills and strategies for planning, drafting, and monitoring. Many of these are based on our knowledge of cognitive processes. Many studies of cognition relate directly to constructing meaning in both reading and writing. In this section, we highlight examples of such instructional research and discuss the ways in which the findings can be used as part of the writing process and used during reading.

### Semantic Mapping and Concept-of-Definition Instruction

Since both writing and reading involve planning and predicting text information, it is not surprising that many of the strategies studied have their basis in understanding how information is organized in our memories as well as in text. Knowledge of organizational patterns or structures is important during planning, as well as during the drafting and monitoring of texts. Two strategies that focus on organizing information are on semantic mapping (Johnson, Pittleman, & Heimlich, 1986) and a related idea, concept-of-definition instruction (Schwartz & Raphael, 1985). These make explicit for students the facts that (1) information can be organized or grouped into categories and (2) grouping such information makes it easier to plan, understand, and remember text.

Johnson and his colleagues (1986) describe semantic mapping as "the categorical structuring of information in graphic form" (p. 779). Semantic maps for a specific story are presented in chapter 5. Broadly defined, a semantic map is a graphic display that visually depicts the relationships among ideas or concepts. These can include class, property, and example relationships. For example, in Figure 8.1 the word *dog* is mapped as a member of the *class* known as "animals." *Collie* is mapped by *properties* such as long hair and pointed ears, and as an *example* of the more general class known as dogs. Johnson and his colleagues have used semantic mapping during vocabulary instruction to facilitate students' identification of information related to new concepts being introduced, arguing that "the procedure of mapping a topic provides students with a means for both activating

**Figure 8.1**   Semantic Map Showing Class, Property, and Example Relationships

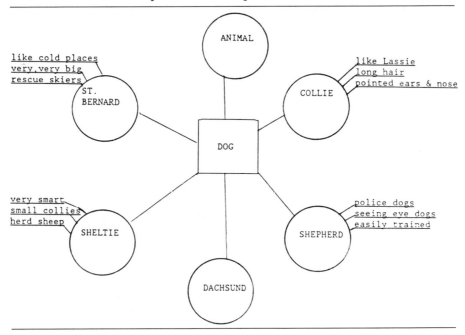

and enhancing their knowledge bases regarding the specific topics and words discussed. . . . [It] results in a categorical structuring of information in graphic form . . . [and helps students to] see the specific relationships among concepts" (p. 780).

This is similar to the brainstorming of ideas, often used during the planning phase in writing a story or informational paper, as writers generate all the ideas they can related to the topic about which they are going to write. Both semantic mapping and brainstorming, however, are associative strategies that can fall short of the students' needs, since some of the ideas generated may be irrelevant, while other categories of information may go unmentioned. A second procedure involves the grouping or structuring of such information (Schwartz, in press; Schwartz & Raphael, 1985).

Schwartz's "concept-of-definition" instruction provides a basis for students to group information they have generated and begins to link the generation of ideas to generating the questions that one wishes to answer during the reading or writing of text. Schwartz and Raphael (1985) suggest that students benefit from learning a set of general questions that can drive the generation of relevant information. For instance, if students are attempting to generate information related to a concept that is a "thing" (e.g., canoes, computers), they may use questions such as What is it? (i.e., To what class of objects does it belong?), What is it like? (i.e., What are some traits or features unique to the item?), and What are some examples? The ability to generate and respond to such questions is the basis for creating a well-organized descriptive passage, as well as for identifying important information in text.

## Cognitive Strategy Instruction in Writing

Both semantic mapping and concept-of-definition instruction focus on brainstorming or organizing information at the concept level. Others have applied similar approaches to the text level, for both stories and informational selections, studying how texts are organized and how this organization can best be conveyed to beginning writers and readers (e.g., Armbruster & Anderson, 1982; Flood, Lapp, & Farnan, 1986; Raphael, Kirschner, & Englert, 1988). Ruth (1987) suggests that text-structure instruction may be particularly helpful in encouraging students to see sequences in text, rather than focusing at the word or clause level.

Englert et al. (1986) developed an approach called Cognitive Strategy Instruction in Writing (csiw), which is based on several of the principles described earlier: frequent and extended writing opportunities, writing for real purposes and audiences, and writing different types of papers. The csiw program combines principles of process writing with principles underlying the teaching of cognitive strategies such as those used during reading and writing. An important thread throughout the program is highlighting (1) the nature of text organization; (2) how this organization can drive the planning, drafting, monitoring, and revising of texts; and (3) how knowledge of text structures can help writers meet the needs of their audience and help readers understand the purposes authors had when the texts were created. A series of "think sheets" forms the curriculum materials used throughout the instruction. These are particularly valuable in providing students with concrete reminders of appropriate strategies to use and of the times when particular strategies may be relevant. This support takes the form of questions and prompts related to each writing subprocess (e.g., planning, organizing, editing).

The first csiw think sheet (see Figure 8.2), for use during planning, guides students to begin by considering their topic, audience, and purpose. Then students are prompted to brainstorm, generating all the ideas they can think of related to their topic. (This process is similar to the generation of ideas when creating a semantic map.) However, to underscore the difference between brainstorming of all related ideas and selecting important ideas to be grouped by category, students are prompted to examine their brainstormed ideas; to find ideas that go together; to examine ideas that do not seem to fit and decide whether (1) they should be dropped or (2) more related ideas should be added to them; and, finally, to organize the ideas into the categories they have identified.

A second think sheet prompts students to consider the next subprocess in which they need to engage. Once ideas are grouped, students must decide which of the ideas their audience should read first; in other words, they must consider how to sequence or organize the ideas they have generated. There are several versions of this second think sheet, each one representative of a different way of structuring categorized information. (Two of these, the think sheets for organizing narrative and comparison/contrast, are shown in Figures 8.3 and 8.4.) For example, if students are writing a narrative, they will probably wish to sequence their information in terms of setting and character information first, followed by an indication of the character's problem in the story and a set of events that relate to the problem, and finishing with an ending that indicates the resolution. The think sheet for narrative contains prompts such as Who is in the story?

**Figure 8.2** Think Sheet for Planning Stage

Author's Name:_____     Date: _____

Topic:_____

WHO:  For whom am I writing?


WHY:  Why am I writing this?


WHAT:  What do I already know about my topic? (brainstorm)

1. _____

2. _____

3. _____

4. _____


HOW:  How do I group my ideas?

**Figure 8.3**   Think Sheet for Organizing Narrative

Who is in the story?

What is the setting?

What is the problem?

What happens first?

What happens next?

Next?

How is the problem solved?

What is the setting? and so forth, derived from story map questions (e.g., Pearson, 1981). In contrast, the prompts for writing comparison/contrast text include, What is being compared/contrasted? On what? and asks for information on how these are alike and different.

Once students have considered how to organize their text, they also need to consider ways of grabbing their readers' attention and providing a context for them as well as potential endings that will provide the reader with a summary or concluding section. Notes may

**Figure 8.4**   Think Sheet for Organizing Comparison/Contrast

What is being compared/contrasted?

On What?

Alike?

Different?

On What?

Alike?

Different?

On What?

Alike?

Different?

be added to the organizing think sheet, or students may consider these factors as they transform the information from the organizing think sheet into a first draft.

Remaining csıw think sheets include one each for (1) self-monitoring or editing, in preparation for a peer-editing conference;

(2) peer-editing; (3) revision; and (4) final draft. (For further description of think sheets and samples, see Englert et al., 1986). Obviously, each writing activity need not involve all subprocesses of writing. As Applebee (1986) states,

> Some tasks would require extensive prewriting activities; ... [others] help with drafting; some would go through a variety of revisions; some would be edited to share with others; some would emphasize competent first-and-final draft performance. Running through all of these variations would be an awareness, on the part of teachers and students alike, that there are many different kinds of writing and many different strategies for approaching each task; and both tasks and strategies would be varied in a principled way. [p. 107]

However, although the procedures may be varied, it is helpful to introduce students to the entire writing process by using the think sheets, which can later serve as reminders of both where students are in the general writing process and what the specific strategies appropriate to that subprocess are. This provides teachers and students with a basis for selecting different subprocesses and strategies for use during basal reading instruction, without neglecting attention to how these fit into the overall picture of composition and comprehension.

For example, assume that students have just completed reading a fictional story about a brother and sister vacationing near the ocean. While playing in the surf, they find a small box containing an ancient set of directions. This leads to the discovery of some very old relics from a sunken ship. There are many different possible writing activities associated with this story, depending upon the lesson goals. The students may rewrite segments of the text, using first-person narrative or dialogue instead of narrative. They may plan a report about sunken treasures. They may create a journal entry that describes one aspect of the children's adventure. The planning think sheet may be used to help students determine the writing activity of their choice and consider the factors of audience, purpose, and content. Students may then share these plans, even though at this point in the lesson they may not necessarily invest the time required to work their ideas into first drafts and final copies. The mere use of the think sheet will underscore for them the subprocess and appropriate related planning strategies in which to engage. The plans may be resurrected at a later time, to be used in another related writing activity. Further, the prompts on the think sheets emphasize the kind of thinking in which the story's author engaged as she or he dealt with similar content and issues in the generation of the original story.

A second example illustrates how the editing think sheet (see Figure 8.5) can be adapted for use during comprehension instruction in a basal reading lesson. One important element of comprehension instruction is teaching students strategies related to comprehension monitoring. The editing think sheet prompts students to indicate their favorite parts in their paper and the parts they find confusing, and to examine whether or not their organization of ideas is clear for their reader (including appropriate information as well as key words and phrases to signal the reader where information can be found). This think sheet can be used both with existing text they have read, as well as for texts they have generated related to the story. They may edit a selection they have read, noting parts that were particularly well written or interesting, or that used language in a way that they might like to try. They may mark areas of the text that left them confused, that made them wonder what the author had in mind. Finally, they could examine the selection to determine if the elements (identified in a story map or text structure) were clearly presented. In this way, the editing think sheet can be used not only to examine their own writing, but to emphasize editing strategies involved in comprehension monitoring as well.

A further application of the editing think sheet involves students' self-examination of their own papers. For example, assume that students have written a brief description of ancient relics or an explanation of how expeditions are conducted in search of sunken ships, or perhaps compared the findings in the story with the findings from a newspaper accounting of a shipwreck discovery. Students may have planned their papers as a group when the assignment was made, yet they may benefit from individually monitoring and evaluating the individual papers they created. The think sheet not only guides them in their monitoring but reminds them of the strategies useful during that subprocess, how these strategies relate to the writing process as a whole, and how strategies used during writing relate to monitoring text comprehension.

Finally, all of the csiw think sheets can provide support as students begin to respond to selections in ways that replace standard tasks such as writing answers to questions. For example, students may have conferences with peers about selections they have read, or they may write entries in dialogue journals. Such activities allow students to link writing activities with their own reading, and the think sheets can guide students to consider the content of the selections and monitor the clarity of the ideas presented.

# Figure 8.5 Think Sheet for Editing Comparison/Contrast

Author's Name_____     Editor's Name_____

### Read to Check Information

What is the paper mainly about?

What do you like best?  Put a * next to the part you liked best and tell here why you like it:

What parets are not clear?  Put a ? next to the unclear parts, and tell what made the part unclear to you:

Is the paper interesting?  Tell why or why not:

### Question Yourself to Check Organization   Did the author:

| | | | |
|---|---|---|---|
| Tell what two things are compared and contrasted? | YES | sort of | NO |
| Tell the things that they are being compared to and contrasted with? | YES | sort of | NO |
| Tell how they are alike? | YES | sort of | NO |
| Tell how they are different? | YES | sort of | NO |
| Use key words clearly? | YES | sort of | NO |

### Plan Revision

What two parts do you think should be changed or revised?   (For anything marked "Sort of" or "NO," tell whether the author should add to, take out, or reorder.)

1. _____

   _____

2. _____

   _____

What could help make the paper more interesting?

**TALK**:  Talk to the author of the paper.  Talk about your comments on this think sheet.  Share ideas for revising the paper

## Integrated Instruction for Narrative Texts

A second program that concerns organization at the text level focuses on integrating writing and reading instruction of narrative texts (Strickland & Feeley, 1985). While the csiw program begins by teaching text elements through writing and then applying them to reading, Strickland and Feeley begin with reading, using published selections to increase students' familiarity with story elements. They then provide students with writing opportunities during which they apply their knowledge of story elements. The specific story structure elements include characters, setting, initiating events, and resolutions—again, these are consistent with story mapping.

The authors suggest a three-step model for sensitizing students to story structures. In the first step, students are exposed to a variety of stories within a particular genre such as fairy tales, mysteries, animal stories, or adventure tales. The stories also can be related by theme (e.g., loyalty to friends) or by topic (e.g., pioneers). Obvious sources include stories from basal readers, stories chosen for sustained silent reading, and stories read aloud by the classroom teacher. Strickland and Feeley (1985) suggest that teachers create questions related to the elements in the story structure (setting, characters, problem/solution, and so forth) and that the teacher expose children to a variety of examples of these elements in the genre of story being examined.

In the second step, story-reading activities are extended through several language-based activities. One example is a discussion using story-based questions designed to stress the features of the genre being studied. For instance, if mystery stories are selected as the genre, story-based questions might focus students' attention on such features as the importance of suspense, of unexpected happenings, and of the authors' attempts to mask important events. Teachers might ask students to consider how a mystery would have been resolved differently if key story elements or events had been added or changed. Creative dramatics are also suggested, specifically activities that focus students' attention on characters and their behavior or on the setting of the story. Story retellings are another suggested type of activity, in which students individually or as a group retell the significant events in a story, using the genre framework to guide the retelling.

The third step involves writing activities related to both the genre and activities just described, beginning with whole-group activities such as story retelling and writing and the creation of stories within the genre studied. In these activities, the teacher serves as scribe. Strickland and Feeley (1985) suggest small-group writing activities next, with a focus on collaborating and sharing the students' created stories. The final step involves individuals writing stories to share with their peers. The authors indicate that these activities help students develop a schema for the genre that enhances both reading and writing.

## WRITING ACTIVITIES FOR BASAL READING INSTRUCTION

Thus far, our understanding of reading and writing instruction gained from current research and informed practice suggests that students should learn strategies for comprehending and writing within a general literate environment. Such an environment should provide (1) frequent writing opportunities for real purposes and audiences, (2) opportunities for extended writing, and (3) opportunities to write and evaluate different types of texts. These writing experiences can and should link directly to the reading activities in the classroom. One means of doing this is through basal reading instruction.

Frequent writing opportunities can be provided by having students write in connection with each basal selection. Each writing activity, however, need not involve the full range of writing subprocesses. Rather, a specific writing activity should be identified in terms of its relationship to the selection's *topic*, its potential for development of a particular writing *strategy*, and its relevance to the overall writing/reading *curriculum*. Many writing activities lend themselves to integration with basal reading selections' topics. These include:

1. Rewriting a story written in the first person, to take the form of a newspaper report
2. Changing an important story element and speculating on an alternative ending that might result from such a change
3. Extending a "slice-of-life" story by using the same characters in a new situation
4. Selecting a favorite character from a story and writing a character sketch
5. Comparing a selection with one previously read, on such features as setting, theme, or problem/resolution
6. Adding information to an informational selection
7. Writing to the selection's author for additional information
8. Making a journal entry reacting to the content, style, or concepts presented in a selection

9. Writing to an authority to request further information about a topic or a place

The first decision to make, in identifying an appropriate writing activity, is what naturally "flows" from the selection read. The next set of decisions involves the strategy on which to focus. The last decisions concern ways of making the activity meaningful in terms of purpose and audience. We use here a chapter from *Amelia Bedelia* by Parish (1963), which appears in a fourth-grade basal reader, to illustrate the nature of the decisions. In the selection, Amelia is hired to do the upkeep of the Rogers's house and is left with a list of household duties. She has a problem in that she interprets everything on her list in a literal way; thus, when asked to "dust the house," she spreads dust on everything. The only factor that kept the Rogers from firing her was that she had baked them the most delicious pie they had ever tasted.

Not surprisingly, several writing activities naturally follow from such a selection. These include generating an extended list of directions that had literal and inferential interpretations, changing the critical element of making the pie and considering resulting alternative endings, or comparing and contrasting Amelia Bedelia's problem with that of a character from a different story. After determining the range of possibilities, the next decision concerns the strategy to develop (i.e., heightening sensitivity to story structure, using the author's craft of humor in misinterpreting phrases, planning a comparison/ contrast character sketch). Assume that the planning of a comparison/contrast character sketch is selected. The next set of decisions for the activity focuses on ways to make it meaningful in terms of real audience and purpose.

Audience factors may arise as students identify their favorite character from another story read and use the comparison/contrast structure (1) to convey information about the new character by comparing him or her to a known character—Amelia Bedelia, (2) to convince their audience that one of the characters is better (e.g., smarter, funnier) than the other, or (3) to entertain their audience. Using a planning think sheet (refer to Figure 8.2) to guide their preparation, students could then identify their purpose and define the audience for whom they are writing. Next they could generate their ideas and organize them, using the organizing think sheet (see Figure 8.3), in terms of what they are comparing and contrasting, traits on which they will compare and contrast, similarities, and differences. They can then share their ideas with a partner, to get feedback prior to writing.

This single activity is an example of the writing opportunities that can be integrated with basal reading. An activity such as this provides students with the opportunity to "play" with a common text structure, to integrate information from different stories they have read, and to consider how authors use structure to meet different purposes. Even though they may not actually write the piece, they have benefited from participating in the development of the planning strategies for comparison/contrast.

This activity could also be developed quite easily into an opportunity for extended writing. Rather than engage in unrelated writing activities following the reading of each subsequent selection in the basal series unit, students may instead extend their character sketch plans to create a story either about Amelia Bedella, about the new character they have introduced, or even about the two characters together. Each time students work on their papers, they focus on a different feature of their story, a feature that relates to those in the selections they are reading. An obvious second activity following the character sketch plan would be to generate a first draft, while a third activity might require the development of a dialogue between the two characters. This would be particularly appropriate following a selection in which effective use of dialogue was modeled. Other relevant activities include embedding the character sketch and dialogue into a story, and finally, publishing a class book for placement in their room and school library.

Within this extended writing project, students will have focused on different types of texts—narratives in the stories read, as well as comparison/contrast in their own papers. They will have had the opportunity to discuss the writing of a professional author as well as the writings of their peers, and they will have seen monitored the development of their paper through planning, drafting, and revising.

## CONCLUSION

The integration of reading and writing is important, not only to improving the literacy instruction in today's schools but also to enhancing the quality of students' thinking. As students write about what they have read, they learn to approach reading as authors. As authors, they are better able (1) to consider the reasons a particular selection was written, (2) to see relationships among different types of texts and genres, and (3) to consider the questions different texts are designed to answer. They also become more aware of important information and more capable of reading beyond the printed page. The ideas presented in this chapter underscore the point that writing and reading can easily be integrated, regardless of materials used in the developmental reading program. In order for integration to take place, however, those who are involved in instruction need a greater understanding of the similarities and differences between the processes of reading and writing, as well as knowledge of ways in which instruction in the two processes can be merged. We are all just beginning to understand both the complexity and the fun of integrating our language instruction.

## REFERENCES

Applebee, A. N. (1986). Problems in process approaches: Toward a reconceptualization of process instruction. In A. R. Petrosky & D. Bartholomae (Eds.), *The teaching of writing (85th yearbook of the National Society for the Study of Education)* (pp. 95–113). Chicago: University of Chicago Press.

Armbruster, B. B. (1984). The problem of "inconsiderate text." In G. G. Duffy, L. R. Roehler, & J. N. Mason (Eds.), *Comprehension instruction: Perspectives and suggestions.* New York: Longman.

Armbruster, B. B., & Anderson, T. H. (1982). *Idea-mapping: The technique and its use in the classroom* (Reading Education Report No. 36). Urbana: University of Illinois, Center for the Study of Reading.

Atwell, N. (1984). Writing and reading from the inside out. *Language Arts, 61,* 240–252.

Beck, I. L., & McKeown, M. G. (1981). Developing questions that promote comprehension. *Language Arts, 58,* 913–918.

Beck, I. L., McKeown, M. G., McCaslin, E. S., & Burkes, A. M. (1979). *Instructional dimensions that may affect reading comprehension: Examples from two commercial reading programs.* Pittsburgh: University of Pittsburgh, Learning Research and Development Center.

Camp, G. (Ed.). (1982). *Teaching writing: Essays from the Bay Area Writing Project.* Montclair, NJ: Boynton/Cook.

de Beaugrande, R. (1982). Psychology and composition: Past, present, and future. In M. Nystrand (Ed.), *What writers know: The language, process, and structure of written discourse* (pp. 211–267). New York: Academic Press.

DeFord, D. E. (1986). Classroom contexts for literacy learning. In T. E. Raphael (Ed.), *The contexts of school-based literacy* (pp. 163–180). New York: Random House.

Durkin, D. (1978/1979). What classroom observations reveal about reading comprehension instruction. *Reading Research Quarterly, 14,* 481–533.

Durkin, D. (1981). Reading comprehension instruction in five basal reader series. *Reading Research Quarterly, 16,* 515–544.

Englert, C. S., Raphael, T. E., Anderson, L. M., Anthony, H. M., Fear, K., & Gregg, S. L. (1986). *Establishing a case for writing intervention: The what and why of teaching expository writing* (Occasional Paper No. 111). East Lansing: Michigan State University, Institute for Research on Teaching.

Flood, J., Lapp, D., & Farnan, N. (1986). A reading-writing procedure that teaches expository paragraph structure. *Reading Teacher, 39,* 556–562.

Fulwiler, T. (1982). The personal connection: Journal writing across the curriculum. In T. Fulwiler & A. Young (Eds.), *Language connections: Writing and reading across the curriculum* (pp. 15–32). Urbana, IL: National Council of Teachers of English.

Gambrell, L. B. (1985). Dialogue journals: Reading-writing interaction. *Reading Teacher, 38,* 512–515.

Graves, D. H. (1983). *Writing: Teachers and children at work.* Exeter, NH: Heinemann.

Graves, D. H., & Hansen, J. (1983). The author's chair. *Language Arts, 60,* 176–183.

Hairston, M. (1982). The winds of change: Thomas Kuhn and the revolution in the teaching of writing. *College Composition and Communication, 33,* 76–88.

Hillocks, G. (1986). What works in teaching composition: A meta-analysis of experimental treatment studies. In N. L. Stein (Ed.), *Literacy in American schools* (pp. 137–174). Chicago: University of Chicago Press.

Johnson, D. D., Pittleman, S. D., & Heimlich, J. E. (1986). Semantic mapping. *Reading Teacher, 39,* 778–783.

Laine, C., & Schultz, L. (1985). Composition theory and practice: The paradigm shift. *Volta Review, 87*(5), 9–20.

Newman, J. M. (1985). *Whole language: Theory in use.* Portsmouth, NH: Heinemann.

Osborn, J. (1985). Workbooks: Counting, matching, and judging. In J. Osborn, P. T. Wilson, & R. C. Anderson. (Eds.), *Reading education: Foundations for a literate America* (pp. 11–28). Lexington, MA: Lexington Books.

Parish, P. (1963). *Amelia Bedelia.* New York: Harper & Row.

Pearson, P. D. (1981). *Asking questions about stories* (Occasional Paper No. 15). Columbus, OH: Ginn.

Pearson, P. D., & Leys, M. (1985). Teaching comprehension. In T. L. Harris & E. Cooper (Eds.), *Reading, thinking, and concept development* (pp. 3–20). New York: The College Board.

Raphael, T. E., Englert, C. S., & Kirschner, B. W. (1986). *The impact of text structure instruction and social context on students' comprehension and production of expository text* (Research Series No. 177). East Lansing: Michigan State University, Institute for Research on Teaching.

Raphael, T. E., Kirschner, B. W., & Englert, C. S. (1988). Expository Writing

Program: Making connections between reading and writing. *Reading Teacher, 41,* 790–796.

Rubin, A., & Bruce, B. C. (1986). Learning from QUILL: Lessons for students, teachers, and software designers. In T. E. Raphael (Ed.), *The contexts of school-based literacy* (pp. 217–230). New York: Random House.

Rubin, A., & Hansen, J. (1986). Reading and writing: How are the first two R's related? In J. Orasanu (Ed.), *Reading comprehension: From research to practice* (pp. 163–170). Hillsdale, NJ: Lawrence Erlbaum.

Ruth, L. (1987). Reading children's writing. *Reading Teacher, 40,* 756–760.

Scardamelia, M., & Bereiter, C. (1986). Research on written composition. In M. C. Wittrock (Ed.), *Handbook of research on teaching* (pp. 778–803). New York: Macmillan.

Schwartz, R. M. (in press). Learning to learn vocabulary in content area textbooks. *Journal of Reading.*

Schwartz, R. M., & Raphael, T. E. (1985). Concept of definition: A key to improving students' vocabulary. *Reading Teacher, 39,* 198–205.

Spiro, R. J. (1980). Constructive processes in prose comprehension and recall. In R. J. Spiro, B. C. Bruce, & W. F. Brewer (Eds.), *Theoretical issues in reading comprehension* (pp. 245–278). Hillsdale, NJ: Lawrence Erlbaum.

Squire, J. R. (1984). Composing and comprehending: Two sides of the same basic process. In J. M. Jensen (Ed.), *Composing and comprehending* (pp. 23–32). Urbana, IL. National Conference on Research in English

Strickland, D. S., & Feeley, J. T. (1985). Using children's concept of story to improve reading and writing. In T. L. Harris & E. J. Cooper (Eds.), *Reading, thinking, and concept development.* New York: The College Board.

Tierney, R. J., & LaZansky, J. M. (1980). The rights and responsibilities of readers and writers: A contractual agreement. *Language Arts, 57,* 606–613.

Tierney, R. J., & Pearson, P. D. (1983). Toward a composing model of reading. *Language Arts, 60,* 568–580.

## RECOMMENDED READING

Altwerger, B., Edelsky, C., & Flores, B. M. (1988). Whole language: What's new? *Reading Teacher, 41,* 144–154.

Chapter 9

# Creating the Bridge
# to Content-Area Reading

DONNA E. ALVERMANN

A large part of any elementary or middle school teacher's day involves helping students learn from text. Because it is inappropriate to think of reading as an isolated subject, teachers at the primary school level as well as those at the intermediate or middle school level are responsible for developing students' ability to read effectively in the content areas.

Primary school teachers lay the foundation for the bridge between basal reading and reading in the content areas when they read aloud from informational books that are organized according to one or more of the common expository text structures, such as cause/effect or comparison/contrast. Intermediate and middle school teachers help build the bridge from basal reading to content-area reading when they help students acquire strategies that increase their independence in learning from a variety of texts.

This chapter is about the different ways teachers in grades K–8 can prepare students to learn from content-area texts by extending what they have learned in basal reading. It focuses on three parts of that preparation: building an anticipatory set, guiding the reading, and helping students integrate and apply what they have learned. The goal of this preparation, or bridging, is to develop within students the ability to read effectively in the content areas. Before discussing the recommended procedures for creating this bridge to content-area reading, however, it is important to establish the background and rationale for such instruction.

## BACKGROUND

Although learning from text is of foremost importance to most educators, we know very little about how classroom teachers use content-area textbooks. The research that does exist is inconclusive. In one study (Rieck, 1977), where teachers did not provide time for discussing content-area reading assignments in class, students reported seeing little purpose in reading their textbooks. Other studies (Ratekin, Simpson, Alvermann, & Dishner, 1985; Smith & Feathers, 1983) suggest that students view their teachers, not their textbooks, as their major source of information. Ratekin and colleagues (1985) attributed this to the fact that the teachers they observed seemed to use the textbook as a "safety net"—a verification of information presented via lectures and lecture-discussions.

In a study that compared elementary teachers to secondary teachers (Davey, 1988), both groups of teachers reported using textbooks to supplement their instruction, rather than as a basis for content learning. Also, both groups reported that they rarely taught students how to use their textbooks. Compared to secondary teachers, elementary teachers were more flexible in their choices of content-area reading materials and they were more apt to allow students time to read their textbooks in class. Elementary teachers, however, unlike secondary teachers, rarely expected students to exhibit the self-monitoring and self-directing practices necessary for completing assignments independently.

In another study, seventh- and eighth-grade teachers who taught social studies, language arts, science, health, and human development were observed encouraging the use of the textbook in a variety of ways during whole-class discussion (Alvermann, Dillon, O'Brien, & Smith, 1985). Sometimes the text was used by teachers and students to verify a point or settle a dispute that arose during class discussion of a homework assignment. At other times, it was used indirectly as a reminder of something that had been read before or as a means of refocusing attention on the topic at hand. Students were frequently observed using their textbook to help them paraphrase their responses to the teacher's questions.

Limited as it is, the research on the use of textbooks in helping students learn from text has several implications for this chapter. First, it suggests that students will not read their content-area textbooks if teachers fail to expect them to learn from text. Second, the research suggests that teachers rarely spend time teaching students how to use their content-area texts. Third, students may perceive a need to learn from text if teachers regularly involve them in discussions of previously assigned material. Each of these implications is addressed in the procedures section of this chapter.

## RATIONALE

To introduce the notion of bridging the gap between basal reading and content-area reading, it is helpful to compare and contrast two lesson frameworks: the directed reading activity (DRA), which is the common lesson framework for basal instruction, and its counterpart in content-area reading, the instructional framework (Herber, 1978).

Both the DRA and the instructional framework assist teachers in structuring lessons that employ the building of anticipatory sets to prepare students to read. Typically, this includes activating relevant background knowledge, introducing new vocabulary, and setting motivational purposes for reading. In basal reading instruction, building the anticipatory set is a highly structured, teacher-guided activity. In content-area reading instruction, the goal is for teachers to demonstrate prereading strategies and then gradually withhold assistance until students are able to perform the strategies independently.

The core of the DRA, guided silent and oral reading, is similar to the guided reading portion of the instructional framework. In the latter, however, the emphasis is on students learning the content presented in the text, with the building of reading skills a secondary goal. Although content is important to the guided reading portion of the DRA, these lessons are primarily focused on building students' reading skills.

The integration/application sections of both the DRA and the instructional framework also share some similarities in form, though not necessarily in function. In the DRA, the teacher's manual usually offers suggestions for integrating and applying newly learned reading skills in the content areas. Workbook exercises and supplemental work sheets frequently simulate this integration/application phase of instruction. For example, students may be required to write the main idea of several short passages that look like science content but are actually found on the page of a workbook or work sheet. The integration/application phase of the instructional framework is also concerned with helping students make use of what they have learned, but it functions somewhat differently. Here students are expected to use the knowledge they have gained from reading a particular content-area text, rather than complete simulated exercises designed to correlate with a particular reading skill. For example, students may be required to use their knowledge of the properties of oxygen to conduct an experiment independently.

To summarize, the DRA and the instructional framework have many similarities. This is helpful for the elementary classroom teacher, who typically doubles as the reading teacher and the content-area teacher. The teacher can show students that what they are learning, through the use of the DRA in their basals, is relevant to reading in their subject-area textbooks. Despite their similarities, however, the DRA and instructional framework differ in at least one important way: Students are expected to develop much greater independence in all phases of the instructional framework than they are in the directed reading activity. This fact presents challenges that this chapter is designed to address.

## RECOMMENDED PROCEDURES

Moving students along a continuum toward independence in learning from content-area textbooks takes time. This process begins in the primary grades of elementary school and extends through the upper grades. Although much of what students learn in their K–8 basal instruction has application to the content areas, providing the bridge so that this application occurs in practice rather than in theory requires careful attention to the three phases of the instructional framework. Each of the recommended procedures described in this chapter was selected on the basis of its potential for helping teachers attend to one of these phases: (1) preparing students for reading through building an appropriate anticipatory set, (2) guiding students' reading as the content is being presented, and (3) helping students acquire strategies that enable them to integrate and apply what they have learned on their own.

As in all lesson planning, teachers will want to make certain that the procedures they select grow out of the objectives they have set. Setting objectives in content-area reading involves both content and process (see chapter 1 for more detail). In setting these objectives, it is helpful to keep in mind that content should determine process (Herber, 1978). For example, in the "anticipatory-set" procedure that will be described presently, the teacher's content objective was to clarify the misconceptions students had about the word *colonist*.

Consequently, the process objective became one of helping students work through a procedure for attaining an accurate concept of *colonist*—a procedure that students could use with other words at other times.

### Preparing for Reading

Frayer, Fredrick, and Klausmeier (1969) developed a procedure for classifying a concept along several dimensions: its relevant and irrelevant properties, examples and nonexamples of the concept, and its relationship to other concepts. This model of concept attainment provides a means of building an "anticipatory set" prior to having students read from their content-area texts. It can be used to introduce new vocabulary or to clarify misconceptions.

This procedure has particular appeal in terms of teaching social studies content, because social studies textbooks have been found to be lacking in the quality of their definitions and the number of examples they provide (Johnson, 1967).

Without adequate concept development, students will begin to experience difficulty in comprehending their content-area assignments. Teachers who view the problem as being the textbook's fault may opt to ignore the text in favor of providing the information to students through other channels. This, in turn, may suggest to students that the teacher does not expect them to learn from text, with the result that they give up trying. One way out of the dilemma is to use Frayer and colleagues' (1969) model to aid concept attainment within the given instructional framework. An example of how this procedure worked with students at the intermediate level follows.

Mr. Jones discovered that his students were having difficulty with the meaning of the word *colonist*. They tended to lump together everyone who lived in North America in the early part of the seventeenth century and to label them as colonists. The students' textbook did not define the word directly. Instead, its authors left it up to the students to infer the meaning of *colonist* from their definition of *colony*: "A *colony* is a settlement made by people who leave their own country and settle in another land. The colony is ruled by the country from which the settlers came" (Schreiber et al., 1986, p. 108).

Using Frayer and colleagues' (1969) model for concept attainment, Mr. Jones engaged in the following dialogue with his students, before assigning them the next few pages to read in their social studies textbook:

MR. JONES: Your textbook defines *colony* for you. Based on that definition, what would be two things about a colonist that would probably always be true?

BETTY: Someone who leaves one country to settle in another country, and . . . (long pause) then is still under the same ruler as in the homeland.

MR. JONES: Good! What could you probably say about the colonist's language and customs?

BETTY: They would be the same as the person's home country?

MR. JONES: Right again! Okay, you've described three things about a colonist that generally will hold true for all colonists. Now I would like someone to think of two things that might not always be true of all colonists.

RICH: Not all colonists come from England, and . . .

SUZETTE: [interrupting] And not all colonists settle in a new land to find religious freedom. The Dutch settled New York because they wanted to set up trading posts.

MR. JONES: All right. You're doing very well in defining what a colonist is and is not. Rich and Suzette even gave us some examples of colonists in America—the English and the Dutch. Let's see if someone else can give a nonexample of a colonist.

KIM: Pocahontas wasn't a colonist, because she was already living in the country she was born in.

KATIE: Neither was Ponce de León, because he didn't come to America to settle here. He only wanted to explore Florida to find the "Fountain of Youth."

MR. JONES: Excellent! What great thinkers I have as students! Here's a tough question for someone. Put your thinking caps on. What did the English and Dutch colonists, Pocahontas, and Ponce de León all share in common?

SEVERAL VOICES: They're all a part of our history . . . our culture . . . but they're not all colonists.

MR. JONES: Yes, and now you should be ready to read about a very special group of colonists. Like the Pilgrims, they came from England. But the Puritans, as these new colonists were called, were different in several ways. Read the next two pages to find out why there were troubles among these newest colonists to come to America.

When Frayer and colleagues' (1969) model is applied to instruction with a younger group of students, adaptations will need to be made, depending on the maturity of the group. For example, discussing concrete concepts (*ball, globe, store*) generally works better than working on abstract concepts (*sky, war, frontier*). Exploring a concrete concept enables young children to use their five senses in determining its relevant and irrelevant properties, examples and nonexamples of it, and its relationship to other, more familiar concepts.

A mature middle school student, on the other hand, might use the model initially as part of an independent prereading activity during the first phase of the instructional framework, and then use it again during the integration/application phase. At the outset, this student's concept of the term *natural resources* might look like the drawing in Figure 9.1. After reading about natural resources, this same student's drawing might be modified to reflect a greatly expanded awareness of the relationship aspect, as shown in Figure 9.2.

To summarize, Frayer and colleagues' (1969) model of concept attainment is a procedure that enhances bridging the gap between basal reading instruction and reading in the content areas in three

**Figure 9.1**  Examples of Initial Concept of the Term *Natural Resources*

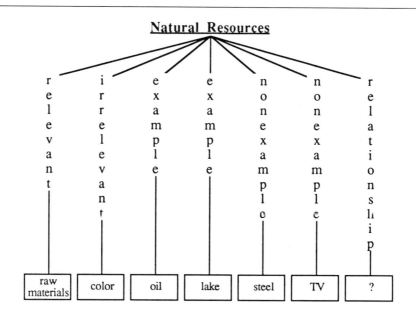

**Figure 9.2** Example of Modified Concept of the Term
*Natural Resources*

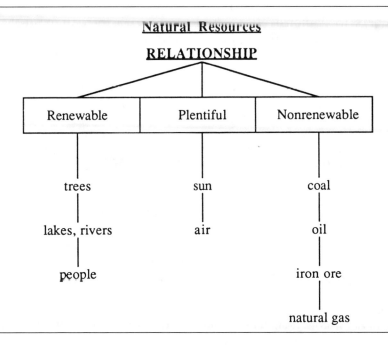

important ways. First, the procedure can be used in one or more of the instructional framework phases, thus providing teachers with an alternative to the instruction, "Open your books to page 13 and read to the end of the chapter." Second, it can be adapted to different ages, with the goal being toward guided independent use of the procedure. Third, it provides a means of structuring poorly written material so that it is comprehensible to students. This feature may be the most important, considering that some of the research shows students rely on their teachers, not their textbooks, when it comes to comprehending subject-matter content.

### Guiding the Reading

K-W-L, an abbreviation that stands for "*K*now, *W*ant to know, *L*earned," is a procedure developed by Ogle (1983) to encourage active reading of expository text. It fits especially well within the guided reading phase of the instructional framework because students who use K-W-L are involved in a continuous cycle of recalling what they know, determining what they want to learn, and identifying what they have learned. Because K-W-L is a procedure that enables teachers to demonstrate to students how their content-area textbooks can be used to acquire new information, it addresses two of the research implications discussed earlier. Students discover that teachers actually do expect them to learn from text, and teachers discover that showing students how to make use of their textbooks pays off.

Following is an example of how K-W-L worked when applied to a section of a science text on electricity. Ms. Berry wanted her group of sixth-grade students to read five pages from their science text, in preparation for an experiment they would conduct in class the next day. The topic was electric current, and the students were going to use a dry-cell battery to demonstrate how current moves in a circuit.

First, Ms. Berry involved her students in a brief brainstorming activity designed to activate their prior knowledge about electricity in general. After three or four minutes, students began to list on individual work sheets what they felt they knew about electricity. This information was recorded in the left-hand column as indicated in the example provided in Figure 9.3. Note that this particular student's knowledge consisted of information that could be categorized as real-world knowledge (i.e., based on fact) and folk knowledge (i.e., based partly or entirely on hearsay).

Second, students predicted categories of information they expected to find in their textbook. To help them with this process, Ms. Berry modeled how she would skim the text to predict the anticipated categories. Then, students used the categories they generated to develop some questions they wanted answered. The student in the example listed *electrical matter, charges, resistance,* and *voltage* in the bottom left-hand corner of her work sheet. Note, however, that the questions she generated in the middle column of the work sheet were a combination of what she wanted to know based on her prior knowledge of electricity and on her anticipation of what the text would present on the topic.

Third, students read their texts, guided by the questions they wanted to have answered. Setting their own purposes for reading was a powerful motivator. Although students were responsible for monitoring their own comprehension, Ms. Berry was available to help those who had difficulty locating answers to their questions. Sometimes difficulties arose because students did not take the time to list the answers to the questions as they found them in the text. Students

**Figure 9.3** Example of a K-W-L Work Sheet

| K (Know) | W (Want to know) | L (Learned) |
|---|---|---|
| Electricity lights our house.<br><br>Electricity can kill you.<br><br>Lightning is caused by electricity.<br><br>Lightning never strikes twice in the same place.<br><br>My hair has electric sparks in it.<br><br><br><br>electrical matter<br>charges<br>resistance<br>voltage | What causes lightning?<br>Are sparks the same as charges?<br>What is electrical matter?<br>What does resistance have to do with light bulbs?<br>How does the ~~battery~~ voltage help make electricity?<br>* How do charges move? | Atoms have electric charges that move.<br><br>Lightning hit one building 8 times.<br><br>Charges jump from one thing to another.<br><br>Lightning is a big spark.<br><br>When charges jump they make sparks.<br><br>The wire in a light bulb glows because it resists the charges moving through it<br><br>Voltage means the push a battery gives to charged atoms. |

discovered that reading to acquire new information from content-area textbooks is often a slow and tedious process. They also discovered, however, the satisfaction that comes with knowing how to apply a newly learned strategy to a particular piece of text in order to answer their own questions.

Note that in the sample work sheet (Figure 9.3) the student has answered not only her original set of questions but an additional question as well. The additional question, marked with an asterisk, arose while she was reading to find answers to her other questions.

Although K-W-L typically concludes with a discussion of what students have learned while reading, for purposes of this chapter the discussion will be delayed and incorporated later as the third recommended procedure.

Depending on the maturity of the group, K-W-L should be adapted so that students are introduced to the procedure in a nonthreatening way. For example, a second-grade teacher might want to turn K-W-L into a guided listening procedure rather than a guided reading procedure, at least for the first few times it is used. To do this, steps one and two would remain the same, except that, rather than having students complete individual work sheets, the teacher might use an overhead projector and transparency to list what the students know and the questions they want answered. The third step, the guided reading portion of K-W-L, would consist of having students listen for answers to their questions as the teacher reads. The teacher would then write the answers on the overhead transparency, and a class discussion would follow in which students might resolve any unanswered questions or unclear answers. By gradually shifting the responsibility to individual students for recalling what is known, what is left to be answered, and what has been learned, this second-grade teacher would be helping students to move along the continuum toward independence in content-area reading.

To summarize, K-W-L helps teachers bridge the gap between basal reading instruction and content-area reading by providing students with a simple but effective way for activating prior knowledge (the know step), setting purposes for reading (the want-to-know step), and guiding comprehension (the learn step). Too frequently students are left with the notion that they don't have to depend on their textbooks to learn content because their teacher will tell them what they need to know. K-W-L turns that kind of thinking around by making it possible for students to take increasing responsibility for their own learning. As a three-step procedure, K-W-L fits nicely within the instructional framework.

We now turn to the last step of K-W-L, which incorporates a postreading discussion of what was learned and corresponds to the integration/application phase of the instructional framework.

## Integrating and Applying What Has Been Learned

Gall and Gall (1976) have classified discussions according to specific instructional objectives. For example, if the objective for holding a class discussion is to facilitate students' abilities to integrate and apply what they have learned from reading their content-area texts, then Gall and Gall would classify that discussion as being a subject mastery discussion. Although one might argue that a discussion by any other name is still a discussion, the point to be made here is that discussions do vary according to the purpose for which they are intended.

Subject mastery discussions are characteristically grounded in the textbook; as such, they provide students with a forum for identifying important concepts, clarifying misconceptions, and interacting with their peers. Encouraging students to read widely and on related topics in other forms of print (e.g., trade books, news magazines, original documents) is one way of enriching subject mastery discussions (Alvermann, Dillon, & O'Brien, 1987). Another way is to show segments of a related filmstrip or videotape. Ms. Berry chose to do the latter for her students' postreading discussion of the five-page assignment on electric current. A portion of that discussion follows.

| | |
|---|---|
| MS. BERRY: | Each of you has a completed K-W-L work sheet on electricity. Let's talk about some of the things that you learned from reading your science textbook. |
| JENNIFER: | Lightning is a dangerous form of electricity. |
| ADAM: | When the electrons get too crowded on one cloud, they move to another cloud or come down to the ground. |
| MS. BERRY: | Yes, both of you found out some interesting facts about lightning. Anything else? |
| LUANN: | Lightning *can* strike the same place twice. It hit one building in New York City eight times! |
| KENNY: | Yeah! I always heard lightning never strikes the same place two times in a row. |
| SUE: | Me, too. But it said in the book the Empire State Building was hit eight times in twenty-four minutes! |
| MS. BERRY: | Okay, we need to move on to some more things that you learned. Yes, Douglas? |
| DOUGLAS: | I found out that the electrons and protons in atoms have an electric charge. |
| KIM: | The proton has a negative charge, and . . . |
| DOUGLAS: | [interrupting] No, the electrons have the negative charges. |
| KIM: | Oh, that's right. |
| MS. BERRY: | How can we help Kim keep them straight? |
| SANDY: | I remember that the electrons have negative charges because they often leave one atom to go to another—I think of them leaving because they are feeling "negative" about something. |

MS. BERRY:   Okay, Sandy has made up a little story to help herself remember.

LUANN:   I thought atoms have electric charges that move, and that's why I don't see how you can ever have any negatively charged atoms like it says in the book. They'd be all gone.

MS. BERRY:   You've raised a good question. Let's see if we can find an answer after we look at this short segment of a videotape that I picked up from the school media center. [The videotape shows what happens to a neutral atom when it loses some of its electrons. Using computer-generated graphics, the videotape next shows how the once-neutral atom becomes positively charged, that is, how it gets more protons than electrons.]

MS. BERRY:   [stopping the videotape momentarily] What do you think would have to happen to make that positively charged atom become negatively charged?

LUANN:   It would have to gain more electrons so that the number of electrons would be more than the number of protons.

MS. BERRY:   You're absolutely right. Now do you see why there can be negatively, as well as positively, charged atoms?

LUANN:   Yeah. That's easy now.

Capitalizing on the technical capabilities at hand, Ms. Berry was able to help LuAnn (and no doubt others in the class) understand the difficult concepts associated with electrical matter. Through discussion, students were able to clarify and summarize what they had learned from reading their science textbook. Although Ms. Berry took an active role in directing the discussion, she did not dominate it. Students were free to comment on other students' responses, and, as LuAnn demonstrated, she felt free to express doubt about something she had read when it did not make sense to her.

To review briefly, using discussion to help students integrate and apply what they have learned from reading their content-area textbooks is one sure way for a teacher to demonstrate that textbooks are a major source of information and that there is an expectation that students will learn from their texts. Because discussion is a natural part of the directed reading activity, it makes creating a bridge between basal reading instruction and content-area reading much easier. Students always do better when they are accustomed to a procedure. Finally, discussions fit nicely within the last phase of the instructional framework and the last step of the K-W-L procedure.

## SUMMARY

Preparing students to read effectively in the content areas is the responsibility of teachers at all levels. Creating a bridge from basal reading instruction to content-area reading is one way to assure that this responsibility is taken seriously and that the goal of helping students learn from content-area textbooks is achieved. Although research on the use of textbooks in content-area reading is limited, the evidence that does exist suggests that students will not read their textbooks if teachers do not expect them to learn from text and/or do not show them how to use their texts efficiently. Three procedures for helping students become increasingly independent in completing their content-area reading assignments have been described, procedures that fit well within the instructional framework. These are Frayer and colleagues' (1969) model for concept attainment, the K-W-L procedure for guiding the presentation of content, and subject mastery discussions for aiding the integration and application of that which has been read.

## REFERENCES

Alvermann, D. E., Dillon, D. R., & O'Brien, D. G. (1987). *Using discussion to promote reading comprehension.* Newark, DE: International Reading Association.

Alvermann, D. E., Dillon, D. R., O'Brien, D. G., & Smith, L. C. (1985). The role of the textbook in discussion. *Journal of Reading, 29,* 50–57.

Davey, B. (1988). How do classroom teachers use their textbooks? *Journal of Reading, 31,* 340–345.

Frayer, D. A., Fredrick, W. C., & Klausmeier, H. J. (1969). A schema for testing the level of concept mastery. *Working paper from the Wisconsin Research and Development Center for cognitive learning* (No. 16). Madison, WI: University of Wisconsin.

Gall, M. D., & Gall, J. P. (1976). The discussion method. In N. L. Gage (Ed.), *Psychology of teaching methods* (*National Society for the Study of Education, Seventy-fifth Yearbook*) (pp. 166–216). Chicago: University of Chicago Press.

Herber, H. L. (1978). *Teaching reading in content areas* (2nd ed.). Englewood Cliffs, NJ: Prentice-Hall.

Johnson, R. M. (1967). *A critical analysis of the treatment given representative social science ideas in leading fifth and eighth grade American history textbooks*. Unpublished doctoral dissertation, Northwestern University, Evanston, IL.

Ogle, D. (1983). K-W-L: A teaching model that develops active reading of expository text. *The Reading Teacher, 39*, 564–570.

Ratekin, N., Simpson, M. L., Alvermann, D. E., & Dishner, E. K. (1985). Why teachers resist content reading instruction. *Journal of Reading, 28*, 432–437.

Rieck, B. J. (1977). How content teachers telegraph messages against reading. *Journal of Reading, 20*, 646–648.

Schreiber, J., Stepien, W., Patrick, J., Remy, R., Gay, G., & Hoffman, A. J. (1986). *America past and present*. Glenview, IL: Scott, Foresman.

Smith, F. R., & Feathers, K. M. (1983). Teacher and student perceptions of content area reading. *Journal of Reading, 26*, 348–354.

# Summary:
# *Improving Basal Reading Programs*

JEAN H. OSBORN

To write a summary of this book is not a simple matter. Each of the book's chapters is about an important aspect of a classroom reading program. The chapters are written by authors who are well grounded in contemporary research about reading, and who, in addition, are researchers in their own right. What's more, these authors are reading researchers with their feet in the real world of classrooms, teachers, and students. They have presented us with a full plate (or, perhaps more accurately, nine full plates) of ideas, information, and instructions that have promise of leading to the improvement of reading instruction in elementary and middle school classrooms. One of the challenges to the readers of this book will be to relate its content to the real world of their own classrooms.

The title, *Improving Basal Reading Instruction*, does not completely convey the full range of the book's message. It is true that the readers of the book will learn ways of expanding upon, adapting, modifying, individualizing, and sometimes even personalizing the content of the teacher's guides and student materials of a basal reading program. In addition, they will read about reading activities that are independent of the content of these programs. Most important, however, they will become aware of the theme that emerges from each chapter—and therefore becomes the thesis of the book. It is first stated in the beginning sentence of Winograd's introduction. His thesis is that "basal reading programs are most effective when they are used flexibly and as part of a comprehensive, balanced program of reading instruction." Furthermore, Winograd asserts that basal reading programs are least effective when they are used as the total reading program and children spend all of their allocated instructional time in reading selections and completing the various exercises of the program.

Winograd proposes that a comprehensive, balanced program of reading instruction must contain more than the selections and exercises of a basal reading program. He supports this proposition by reviewing what modern research about reading has revealed about the reading process and about the effects of a reader's purpose on comprehension. He also describes the importance to comprehension of the personal knowledge a reader brings to a text and some of the strategies successful readers possess. He then describes how this improved understanding of the process of reading has affected ideas about reading instruction. Many of these ideas are illustrated in the chapters that follow his, and suggestions and procedures are given for their incorporation into classroom reading programs.

Each one of the chapters examines important aspects of a "comprehensive, balanced program of reading instruction." Karen Wixson and Charles Peters (chapter 1) discuss how teachers can evaluate and modify lessons to fit their students better. Mary Shake (chapter 2) discusses two very practical topics—grouping and pacing—and offers practical advice, based on several decades of research, about how to organize students for instruction and orchestrate that instruction so that students will make optimal progress in learning to read. Judith Scheu, Diane Tanner, and Kathryn Au, in chapter 3, describe the development of workbook activities that integrate seatwork with reading instruction, rather than isolating it. Thus, children benefit fully from the time they spend working independently. Marjorie Lipson and Karen Wixson (chapter 4) review a number of important aspects of student evaluation and describe how teachers can improve this crucial aspect of reading instruction. In chapter 5, Marjorie Lipson describes many practical and useful ways of individualizing instruction and thereby making it more appropriate to the needs of all students.

Connie Bridge (chapter 6) focuses her attention on ways that teachers can extend basal reader instruction and create a literate environment in which young children will find the incentive and assistance they need to develop into fluent and motivated readers. In chapter 7, Lesley Morrow points up the importance of the availability of literature (both read to and read by students) to the development of reading skills and interest in reading. Next, in their chapter, Taffy Raphael and Carol Sue Englert underscore the idea that writing and reading can easily be integrated and point out the need for teachers to have knowledge of the processes of reading and writing, as well as knowledge of ways in which instruction in the processes can be merged. Finally, Donna Alvermann (chapter 9) offers many suggestions that will aid teachers in helping students to transfer the skills and strategies they are learning in their basal readers to the textbooks and trade books in the content areas.

## IMPLEMENTING THE RECOMMENDATIONS: THE TIME FACTOR

The recommendations for practice that fairly tumble out of these pages are not only well grounded in research, they are practical as well. But teachers and administrators should take warning: Although the recommendations are practical, the translation of any group of them into action will involve a good amount of time. Like many other of life's precious commodities, the concept of *time* has many facets of meaning. In this case, time will be needed to study each chapter seriously. Those readers who do so will probably determine they want to introduce some of the book's recommendations into their own reading programs. So, one time-consuming step will be to identify which of the recommendations are important and most applicable to one's own situation, whether it be a classroom, a school, or an entire district. Getting good ideas translated into action, as everyone knows, takes lots of planning and lots of work—which, of course, take lots of time. For every specific idea, procedure, or technique selected, time will have to be spent figuring out just how to adapt these changes for use in existing instructional programs. More time will have to be spent determining how the changes can be smoothly integrated into these programs. And of course, classroom time will have to be allocated to each of the ideas, procedures, or techniques used. Finally, additional planning time will have to be spent devising procedures for evaluating the impact, on classroom practice and student achievement, of the recommendations that are being implemented.

Many of the recommendations in these chapters are worthy of extended inservice programs. Administrators and teachers may well want to organize workshops for planning how to put into action the recommendations they want to implement. For example, teachers interested in adapting the Framework for Evaluation described in the Lipson and Wixson chapter will need opportunities to discuss and try out the many procedures described in the chapter, as well as time to prepare and share the record-keeping forms and other materials needed for some of the procedures. And, as the teachers start working with the framework, they should be given opportunities to discuss and evaluate their efforts.

Although putting any of these recommendations into action will involve the expenditure of time—for thinking, planning, practicing, implementing, and evaluating—there is a more than reasonable chance that the return on such an effort will be significant improvements in the reading programs of classrooms, schools, and school districts. Why do the recommendations in these chapters warrant the expenditure of time and the anticipation of success? In part it is because they emanate from some of the most compelling research of the past fifteen years, and because they have been successfully used in classrooms by a number of teachers in a number of different schools.

## AUTHENTIC VERSUS CONTRIVED
## READING ENVIRONMENTS

A major theme of this book is that the expansion and adaptation of basal reading programs is essential to the successful teaching of reading. Another closely associated theme has to do with the relevance or "authenticity" of the classroom reading environment, and of the reading materials within that environment. In the introduction, Winograd cites studies that indicate that students spend a great deal of time doing work sheets and skill sheets and reading texts that have been written to conform to readability formulas or "manufactured to provide exercises in specific skills." He describes this kind of reading as *contrived*. In contrast, *authentic* texts would include trade books, magazines, reference books, posters, letters, and newspapers. Authentic purposes for reading would include reading—and often writing—for pleasure, discussion, information, and sharing.

The theme of authenticity becomes apparent when the nature of many of the recommendations in this volume is considered. The authors, as well as a number of other researchers and practitioners concerned with reading instruction (Goodman, Freeman, Murphy, & Shannon, 1987; Roehler & Duffy, 1984; Shannon, 1983), are worried about the contrived situations that are so typical of basal instruction, as well as the contrived tests (described by Winograd as "ends") that have been devised for evaluating the effectiveness of instruction. They are equally concerned with the contrived materials that have been developed for children to read in their student readers and to practice in their student workbooks. Teachers are advised to organize additional reading opportunities so that students spend time reading authentic texts for authentic purposes and do so in instructional situations that are less contrived—and also less competitive. Also advocated are assessment procedures that more adequately reflect and measure the real processes of reading, rather than a student's ability to read isolated paragraphs and respond to multiple-choice questions.

Basal reading programs seem, almost by definition, to be more contrived than authentic. They consist of graded and sequenced instructional plans for teachers and graded and sequenced textbooks and other practice materials for students. They also include a number of other supplemental products, for example, ditto masters for additional seatwork, audiovisual tapes and filmstrips, word drill cards, and supplementary readings, as well as management systems and testing programs. All of these materials have been contrived; that is, they have been developed as instructional plans and practice materials for teachers and students to use in classroom reading programs.

## EXAMINING THE RATIONALE FOR BASAL PROGRAMS

The demands for a less contrived and more authentic reading environment can, without much trouble, bring to mind a somewhat burning question: Do we really need basal reading programs? This question is somewhat inflammatory because it threatens both habit and tradition. Most children in American schools are taught to read by teachers who use basal reading programs, and, what's more, most teachers in American schools learned to read in classrooms in which basal reading materials were an important part of the reading program. Basal reading programs have been extensively used in American classrooms since the 1920s, which is when, according to one analysis of their history (Goodman et al., 1987), the directions to teachers were first compiled into separate teacher's manuals. Before that, graded student materials, such as the McGuffey readers, were used extensively in the classrooms of American public schools.

The estimates of how many of the American elementary schools of the late twentieth century use basal reading programs as the core of their reading instruction vary (Fisher et al., 1978; Mason & Osborn, 1982; Shannon, 1983), but it is probably safe to say that sets of one or more basal reading programs are found in essentially every elementary school in the United States. It is also probably safe to say that in some of these schools the content and materials of basal reading programs are the entire reading program.

How extensively and with what fidelity these programs are followed is a topic that will presently be discussed in more detail; however, a rough estimate taken from classroom studies is that the materials provided by basal reading programs account for from 75 to 90 percent of the time spent during the periods allocated to reading instruction in elementary schools.

## What Do Programs Offer?

What do basal reading programs offer school districts, teachers, and students? One of the most evident features of basal reading programs is their capacity to serve as an organizing framework for reading instruction. Such a framework can unify reading instruction in a single classroom, as well as from grade to grade within a school. When an entire school district adopts a single basal reading program, the program can also contribute to unifying the reading instruction in that district.

An almost equally evident feature of basal reading programs is their convenience. As mentioned earlier, one of the most precious commodities in the life of a teacher is time. The student textbooks, workbooks, skill sheets, wall charts, and other ancillary materials of a basal reading program provide classroom teachers with an organized and sequenced set of materials to use with their students. Such a set of materials would take most teachers an enormous amount of time to prepare and also require that they have access to a number of resources.

Another evident feature of basal reading programs is the coordination of their student materials with the instructions for their use in the teacher's manuals. The organized lessons of the teacher's manuals are a central feature of all basal reading programs. It is this feature, however, that is the cause of some concern. This concern has to do with what lots of people believe should be happening somewhere else, that is, in the teachers' heads. All basal reading programs are accompanied by teacher's manuals. These very thick manuals provide teachers with advice, usually accompanied by very specific lesson plans as well as some very detailed steps for the teachers and students to follow.

## Why Are They Used, and How Much?

In recent years a number of researchers and practitioners have taken up worrying about why teachers follow the advice in teacher's manuals instead of following their own instincts and creating their own plans. Why do teachers continue to do this, even in the face of a growing number of researchers and practitioners who are so visibly and audibly (in print and also at national and regional meetings of reading organizations) worried about their doing so? A number of explanations are offered by researchers who have spent time observing in classrooms.

Several studies indicate that teachers follow the sequence of suggested teaching in basal reading programs because they are required to do so by the administrators of their schools or districts (Duffy, Roehler, & Wesselman, 1985; Shannon, 1983). Other studies (Shannon, 1983, 1987) found that both teachers and administrators believe that the programs are written by experts and thus are better than what teachers alone could produce. In fact, Shannon (1987) observed that teachers "treat the directives in teacher's manuals as the science of reading instruction" (p. 314) and expressed concern that this type of thinking moves the focus of reading instruction away from a human undertaking and toward a scientific undertaking.

How extensively and precisely do teachers and students actually use these materials? Several classroom observation studies indicate that teachers follow rather closely both the intent and the content of basal reading programs. Duffy and McIntyre (1982) found that teachers relied heavily on commercial reading materials (especially the teacher's manuals) for planning and conducting reading instruction. They observed that typical teaching routines consisted of asking the questions provided in the teacher's guides, eliciting answers from students, and assigning workbook pages. Establishing background, purpose-setting, and other forms of assistance was often omitted. These researchers concluded that teachers were task monitors and managers, rather than active decision makers and instructors.

Duffy, Roehler, and Putnam (1987) observed that, regardless of the grade level, "many teachers of reading simply follow instructional materials and make few decisions about what to teach or how to teach it" (p. 359). These observers pointed out that teachers' reliance on basal reading programs has a lot to do with the time constraints of the classroom and the difficulty of designing effective instructional materials and making effective instructional decisions.

We suggest, however, that time constraints result in teachers using what is readily available rather than designing their own instructional programs. Experienced teachers point to the enormous amounts of time needed to create even simple work sheets and games, let alone to develop materials for a complete reading program. The teaching of reading is a complex undertaking, one that requires the balancing of many factors. The organized, sequenced lessons of basal reading programs are available to help teachers "put it all together," and, as a matter of fact, there is a lot to put together. Both the authors and the readers of this book would certainly have no trouble agreeing that teachers are being continuously urged to put *lots* of things together when they teach reading. Students must, for example, learn to decode fluently, develop useful comprehension strategies; find the main ideas; acquire large vocabularies; catch on to structural analysis, syllabication, and punctuation skills; appreciate quality literature; read expository prose with understanding; develop thinking skills; write frequently; and practice listening.

### How Are Programs Developed?

How do the publishers of basal reading programs go about putting all of these aspects of reading instruction into an organized and logical sequence? In most publishing houses, basal reading programs are developed rather than written; that is, no single author writes and then organizes the quantities of directions in the teacher's guides and the exercises in the practice materials. Rather, these materials are written and organized by teams of in-house editors and writers, as well as the editors and writers of the companies the publishing houses contract with to do much of their developmental work. Authors most often work in an advisory capacity with these teams of editors and writers, with the resulting student textbooks being anthologies of fictional and expository selections. Some of these selections are written especially for a particular program, but frequently selections are chosen from well-known children's stories and books. Often these selections are abridged and rewritten to conform to the space and readability requirements of a specific grade level.

A great deal of effort, time, and money is devoted to the development of a basal reading program. The preparation of a new edition in the late 1980s probably cost its publisher in excess of $30 million, and its staff probably devoted at least five years of intensive work to the project.

## Research About Basal Reading Programs

How effective are basal reading programs? What do the researchers say about their quality? Interestingly enough, despite their heavy use, it is only during the past decade that researchers have begun to analyze the content of the various components of basal reading programs. The work of a number of different people who have looked at, analyzed, and written about the student textbooks, teacher's manuals, and workbooks associated with basal reading programs will be reviewed in this section.

What are the characteristics of the basal textbooks that students use as they learn to read? If basal reading programs are considered preparation for reading authentic texts, then how well do the books in these programs prepare students to read authentic short stories, novels, expository articles, reference books, content-area textbooks, directions, and instructions? In a study comparing characteristics of basal textbooks stories with those of trade books stories, Bruce (1984) found a number of differences and concluded that publishers of basal programs should expand the range of story types they include in their student textbooks. Barring this, teachers should be made aware that children reading from basal textbooks are not exposed to many of the story types they will encounter in authentic materials; thus, teachers should supplement the textbooks with trade books. Another investigation (Liebling, 1986) found basal textbook narratives lacking in "interior voice" and recommended more use of trade books in classrooms. These observations are certainly consistent with the recommendations of Lesley Morrow in chapter 7.

Investigations into the quality of stories in basal reading programs have been carried out for a number of years, but there has not been as much investigation of the expository writing in these programs. An exception is the work of one group of researchers (Beck, McKeown, & Gromoll, 1986), who examined the expository selections in four basal reading programs. They looked at the content of the selections, the amount of prerequisite knowledge they implied, and their structural aspects. In this latter category, they were particularly concerned with the coherence of the selections. They defined coherence as "the extent to which the sequence of ideas in a text makes sense and the extent to which the language used in discussing those ideas makes the nature of the ideas and their relationships apparent. In other words, a coherent text all fits together, seems of a whole" (p. 22). They found that, "more often than not, selections lacked coherence" (p. 42). They also found that many of the selections covered content that was likely to be difficult for many students, in part because they assumed prerequisite knowledge the students were not likely to possess.

One examination of the expository prose in content-area textbooks provides a basis for concern about the quality of the expository prose in basal readers. An analysis of the text structure, text coherence, text unity, and audience appropriateness in social studies and science texts revealed many examples of unclear writing (Anderson, Armbruster, & Kantor, 1980). The researchers pointed out that the effect of such writing on how much content-area knowledge students acquire in the early elementary grades may, in fact, *not* be very great, because many teachers do not use these textbooks as the primary learning source. In the intermediate grades, however, they suggested that unclear texts may have a significantly negative effect on how students learn *how to comprehend* information from content-area texts. A more recent study about how the quality of writing in student textbooks affects student comprehension found that textbooks rewritten by skilled journalists to be "interesting" were not only more enjoyable to read but were also easier to learn from (Graves & Slater, 1986).

One of the problems writers and editors encounter when they try to increase the appeal of stories and informational articles has to do with text difficulty. The difficulty of the stories and articles in basal reading programs is typically measured by standard readability formulas. These are measures of sentence length, word length, and the degree of familiarity of vocabulary. Everybody—teachers, adoption committee members, writers, and editors—can assess the difficulty of textbooks by using one or more of these formulas. How the comprehensibility of text is affected when these formulas are used as a basis for either writing or rewriting stories and articles is the topic of several important studies conducted during the past decade. In one study (Davison, 1984), original texts from magazines and books were compared with the same texts rewritten to be less difficult and to achieve an appropriate readability score at a given grade level. The linguists conducting this study found that the rewritten texts that were supposed to be easier were frequently more difficult to comprehend than the original texts, which had longer sentences and more difficult words. They pointed out that, although rewritten texts frequently lower vocabulary demands and sentence length, the resulting simplifications are sometimes made at the expense of important contextual and factual information.

For example, when longer sentences are made into shorter sentences, connecting words or phrases are frequently dropped. Thus the sentence, "The boy went to the store because his mother needed some flour" can become, "The boy went to the store. His mother needed some flour." Dropping the connecting word *because* requires the reader to infer why the boy went to the store.

The practice of substituting "easy" words for "hard" words can lengthen sentences considerably as well as add subordinate clauses to them. For example, if *mansion* is deemed too infrequent a word for the desired readability of a selection, the phrase "very big house where very rich people live" certainly would add to the length of any sentence in which *mansion* would be used. The evidence presented by Davison (1984) strongly suggests that making changes in text solely on the basis of potential readability scores can have harmful effects on its comprehensibility.

Studies about varying aspects of the student textbooks in basal reading programs are fairly numerous. Only one researcher, however, has done a significant examination of the teacher's manuals associated with basal reading programs (Durkin, 1984). In her analysis of comprehension instruction in five basal reading programs, she organized the suggestions to teachers she found in the manuals into four categories: instruction, review, application, and practice. She recorded the number of suggestions in each category and gave examples of their quality. She found, for example, that when manuals specified comprehension instruction, the instructions were often vague. In addition, she found that the manuals offered precise help (for example, obvious answers to assessment questions) when it was least needed, but that they were "obscure to silent" when specific help was likely to be required (p. 31). Regarding review, her observations were that "the frequency with which information or a skill is reviewed appears to have no connection with difficulty or importance for reading. Instead, the amount of review in all the series seemed more like the product of random behavior than of a pre-established plan" (p. 35). Her findings about application and practice were equally grave.

Student workbooks have also been analyzed. The quality of workbooks becomes a matter of importance when it is realized how much they are utilized in classrooms. Several classroom observation studies have revealed that students spend up to 70 percent of the time allocated for reading instruction working in workbooks and other practice materials (Anderson, 1984; Mason & Osborn, 1981).

In an analysis I did of workbooks associated with basal reading programs, I commented on many aspects of workbook tasks, including the relationship of workbook tasks to the rest of the program, vocabulary and concept level, instructional design, amount of practice, student response modes, number of task types, art, layout, quality of content, and clarity of instructions (Osborn, 1984). I found that workbook tasks in some programs had little or nothing to do with the rest of the program; that instructions were often unclear, obscure, or unnecessarily lengthy; that the vocabulary of the workbooks was sometimes more complex than that of the rest of the program; and that the art and page layouts were often confusing. In addition, I found that, although many tasks had little to do with reading or writing, some of the most important tasks occurred only once or twice in an entire workbook. Although I found many examples of well-constructed tasks, I concluded that "workbooks are the for gotten children of basal programs" (p. 55) and urged publishers and teachers to attend to the problems inherent in these practice materials.

### Publishers' Response to Criticism

It should be noted that the publishers of most basal reading programs—and their editors and authors—pay a great deal of attention to research about reading. They attend meetings, read the journals, and frequently consult with (and sometimes work with) people engaged in research about reading. For example, administrative officers and editors of essentially every major educational publishing company involved with the development of reading programs have attended the meetings the Center for the Study of Reading has organized for publishers. Three meetings of several days' duration have been held during the past eight years. The goal of these meetings has been to communicate to the publishers of these programs the findings of research with relevance for reading programs. I took part in each of these meetings and will report that the response of the publishers was cautious but positive. I believe the caution comes from wanting to produce programs that reflect what is known about reading instruction and that are, at the same time, perceived by their customers as useful and relevant to their needs.

During the next decade a number of new basal reading programs and major new versions of the established programs will be available. Will the programs of the last decade of the twentieth century reflect some of the new knowledge about the process of reading? How will these programs deal with issues of prior knowledge and purpose for reading? Will they be more authentic and less contrived? We suspect they will, but we urge the teachers and administrators who examine these programs to be cognizant of what to look for and to be knowledgeable judges of the potential effectiveness of what they see.

## SOME ANSWERS TO THE QUESTION

Earlier in this chapter, I asked the question, Do we really need basal reading programs? The discussions that followed included information about how basal reading programs are used in classroom reading instruction, what they offer teachers and students, and how they are developed. I also reviewed some of the analyses that have been made of student textbooks, teacher's manuals, and workbooks and described how publishers have responded to their critics.

These discussions were intended to point up the difficulty of providing an easy answer to our question. Our information, in brief, says that basal reading programs are used, they are the products of teams of people who expend both time and money on their development, they are not perfect, and they are subject to change. But the question remains.

Are there alternatives to basal reading instruction? Certainly they do exist, and they include teacher-, school-, and district-developed plans and materials that do not include basal reading programs. We suggest that teachers and administrators embarking on any such effort allocate an enormous amount of time and effort to it. Some—but certainly not all—of the issues that would have to be dealt with include the following: how teachers will work (both in and out of their classrooms) to formulate and expedite the new plan, how student reading materials will be selected and purchased, how teachers unpracticed in the plan will be trained and provided with classroom help, how the implementation of the plan will be monitored, and how student achievement will be evaluated. Furthermore, we suggest that this alternative should not be undertaken unless a careful analysis is made of the present role basal reading programs hold in the reading curriculum of a district.

Although the researchers who have studied how basal programs are used in classrooms offer a number of explanations for their heavy use (as discussed earlier), one explanation remains to be mentioned. It has to do with the communication of information. It is obvious that the student materials and teacher's manuals of basal reading programs are convenient to use. What is perhaps less obvious is that these programs communicate information about reading instruction to teachers and that, in doing so, they shore up some fairly inconsistent and often inadequate educational structures found in pre-service and inservice training programs. Common complaints about pre-service teacher training at colleges and universities and inservice education in school districts include their insufficiency, their lack of specificity, and their failure to focus on the real problems of instruction and learning.

Basal reading programs are attempts to communicate a large amount of specific information about the teaching of reading to teachers; in fact, the teacher's manuals of these programs can be viewed as daily, applied inservice training for teachers. We suggest that how much the manuals are relied upon is a function of the kind of pre-service training new teachers have had and the amount and quality of inservice training available to both new and experienced teachers in a district. This view of basal reading programs as conveyors of information about reading instruction contrasts, but does not necessarily conflict, with some of the explanations proposed about their use in the research reports described earlier. We believe this view is worth considering when attempting to answer the question, Do we really need basal reading programs?

I also propose another view of the role of basal reading programs, and that is their potential for practicality and for being up-to-date. If it is agreed that there is a great deal to "put together" when planning a reading program, and if it is also agreed that the research of the past decade has implications for reading instruction, then it seems reasonable to expect that a basal reading program that organizes the many elements of reading instruction and utilizes the implications of research for reading instruction could be of practical use. Such programs could be of use to administrators as they plan flexible and comprehensive reading programs and to teachers as they go through the daily tasks of conducting reading instruction.

A final caution must be added to this discussion of practicality and being up-to-date. It has to do with the necessity for "reinventing the wheel." Ideas for good instruction developed by specialists can be communicated in writing as well as "invented" by individual teachers. In a number of occupations, busy professionals responsible for dealing with difficult and complex tasks often look to other, more specialized professionals for help, so that these busy professionals have more time to deal with the complexities of their own jobs. The demands upon the time and energy of teachers are well known. When the instructional ideas in teacher's manuals and the content of the student materials are useful and effective, they can be considered professional help. As professionals, teachers can take advantage of this help—and then modify it, expand upon it, and individualize it—to meet the demands of the situation in which they are working.

My answer to the question, Do we need basal reading programs? is yes, but it is not a simple yes. Rather, it is a yes that is very consistent with the thesis of this book: Basal reading programs should be used flexibly and as part of a balanced program of reading instruction. I propose that the effectiveness of a balanced program of reading instruction will depend not only upon the appropriateness and effectiveness of all of its elements, but also upon the quality of the basal reading program being used. How to evaluate basal reading programs better is therefore the topic of the next section of this chapter.

## EVALUATING BASAL READING PROGRAMS

If it is determined that basal reading programs are important to a comprehensive, balanced program of reading instruction in a district, the next question is some variation of, How can teachers and administrators determine the special features and overall quality of basal reading programs so as to select the program or programs that will best meet the needs of the students in their school district? Or, more succinctly, What about textbook adoption?

The heart of any textbook adoption process is what the members of the adoption committee do, particularly how they go about examining the programs they are considering. This process has been analyzed in recent years and rather severely criticized by several researchers (Dole, Rogers, & Osborn, 1987; Farr, Tulley, & Powell, 1987a,b; Powell, 1986). The consensus is that textbook adoption is an overwhelming task that frequently leads to a superficial assessment of the basal reading programs being examined.

Dole and I, as two researchers who have spent several years working with committees who wanted to improve their adoption process, have observed that, although the procedures, membership, and policies of adoption committees differ, most committees have a similar mandate: to choose the programs that will be used in the classrooms of their districts (Dole & Osborn, in Wepner, Feeley, & Strickland, in press). We also have noted that, to accomplish this task, adoption committees use some variation of the following steps:

1. The leader and other committee members gather reports of information about reading research.

2. They arrange (usually with publishers' representatives) to hear presentations about programs and to obtain examination copies.
3. They meet to establish criteria.
4. They examine and evaluate programs.
5. They select the programs that best match their criteria.

We (Dole & Osborn, in press) offer some ideas, derived from working with several groups, for adoption committees to consider as they follow these steps. For example, we have found that members of committees often want to update their own knowledge before they begin to evaluate new programs. They do so in a variety of ways, such as (1) small groups of committee members are assigned to report on research on given topics; (2) local reading experts, such as reading coordinators and reading teachers particularly interested in research, are invited to report on research about topics of particular interest to the committee; or (3) consultants from outside the school district present research reports to the committee.

We have also found that the criteria that committee members develop determine what they will look at as they evaluate programs. We suggest that committee members develop criteria that emphasize both research-based information about effective instruction and practice-based information that reflects the instructional needs of the students in the district, as well as the experiences of the committee members and the teachers they represent.

We also suggest that, once committee members decide on the criteria they will use for evaluating programs, they develop a systematic procedure that (1) will evaluate the correspondence between the criteria and the programs and (2) will focus on the content of the materials rather than on the appearance of labels in scope-and-sequence charts.

I have also been working on a project involving textbook selection at the Center for the Study of Reading at the University of Illinois. A set of booklets, *A Guide to Evaluating Basal Reading Programs*, has been developed to provide information about reading research to members of adoption committees. The booklets contain reviews of research about topics important to reading instruction, as well as work sheets for use in assessing how these topics are treated in teacher's manuals, student textbooks, and workbooks. The booklets require committees to make a commitment of both time and effort, and the emphasis is on the in-depth examination of program lessons. (See Dole et al., 1987, for a description of this effort.)

The procedures that I will now describe are derived from the more extensive procedures available in these booklets. They can be used as a "first-pass" screening device to reduce the number of programs that will be examined in greater detail and depth.

## General Features of a "First-Pass" Examination

For each basal reading program to be examined, randomly select at least four complete lessons at each grade level of a program. Identify the lesson parts in the teacher's manuals, student textbooks, and workbooks. These listed lessons will first be used to examine the following three topics: instructional activities, instructional design, and adaptability.

INSTRUCTIONAL ACTIVITIES
1. Determine lesson objectives and write them down.
2. Look at the instructional activities for each objective.
    a. Do the activities match the objectives?
    b. Are the most important objectives supported by a sufficient number of activities? Justify this answer.
3. Try out (role play) several of the activities.
    a. Are the directions easily followed?
    b. Are the activities instructionally adequate; that is, do you think the students will learn from them?
4. Describe an activity designed to teach something that is likely to be new learning for the students in the program.

INSTRUCTIONAL DESIGN
1. To examine sequencing of instruction, choose activities from the two lessons that follow the listed lesson. Highlight any activities that begin in one lesson and are continued in subsequent lessons.
2. Determine which of the highlighted activities listed are *introductory, review, integration,* or *generalization* activities.
    a. *For introductory activities:* Describe and evaluate the effectiveness (for the students likely to be using the program) of any activities designed to present new learning.
    b. *For review activities:* Describe and evaluate the effectiveness of any activities designed to review previous learning.
    c. *For integration activities:* Describe and evaluate the effectiveness of any activities designed to help students combine, or integrate, new learning with previous learning.
    d. *For generalization activities:* Describe and evaluate any activi-

ties designed to help students apply what they are learning to new situations.

## ADAPTABILITY

1. Describe the suggestions for managing and coordinating the activities of the lessons. Do these seem workable?
2. List some of the procedures offered for individualizing the program, for example, the reteaching or alternative teaching of students who need either more help or more challenge.

## SUMMARY

Use the information obtained in the preceding three lists to describe briefly the instructional philosophy and the types of instructional strategies most typical of each program.

### Specific Content of a "First-Pass" Examination

The same listed lessons can be used to examine some of the specific content of the programs being considered.

## DECODING (WORD IDENTIFICATION) INSTRUCTION

1. Describe the approach to the teaching of beginning reading.
2. Is this approach consistent with the needs of the students in the district? Explain.
3. For beginning reading, is systematic instruction in phonics, as well as a variety of other strategies, included in the instruction? Describe the different strategies.

## VOCABULARY (WORD-MEANING) INSTRUCTION

1. Identify the vocabulary (word-meaning) activities of each lesson.
2. Read through the reading selection in the student textbook.
3. Look at the word-meaning activities in the teacher's manual.
   a. *Words*: Do the words identified for vocabulary instruction in the teacher's manual meet the needs of the students who would be reading this selection? List words you would omit; words you would add.
   b. *Expressions*: Describe how the meanings of special expressions, for example, idioms and figurative language, are presented.
4. Describe the most frequently used procedures (definitions, context, special vocabulary activities) for teaching the meanings of new words and language expressions. Do you think these proce-

dures will be effective with the students who would be using this program? Justify this answer.

## COMPREHENSION ACTIVITIES
1. Identify the comprehension activities in each lesson.
2. Describe the comprehension, thinking, and skill and strategy activities of the lesson.
3. Will the suggestions made for the presentation of these activities be effective for the students who will use the program? Justify the answer.
4. Do these activities emphasize that students should—depending upon what they are reading—selectively use a variety of comprehension skills and strategies?
5. Will these activities move the students toward the independent use of comprehension skills and strategies? Justify the answer.

## PREREADING AND PURPOSE-SETTING ACTIVITIES
1. Identify the prereading and purpose-setting activities of the lessons.
2. *Importance:* Do these activities focus on the important concepts and ideas of the selection in the student textbook? Comment.
3. *Tying into prior knowledge:* Do these activities tie into the students' prior knowledge about the topic of the selection? Comment.
4. *Using prior knowledge:* Do these activities encourage the students to use their prior knowledge of the important concepts and ideas in the selection? Comment.
5. *Developing knowledge:* Do these activities provide for the development of new knowledge relevant to the selection? Comment.
6. *Evaluation:* Would you evaluate these activities as both efficient and effective? Are they likely to have a positive effect on the comprehension of the selection? Comment.

## READING THE SELECTION
1. *Procedures:* Briefly describe the procedures for guiding the reading of the selection.
2. *Application of the content:* Are there provisions for helping students apply the skill or strategy of the lesson as they read the selection? If yes, give a couple of examples.
3. *Oral/silent reading:* Describe the suggested procedures for oral and/or silent reading of the selection. Are they appropriate to the students who will be in the program?

4. *Questions:* Read through and evaluate the questions provided for the selection.
   a. Do they focus on important aspects of the selection?
   b. Do they help students develop an understanding of the entire selection?

FOLLOW-UP AND RELATED ACTIVITIES
1. Describe the suggested follow-up and related activities.
   a. Would these activities help students develop an integrated understanding of the selection? How?
   b. Would these activities give students the opportunity to combine information from previous selections with what they have just read? Give an example.
2. *Extending:* What suggestions are there for extending the content of the lesson?
3. *Listening and speaking:* Do these activities provide opportunities for students to relate listening and speaking with reading and writing? Give some examples.
4. *Writing:* List the provisions made for student writing. Are these integrated with the reading activities?
5. *Additional reading:* List the suggestions given for additional reading.
   a. Are there suggestions for stories, articles, and books the students can read independently?
   b. Are there suggestions for stories teachers can read to the students?

THE STUDENT READER
1. Examine the listed lesson, the four lessons immediately preceding it, and the four lessons immediately following it. List the selections in this nine-lesson sequence.
   a. *Selection types*
      How many narratives are there?
      How many informational articles?
      List any other types of selections.
   b. *Quality of selections*
      Are the selections sufficient in length for the age, ability, and interest of the students who will read them?
      Do you think the selections will be interesting to the students who will read them?
      Do any of the selections relate to previous (or subsequent) selections?
      Are there both contemporary and classic selections?

Is a variety of ethnic and cultural groups represented in the selections?

Are the selections and their illustrations free of culturally or socially inappropriate allusions?

2. Examine the graphics, layout, and illustrations.

a. Is the print clear and of appropriate size? Are the breaks between pages reasonable?

b. Do the illustrations support the text? Are there an appropriate number of illustrations?

WORKBOOKS

1. Examine the workbook tasks in a lesson.

a. Do they reflect what is being taught in the rest of the lesson?

b. Do the tasks focus on the most important aspects of the lesson?

c. Is the purpose of each task clear to the students?

d. Can the students follow the directions?

e. Is the layout of the page functional?

f. Do the tasks require the student to do an adequate amount of reading and writing?

2. Examine the tasks for the listed lesson as well as those for the two lessons immediately preceding it.

a. Are there any tasks that continue from one lesson to the next?

b. Are there tasks that review previous learning?

c. Are there tasks in which new and previous learning are combined?

The examination of programs implied by this procedure will reveal a great deal of precise information about the content of basal reading programs. This information will provide a basis for further discussion and a means for making decisions about which programs to examine in greater depth. Such analyses of programs are far different from the flip-test and checklist investigations that Farr and his associates (1987a,b) found to be so prevalent in the committees they observed. These procedures take time and effort. The reward is increased knowledge about the strengths and weaknesses of the basal reading programs being considered for use in a district.

## LOOKING TOWARD THE FUTURE

Modern research about reading has perhaps enlightened us, but it has also doubtlessly strengthened many of our fundamental instincts about the reading process and reading instruction. As the National Commission on Reading states, "The new knowledge about reading and schooling contains some surprises, but more often it confirms old beliefs" (Anderson, Hiebert, Scott, & Wilkinson, 1983, p. 4). Some of the new knowledge and many of the old beliefs have been described by the authors of the chapters of this book. Their recommendations are not in the category of "ivory tower thinking" or "armchair advice"; rather, they represent a synthesis of new and old that has been verified in classroom practice.

The foundation for much of what they discuss is the research of the past decade and a half. The strong interest in reading research continues, and it should be noted that not only is there a lot of it, but research about reading is emanating from a number of disciplines, including cognitive psychology, psycholinguistics, ethnography, and artificial intelligence, as well as reading education and educational psychology. This community of researchers is adding to what we know about the reading process, how people learn to read, and how instruction can positively affect the process of learning to read.

Reading research, like research in many other fields, can be categorized as either basic (seeking to understand the fundamental principles organizing a field) or applied (seeking verified information about how to put knowledge derived from basic research into practice most effectively). Of particular interest is that much of the knowledge gained from recent basic—as well as applied—reading research has had obvious and evident implications for classrooms. For example, both schema theory and metacognition, concepts which have had a great deal of application in the preparation of new basal reading programs (as well as in classroom practice), originated in the realm of basic research.

Many ideas and hunches, as well as some carefully researched procedures for and approaches to reading instruction, are evolving from this burgeoning body of both basic and applied research. It must be acknowledged, however, that reading research brings us to nowhere near the kind of certainty that is available to researchers and practitioners working in other areas. In physics, for example, everyone agrees that matter is composed of atoms and molecules. This agreed-upon knowledge permits the investigation of some even more elusive qualities of matter, for example, the quarks that modern physicists talk about. Another example from physics is the newest work in superconductivity, which in the not-too-distant future will probably save consumers a lot of money in electrical costs. This progress is possible because of the enormous amount of knowledge, verified and agreed upon by the experts of the field, about how heat and energy are conducted.

Research about reading has not brought us to that kind of certainty, and it is not likely to do so in the near future. On the contrary, the field of reading, as is the case with other fields that do not rest solidly upon a body of agreed-upon knowledge, still has its share of differences. People who *do* reading instruction are often governed by strongly held beliefs and opinions that are based on their own experiences. Sometimes these beliefs and opinions fly in the face of research-based knowledge. It must also be acknowledged, however, that one of the reasons that beliefs and opinions are relied upon as the primary source of knowledge about a field is the perception that the research basis of the field is confusing and incoherent. Certainly, as a field, reading is typified by a good amount of incoherence, ambiguity, and confusion, much of which has yet to be resolved convincingly.

As the Commission on Reading states in its report, *Becoming a Nation of Readers* (Anderson et al., 1983), "While there is more consensus about reading than in the past, there are still important issues about which reasonable people disagree" (p. 4). Reasonable people still find it easy to disagree about a number of the important topics associated with reading. It is still easy, for example, for practitioners and researchers to have some very big arguments about how beginning reading should be taught, about what students should read, and about how best to organize reading instruction in classrooms. And it is still all too easy for reading enthusiasts to make fervent claims for their approaches to a particular aspect of reading (whether it be literary appreciation, intensive phonics, meaningful writing, whole language, or high-level thinking skills) as "the answer" for teachers of reading. The lack of a body of agreed-upon knowledge in the field of reading means not only that the arguments can last a long time but that various kinds of extravagant claims can continue to be made. This lack of a firm base of knowledge probably has a lot to do with the swings and fads for which the reading field is known.

On the other hand, the presence of some confusion and incoherence in the research base of reading should not be viewed in the same way as another aspect of its research base, namely, its efforts to address complexity. One of the most agreed-upon conclusions of modern research about reading is the complexity of the reading process. The effect of complexity upon what we know about the teaching and learning of reading is nicely described in *Becoming a Nation of Readers* (Anderson et al., 1983):

Based on what we now know, it is incorrect to suppose that there is a simple or single step which, if taken correctly, will immediately allow a child to read. Becoming a skilled reader is a journey that involves many steps. Similarly, it is unrealistic to anticipate that some one critical feature of instruction will be discovered which, if in place, will assure rapid progress in reading. Quality instruction involves many elements. Strengthening any one element yields small gains. For large gains, many elements must be in place. [p. 4]

With the numerous bows to reality that have been put forth in this summary, and with the full acknowledgment of the still-limited claims that can be made about the developing body of knowledge about reading, we nevertheless believe a considerable amount of the new research conveys a number of strong messages to classroom teachers and administrators of reading programs. The chapters in this book convey many of these messages.

The reading research of the past fifteen years has reduced the confusion and incoherence and increased the knowledge base. A book such as this can help teachers and administrators combine current reading research with some of the successful practices in place in their classrooms. Surely, when the best of what can be learned from the new research is combined with the wisdom that comes from experience, we can anticipate dramatic improvements in the reading achievement of all the students in American schools. To quote again from the Commission on Reading (Anderson et al., 1983):

The knowledge is now available to make worthwhile improvements in reading throughout the United States. If the practices seen in the classrooms of the best schools could be introduced everywhere, the improvements would be dramatic. [p. 3]

## REFERENCES

Anderson, L. (1984). The environment of instruction: The function of seat-work. In G. Duffy, L. Roehler, & J. Mason (Eds.), *Comprehension instruction: Perspectives and suggestions* (pp. 93–115). New York: Longman.

Anderson, R. C., Hiebert, E. H., Scott, J. A., & Wilkinson, I. A. (1983). *Becoming a nation of readers: The report of the Commission on Reading.* Urbana, IL: Center for the Study of Reading.

Anderson, T. H., Armbruster, B. B., & Kantor, R. N. (1980). *How clearly written are children's textbooks? Or, of bladderworts and alfa* (Reading Ed. Rep. No. 16). Urbana: University of Illinois, Center for the Study of Reading.

Beck, I. L., McKeown, M. G., & Gromoll, E. K. (1986). Issues concerning content and structure of expository text for young readers. Unpublished manuscript.

Bruce, B. (1984). A new point of view of children's stories. In R. C. Anderson, J. Osborn, & R. J. Tierney (Eds.), *Learning to read in American schools* (pp. 153–174). Hillsdale, NJ: Lawrence Erlbaum.

Davison, A. (1984). Readability—Appraising text difficulty. In R. C. Anderson, J. Osborn, & R. J. Tierney (Eds.), *Learning to read in American schools* (pp. 121–140). Hilldale, NJ: Lawrence Erlbaum.

Dole, J., & Osborn, J. H. (in press). Reading materials: Their selection and use. In S. B. Wepner, J. T. Feeley, & D. Strickland (Eds.), *The administration and supervision of reading programs.* New York: Teachers College Press.

Dole, J. A., Rogers, T. R., & Osborn, J. (1987). Improving the selection of basal reading programs: A report of the Textbook Adoption Guidelines Project. *Elementary School Journal, 8*(7), 283–298.

Duffy, G., & McIntyre, L. (1982). A naturalistic study of instructional assistance in primary-grade reading. *Elementary School Journal, 83,* 15–23.

Duffy, G., Roehler, L., & Putnam, J. (1987). Putting the teacher in control: Basal reading textbooks and instructional decision making. *Elementary School Journal, 87,* 357–366.

Duffy, G., Roehler, L., & Wesselman, R. (1985). Disentangling the complexities of instructional effectiveness: A line of research on classroom reading instruction. In J. Niles & R. Lalik (Eds.), *Issues in literacy: A research perspective (34th Yearbook of the National Reading Conference).* Rochester, NY: National Reading Conference.

Durkin, D. (1984). Do basal manuals teach reading comprehension? In R. C. Anderson, J. Osborn, & R. J. Tierney (Eds.), *Learning to read in American schools* (pp. 29–38). Hillsdale, NJ: Lawrence Erlbaum.

Farr, R., Tulley, M. A., & Powell, D. (1987a). The evaluation and selection of basal readers. *Elementary School Journal, 87,* 267–282.

Farr, R., Tulley, M. A., & Powell, D. (1987b). Selecting basal readers: A comparison of school districts in adoption and nonadoption states. *Journal of Research and Development in Education, 20,* 59–72.

Fisher, C. W., Berliner, D., Filby, N., Marliave, R., Cohen, L., Dishaw, M., & Moore, J. (1978). *Teaching and learning in elementary schools: A summary of the beginning teacher evaluation study.* San Francisco: Far West Regional Laboratory for Educational Research and Development.

Goodman, K. S., Freeman, Y., Murphy, S., & Shannon, P. (1987). *Report card on basal readers.* Urbana, IL: National Council of Teachers of English, Commission on Reading.

Graves, M., & Slater, W. (1986). Could textbooks be better written and would it make a difference? *American Educator, 10,* (1), 36–44.

Liebling, C. R. (1986). *Inside view and character plans in original stories and their basal reader adaptations* (Tech. Rep. No. 397). Urbana: University of Illinois, Center for the Study of Reading.

Mason, J., & Osborn, J. (1981). *When do children begin "reading to learn"? A survey of classroom reading instruction practices in grades two through five* (Tech. Rep. No. 261). Urbana: University of Illinois, Center for the Study of Reading.

Osborn, J. (1984). The purposes, uses and contents of workbooks and some guidelines for publishers. In R. C. Anderson, J. Osborn, & R. J. Tierney (Eds.), *Learning to read in American schools* (pp. 45–112). Hillsdale, NJ: Lawrence Erlbaum.

Powell, P. A. (1986). *Retrospective case studies of individual and group decision making in district-level elementary reading textbook selection.* Unpublished doctoral dissertation, Indiana University, Bloomington.

Roehler, L., & Duffy, G. (1984). Direct explanation of comprehension processes. In G. G. Duffy, L. R. Roehler, & J. Mason (Eds.), *Comprehension instruction: Perspectives and suggestions* (pp. 265–200). New York: Longman.

Shannon, P. (1983). The use of commercial reading materials in American elementary schools. *Reading Research Quarterly, 19,* 68–85.

Shannon, P. (1987). Commercial reading materials, a technology, an ideology and the deskilling of teachers. *Elementary School Journal, 87,* 307–329.

# About the Editors
# and the Contributors

**Donna E. Alvermann** is an associate professor in Reading Education, and a fellow in the Institute for Behavioral Research, at the University of Georgia. She received her Ph.D. in reading education from Syracuse University in 1980. She has taught public school in Texas and New York, and is the author of *Using Discussion to Promote Reading Comprehension* and *Research Within Reach: Secondary School Reading*. In addition, she has published in *Reading Research Quarterly, Journal of Reading Behavior, Journal of Teacher Education, Journal of Reading,* and *The Reading Teacher*. Donna serves on the Board of Directors of the National Reading Conference, and is a senior author with D. C. Heath and Company.

**Kathryn H. Au** received a Ph.D. in education from the University of Illinois in 1980. Currently an educational psychologist with the elementary program of Hawaii's Kamehameha Schools, she is also co-author of an introductory reading methods textbook—*Reading Instruction for Today*—and has written journal articles and book chapters on effective reading instruction for cultural minority students. Kathy is an author with the Houghton Mifflin Reading Program.

**Connie A. Bridge** is currently a professor in the Department of Curriculum and Instruction at the University of Kentucky, where she teaches graduate and undergraduate courses in reading and language arts. In 1976, she received her Ed.D. in reading from the University of Arizona. She taught elementary and special reading classes before entering teacher education, and has published articles in the *Reading Research Quarterly, Journal of Reading Behavior, The Reading Teacher, Language Arts,* and *The Elementary School Journal*. Connie is a senior author with D. C. Heath and Company.

**Carol Sue Englert** received a Ph.D. in education from Indiana University. Presently, she is an associate professor in the Department of Counseling, Educational Psychology, and Special Education at Michigan State University, and senior researcher with the Institute for Research on Teaching. She has published in a variety of journals in general and special education, including the *Journal of Educational Psychology, The Reading Teacher, Journal of Educational Research, Exceptional Children, Learning Disability Quarterly,* and *Remedial and Special Education.*

**Marjorie Y. Lipson** (Editor) received a Ph.D. in Education from the University of Michigan in 1981, and is an associate professor at the University of Vermont in Burlington. Marge has published in a number of journals, including *Reading Research Quarterly, The Reading Teacher, Journal of Reading,* and *Review of Educational Research.* Currently, she is working with co-editor Karen Wixson on a textbook in the assessment of reading problems, and is an author with Houghton Mifflin and Company.

**Lesley Mandel Morrow** received her Ph.D. in Education from Fordham University in New York City. She is currently Associate Professor and Coordinator of the Early Childhood/Elementary Programs at the Graduate School of Education at Rutgers University. Lesley's area of research deals with early childhood literacy development, and specifically focuses upon promoting voluntary reading and comprehension of stories through the use of children's literature. She has published in *Reading Research Quarterly, Research in the Teaching of English, Journal of Reading Behavior, Elementary School Journal* and *Reading Teacher,* and is the author of several monographs, book chapters, and *Literacy Development In the Early Years: Helping Young Children Read and Write.*

**Jean H. Osborn** is Associate Director of the Center for the Study of Reading at the University of Illinois. She received a master's degree in special education from the University of Illinois, and has taught preschool, kindergarten, elementary, and middle school. For 15 years she was a field staff member of the United States Department of Education Follow-Through Study, where she worked on training programs with hundreds of teachers, administrators, and students across the country. She has co-authored several instructional programs in language and reading. Her work has included analyses and critiques of the workbooks that accompany reading programs; a series of booklets about reading research for committees adopting basal reading programs to use as they evaluate programs; and two edited volumes, *Learning to Read in American Schools,* and *Foundations for a Literate America.*

**Charles W. Peters** is currently a reading consultant for the Oakland Intermediate School District in Pontiac, Michigan where he provides staff and professional development training for administrators and teachers in the 28 school districts he serves. He received his Ph.D. in reading from the University of Wisconsin—Madison and has taught at the middle school, high school, and university levels. In addition, he has authored articles dealing with theory, research, and practice which have appeared in *Reading Research Quarterly, Journal of Reading, Reading Teacher,* and *Educational Psychologist.* He has been on the editorial review board of several national journals and was editor for the *Michigan Reading Journal.* Charles' current interests include applying current theories on reading comprehension to assessment practices and content instruction.

**Taffy E. Raphael** received her Ph.D. from the University of Illinois, studying at the Center for the Study of Reading. She is currently an associate professor in the Departments of Teacher Education and Educational Psychology at Michigan State University, and senior researcher with the Institute for Research on Teaching. Taffy has published in *Reading Research Quarterly, American Educational Research Journal, Journal of Reading Behavior, Journal of Reading, The Reading Teacher,* and *Learning Disability Quarterly.* She is on the Board of Directors of the National Reading Conference, and has been actively involved on committees for International Reading Association. Taffy is an author with the new Holt, Rinehart and Winston basal reading series.

**Judith A. Scheu** received an M.Ed. in early childhood education from the University of Illinois in 1969. She is currently a curriculum developer at the Kamehameha Schools' Center for the Development of Early Education in Honolulu, Hawaii. Judith has published in *The Reading Teacher.*

**Mary C. Shake** received an Ed.D. in Reading Education from the State University of New York at Albany in 1984. She is currently Assistant Professor in the Department of Curriculum and Instruction at the University of Kentucky in Lexington. Mary has published articles in *The Reading Teacher, Questioning Exchange, Journal of Reading Behavior, Topics in Learning and Learning Disabilities,* and *Reading Research and Instruction.*

**Diane K. Tanner** received a B.A. in elementary education from the University of Hawaii in 1978. She is currently a second-grade teacher at Kamehameha Elementary School in Honolulu, Hawaii. Diane has published in *The Reading Teacher.*

**Peter N. Winograd** (Editor) is an associate professor in the Department of Curriculum and Instruction at the University of Kentucky in Lexington. He received his Ph.D. in education from the University of Illinois at Urbana-Champaign, in 1981. Peter has published in *Reading Research Quarterly, The Reading Teacher, Journal of Educational Psychology, Journal of Reading Behavior, Educational Psychologist, Educational Leadership*, and *Topics in Language Disorders*. He is a senior author with D. C. Heath and Company.

**Karen K. Wixson** (Editor) is an associate professor of Education at the University of Michigan. Prior to receiving her doctorate in reading at Syracuse University in 1980, she was a remedial reading and learning disabilities teacher. Karen conducts research and publishes in the areas of reading assessment and instruction; her awards include the IRA Elva Knight Research Award, the AERA Professional Service Award, and the MRA Reading Researcher Award. Karen is currently a co-author, with Marjorie Lipson, of a forthcoming diagnosis and remediation text for Scott, Foresman, a co-author of the Scribner Reading Series, and co-director of a project with the Michigan Department of Education and the Michigan Reading Association to revise statewide objectives and tests in reading.

# Index